PAGE 21

SONGS
of
GLORY

SONGS
of
GLORY

*Stories of 300 Great Hymns
and Gospel Songs*

William J. Reynolds

Zondervan Books
Zondervan Publishing House
Grand Rapids, Michigan

Songs of Glory: Stories of 300 Great Hymns and Gospel Songs
Copyright © 1990 by William J. Reynolds

First edition

Zondervan Books
are published by Zondervan Publishing House
1415 Lake Drive, S.E.
Grand Rapids, MI 49506

Library of Congress Cataloging-in-Publication Data

Reynolds, William Jensen.
    Songs of glory : stories of 300 great hymns and gospel songs /
    p.   cm.
    ISBN 0-310-51720-6
    1. Hymns, English—History and criticism. I. Title.
BV315.R49   1989
264'.2—dc20   89–37121
                                                                   CIP

Printed in the United States of America

90 91 92 93 94 95 96 / DH / 10 9 8 7 6 5 4 3 2 1

To Mary Lou
whose spiritual discernment, unfailing love, gentle patience,
warm companionship, unbiased counsel, and penetrating
insights have brought strength, understanding, beauty, and
abounding joy

Preface

The singing of hymns is a part of our national heritage and is a common experience in every community throughout our nation. In 1562–65 Huguenot immigrants to the coasts of South Carolina and Florida sang metrical psalms in French, and in June 1579 Sir Francis Drake's men sang English psalms on the coast of northern California. The Pilgrims, landing on Plymouth Rock in 1620, and the Puritans, landing near Boston a decade later, brought their songs of praise. Each wave of immigrants from England, Ireland, Wales, and the European continent came singing their songs of faith and Christian pilgrimage. Each new generation found ways to sing God's praise, to proclaim in song the gospel of Jesus Christ, and to give expression to their Christian faith.

The hymns and gospel songs discussed in this volume represent those sung in churches, in homes, and in other places where Christians meet. The stories are intended to help make understandable the circumstances that produced these songs and the individuals who wrote, arranged, recorded, and preserved them. Written for the weekly church page in local newspapers (beginning a decade ago in the *Nashville Banner* [Tennessee]), these stories have appeared in *The Akron Beacon Journal* (Ohio), *Alexandria Daily Town Talk* (Louisiana), *Foothills View* (North Carolina), *Greensboro Daily News* (North Carolina), *Indianapolis News* (Indiana), *Lyons Progress* (Georgia), *Macon Telegraph and News* (Georgia), *National Christian Reporter* (Texas), *Shreveport Times* (Louisiana), *United Methodist Reporter* (Texas), and *Waco Tribune-Herald* (Texas).

Each selection begins with the first stanza of the hymn. The reader may want to refer to a hymnal and read additional stanzas to have a greater understanding of the complete hymn. Pertinent information about authors and composers is included, along with what is known about the occasion or experience that prompted the writing of the hymn.

The hymns presented here represent a wide diversity of Christian song, ranging from English translations of Latin hymns of the early church to contemporary Christian songs of this decade. Some hymnwriters are well known, but many others were obscure, devout Christians who were inspired to write words that have endured the test of time and have become dearly loved.

To copyright owners who have graciously permitted some stanzas of their copyrighted hymns to be quoted, a word of gratitude is expressed. Every effort has been made to acknowledge ownership of the material that has been used.

William J. Reynolds
January 1989
Fort Worth, Texas

KEEP THE CHARGE OF THE LORD

A charge to keep I have,
A God to glorify
Who gave his Son my soul to save,
And fit it for the sky.

These words of Moses to Aaron and his sons provide the basis for the hymn: "Therefore shall ye abide at the door of the tabernacle of the congregation day and night seven days, and keep the charge of the Lord, that ye die not: for so I am commanded" (Lev. 8:35).

Charles Wesley wrote the hymn and published it as "Keep the Charge of the Lord" in 1762 in the Wesley collection *Short Hymns on Select Passages of Holy Scriptures.*

John and Charles Wesley often met vicious opposition and persecution. Church of England clergy accused the Wesleys of blasphemy and urged the people to have them run out of town. Not only the Wesleys and their fellow ministers, but also those who had been converted in their meetings were treated shamefully.

The strong faith of these early Methodists shines in the lines of this hymn. Trials and tribulations faced them daily, yet they confronted life with assurance and confidence and faced the certainty of death with faith in the Lord.

John and Charles Wesley preached in factories, mines, prisons, anywhere they could find a listening congregation. Charles, the gifted hymnwriter, wrote more than 6,500 hymns. John, the preacher and administrator, was the careful planner and provider. He was the "methodist." John had high regard for congregational singing in their meetings and in 1761 published instructions for singing. He said, "learn these tunes before any others . . . sing them as they are printed here . . . sing everyone . . . sing lustily and with good courage . . . sing modestly; do not bawl . . . sing in time; do not run before or stay behind . . . above all sing spiritually. Have an eye to God in every word you sing. Aim at pleasing Him more than yourself." Today, Wesley's admonition needs our attention.

THE HYMN OF THE REFORMATION

A mighty fortress is our God,
A bulwark never failing;
Our helper he, amid the flood
Of mortal ills prevailing:
For still our ancient foe
Doth seek to work us woe;
His craft and pow'r are great,
And, armed with cruel hate,
On earth is not his equal.

Martin Luther was a disappointment to his father, Hans Luther, who had expected that his son would be a lawyer. He was quite upset when Martin, at age twenty-two, entered a monastery, never dreaming that his son would one day be far better known than any lawyer in Germany.

Martin Luther was ordained a priest in 1507 and the following year began teaching at the University of Wittenberg. It was there, on October 31, 1517, that Luther posted his now famous theses, or articles, against papal abuses and corruption. Two years later he denied the pope's supremacy, an action that resulted in papal condemnation of Luther and his writings.

Luther's greatest literary achievement was his scholarly translation of the Bible into the German language, giving to his people God's Word in their own tongue.

Under Luther's leadership congregational singing became a vital part of the church service. In the Roman Catholic Church, singing had been monopolized by the clergy, and the German people were ready to sing their own songs. So Martin Luther wrote hymns, composed tunes, and adapted tunes from secular sources without apology. He believed and preached that music was a gift from God and should be used in doing the work of God.

His greatest hymn is "Ein feste Burg ist unser Gott," written in 1529. Churches in England sing a translation by Thomas Carlyle that begins, "A safe stronghold our God is still." Churches in America sing a translation by a New England Unitarian minister, Frederick H. Hedge, which begins, "A mighty fortress is our God."

The hymn, based on Psalm 46, was written during a conflict in Luther's struggle against the Roman Catholic Church. It was his confident expression of victory in that crisis. Imagine him singing out the final lines:

> Let goods and kindred go,
> This mortal life also
> The body they may kill:
> God's truth abideth still,
>   His kingdom is forever.

This hymn has been called "the greatest hymn of the greatest man of the greatest period of German history."

A HURRIED COLLABORATION

A pilgrim was I and a-wand'ring;
  In the cold night of sin I did roam,
When Jesus the kind Shepherd found me,
  And now I am on my way home.
Surely goodness and mercy shall follow me
  All the days, all the days of my life.
And I shall dwell in the house of the Lord forever,
  And I shall feast at the table spread for me.*

Alfred B. Smith studied music at the Juilliard School of Music in New York City, at Moody Bible Institute in Chicago, and at Wheaton College. While a student at Wheaton, Smith roomed with Billy Graham and later became his first song leader. Smith began his first music publishing efforts in 1941 under the name Singspiration. In 1954 he employed John W. Peterson as music editor.

One day in 1958 Peterson was sitting in his office improvising at the piano when Smith walked in. As he continued aimlessly playing, a melody emerged. It caught Smith's attention and soon both men added phrases and words until "Surely Goodness and Mercy" had taken shape in a song based on Psalm 23, the Shepherd Psalm.

Later Peterson commented, "Rarely have I collaborated with others in such a way in the writing of a song, but in this instance it was a successful effort, for God has greatly used the song." It was a favorite during the second Billy Graham London Crusade. Cliff Barrows reported that if he failed to use it on a given night he got notes from the crowd.

INSPIRED BY THE WORDS OF JESUS

A ruler once came to Jesus by night
To ask him the way of salvation and light;
The Master made answer in words true and plain,
"Ye must be born again."

Refrain:
*   "Ye must be born again,*
*   Ye must be born again,*
*   I verily, verily say unto thee,*
*   Ye must be born again."*

In August 1877 evangelist George F. Pentecost was engaged in revival services in Worcester, Massachusetts. One evening, in his sermon on the "new birth," Dr. Pentecost quoted the words of Jesus spoken to Nicodemus, "Verily, verily, I say unto thee, ye must be born again" (John 3:3, 7). The words caught the attention of George C. Stebbins, the music leader for the revival. A talented musician, Stebbins had already written several gospel songs and was struck by the rhythm of the words. It occurred to him that by rearranging the first line so that it would read "I verily, verily say unto thee, ye must be born again," he would have a singable line.

A day or so later Stebbins spoke to William T. Sleeper, one of the ministers participating in the revival. Sleeper had written several hymns and the suggestions of Stebbins had captured his imagination. In a few days he handed Stebbins the stanzas to support this "rearranged" Scripture verse.

William Sleeper, a native of New Hampshire, was ordained to the Congregational ministry following his graduation from the University of Vermont and Andover Theological Seminary. In 1876 he became pastor of the Summer Street Congregational Church in Worcester, where he served faithfully for more than thirty years.

For more than twenty-five years George C. Stebbins worked with Dwight L. Moody and his associates. He led the music in the meetings, organized city-wide choirs, and rehearsed with them for the large tabernacle services. A talented and skillful musician, his abilities were great assets in these evangelical enterprises. He wrote many gospel songs, the best known of which are "Have Thine Own Way, Lord," "Jesus Is Tenderly Calling Thee Home," "Take Time to be Holy," and "Savior, Breathe an Evening Blessing."

A WALK BY THE SEASIDE

Abide with me: fast falls the eventide;
The darkness deepens; Lord, with me abide:
When other helpers fail, and comforts flee,
Help of the helpless, O abide with me.

For twenty-three years Henry Francis Lyte, a frail village minister, had lived in Lower Brixham, Devonshire, England. He had preached to the congregation, read the marriage vows for their young people, comforted the bereaved when loved ones died, and ministered to the families of the community in times of joy and sorrow. Early on he had learned to live with his own frail health.

Now at age fifty-four he had been advised by his physician to leave the moist climate by the sea and seek a drier atmosphere in Italy. This Sunday afternoon, September 4, 1947, would be his last in the village he loved. Earlier in the day he had administered his last Communion and preached his last sermon. His mind was flooded with memories of the years, and he had a deepening awareness of his own physical condition. The lines of "Abide With Me" took shape, and he hurriedly penciled them in his notebook. That evening he gave the poem to a dear friend and thought no more of it.

A few days later, Lyte crossed the English Channel and

began a leisurely trip to Italy. But he never reached his destination, for in a few weeks he died in Nice, France.

Several years later William H. Monk, an English church musician and composer, wrote the tune for Lyte's text that bears the name "Eventide." Monk published the words and music in 1861. Widely used, the hymn has been especially helpful to Christians in times of trial and distress.

For her wedding to Philip Mountbatten on November 21, 1947, the future Queen Elizabeth II selected "Abide With Me" as the opening hymn in the ceremony at Westminster Abbey. It also had been the opening hymn at the wedding of her parents, King George VI and Queen Elizabeth.

Edith Cavell, an English nurse and heroine of World War I, sang the hymn as she faced the firing squad in Brussels on October 12, 1915, for assisting Allied soldiers to escape from German-occupied Belgium.

IN CONTEMPLATION OF THE CRUCIFIXION

Alas, and did my Savior bleed
And did my Sovereign die?
Would he devote that sacred head
For sinners such as I?

Under the heading "Godly Sorrow Arising From the Sufferings of Christ," the hymn appeared in a collection of hymns by Isaac Watts published in London in 1707.

A congregation singing the hymn shares with Watts in contemplating the crucifixion of Christ with amazement and wonder. In response to a full awareness of the event of Calvary "for man, the creature's sin," the final stanza becomes an expression of total commitment:

Here, Lord, I give myself away,
'Tis all that I can do.

Over more than two and a half centuries, editors of hymnals have altered some of the lines. The fourth line of the first stanza as Watts wrote it was "for such a worm as I." The descriptive language was intended to contrast the greatness of God with the insignificance of humankind. The terminology is based on Psalm 22:6, "But I am a worm, and no man; a reproach of men, and despised of the people." Over the last century, the line "for sinners such as I" has become almost universal, reflecting the apostle Paul's statement: "Christ Jesus came into the world to save sinners; of whom I am chief" (1 Tim. 1:15).

The tune used for Watts's text was composed by Hugh Wilson, a native of Fenwick in Ayrshire, Scotland. A shoe-maker by trade, Wilson led the psalm singing in his church. He supplemented his income by teaching classes in reading, arithmetic, and music for the villagers. One of his hobbies was designing sundials, one of which may still be seen in Fenwick, about fifteen miles southwest of Glasgow. The year after Wilson's death in 1824, this tune was published in Edinburgh with the notation "as sung at St. George's Church." Because Wilson's name was not given, his heirs brought suit and won judgment in court establishing his claim as the composer.

A REVISED VERSION OF
AN OLD HYMN

Alas, and did my Savior bleed,
And did my Sovereign die?
Would he devote that sacred head
For sinners such as I?
At the cross, at the cross where I first saw the light,
And the burden of my heart rolled away,
It was there by faith I received my sight,
And now I am happy all the day.

In 1885 Ralph E. Hudson used the stanzas of Isaac Watts's "Godly Sorrow Arising from the Sufferings of Christ," written in 1707, added a refrain, wrote a new tune, and published it as a gospel song titled "At the Cross." Hudson's music, well-known by evangelical Christians, has the flavor of American evangelism of the late nineteenth century. A licensed minister in the Methodist Episcopal Church, Hudson devoted most of his time to evangelistic work but was also active in songwriting and songbook publishing. He lived in Alliance, Ohio.

There is great similarity between Hudson's version and a song titled "Take Me Home," which appeared in the middle of the nineteenth century. The opening lines of the text are:

Take me home to the place where I first saw the light,
To the sweet sunny South take me home,
Where the mockingbird sung me to rest every night,
Ah, why was I tempted to roam.

Hudson apparently liked the song, borrowed the phrase "where I first saw the light," and changed "the sweet sunny South" to "at the cross" for the opening of the refrain.

For over a century Hudson's song has grown in popularity so much that Isaac Watts would probably be surprised at the widespread usage of his hymn. But if today's usage is any measure of endurance, Hudson's version will be around for quite some time.

A CANTICLE OF THE CREATURES

All creatures of our God and King,
Lift up your voice and with us sing
Alleluia!
Thou burning sun with golden beam,
Thou silver moon with softer beam,
O praise him, Alleluia!

During the hot summer of 1225 in San Damiano, Italy, Francis of Assisi was afflicted with illness and temporary blindness. He sought refuge from the heat in a straw hut. Added to the heat and his physical discomfort was the presence of field mice who wanted to share his hut.

It is hard to believe that under such circumstances Francis could praise God. But he wrote a magnificent poem entitled "Canticle of the Creatures," which became the basis for the English translation "All Creatures of Our God and King."

The son of a wealthy Italian cloth merchant, Francis was

born in Assisi in 1182. As a young man he had a number of unusual experiences. He saw visions and heard voices that others did not see or hear. Once while visiting the ruins of a church, he heard a voice from the crucifix say, "Repair my house." Francis returned home and, without his father's knowledge, took cloth from his father's warehouse, sold it, and repaired the ruined church.

Renouncing material goods and family ties, Francis embraced a life of poverty. He loved all nature and found great joy in the handiwork of God. Birds and animals were his friends and he called them his "brothers" and "sisters." In 1209 Francis founded the Franciscan Order with twelve followers who were called friars. These were actually street preachers who owned no possessions. The early rule for the Franciscans was "to follow the teachings of our Lord Jesus Christ and to walk in his footsteps."

In the little village of Grecchio in Italy in 1223, Francis sought a more vivid way to portray the Christmas story. He built a life-size manger, placed a statue of the Christ child on the hay, and placed farm animals around him, creating a living picture of what occurred at Bethlehem. Two years after Francis' death in 1226, he was canonized by Pope Gregory IX.

The English version of Francis' hymn is a paraphrase made in 1926 by the Reverend William H. Draper for the Children's Whitsuntide Festival at Leeds, England.

A PROCESSIONAL HYMN FOR PALM SUNDAY

All glory, laud, and honor,
To thee, Redeemer King,
To whom the lips of children
Made sweet hosannas ring:
Thou art the King of Israel,
Thou David's royal Son,
Who in the Lord's name comest,
The King and blessed One.

The Latin hymn "Gloria, laus, et honor" was written by Theodulph of Orleans during his imprisonment, probably in 820. Born of a noble Italian family, Theodulph entered a monastery at Florence as a young man. Charlemagne, the king of the Franks, discovered him there, brought him to France in 781, and made him Bishop of Orleans. He became an influential person in Charlemagne's court, but later was accused of conspiring against King Louis the Pious and was put in prison in Angers. He died there three years later.

Palm Sunday at Orleans was a time of great celebration. There was a solemn blessing by the bishop, a distribution of palm branches to the people, and then a colorful procession. The procession began outside the city with the Gospels, the Cross, and many banners. Next came a living representation of Jesus seated on a donkey, followed by the people waving palm branches and singing hosannas.

At the city gates, the Gospel was read and a prayer was offered up for the people of the city. The children began singing "Gloria, laus, et honor," then everyone else joined them. The procession ended at the cathedral.

Today Theodulph's hymn is sung in many languages on Palm Sunday. The beautiful story of the triumphant entry of Christ into Jerusalem as related in Mark 11:1–10 is told in the stanzas of the hymn.

The English translation of the Latin text most commonly found in our hymnals is that made by John Mason Neale in 1851. In many cathedrals the hymn is partly sung by a group of choir boys positioned high up in a gallery to dramatize the imprisoned Theodulph.

CROWNING JESUS LORD OF ALL

All hail the power of Jesus' name
Let angels prostrate fall;
Bring forth the royal diadem,
And crown him Lord of all.

The hymn about the coronation of Jesus, not surprisingly, was written by an Englishman. Magnificent pageantry and historical remembrance are involved in a coronation. The lines of the hymn contain suggestions of royal pageantry with imagery from both Old and New Testaments.

Edward Perronet, a descendant of Huguenot refugees and the son of an Anglican minister, wrote the hymn in 1779. First published that year in an evangelical magazine, the hymn was later altered by John Rippon, an English Baptist minister, who added two new stanzas. Most American hymnals use Rippon's version of Perronet's hymn.

Three tunes are associated with this hymn. The first, "Miles Lane," composed by William Shrubsole, an English church organist, appeared with Perronet's hymn when it was first published. In many parts of the world, especially in England and Europe, it is the sole tune for the hymn.

"Coronation," the tune most used in America, was composed in 1792 by Oliver Holden. A carpenter by trade, Holden helped rebuild Charleston, Massachusetts, after it had been burned by the British in the Revolutionary War. He later ran a general store, taught singing in schools, and published several collections of songs. His tombstone in a Boston cemetery is inscribed with the first stanza of this hymn.

"Diadem," the third tune, was composed in 1838 by James Ellor, a hatmaker by trade. He took it to the hat factory in Droylsden, England, where it was enthusiastically sung by all the workers. In parts of England and America, the tune may still be heard, and it is widely known in South America, where it is sung to this text in Portuguese and Spanish.

A METRICAL PSALM OF PRAISE

All people that on earth do dwell,
Sing to the Lord with cheerful voice;
Him serve with fear, his praise forth tell;
Come ye before him and rejoice.

This poetic stanza encompasses the first two verses of Psalm 100. The prose has been transformed into stanzas of four poetic lines of equal length, with alternate lines rhyming. The content of the psalm is intact—nothing deleted and nothing added.

In the sixteenth century, John Calvin allowed only Scripture to be sung in his church in Geneva, Switzerland. He urged those with poetic gifts to convert the Hebrew psalms of the Old Testament into French poetic verse.

Calvin's chief musician was Louis Bourgeois, music director at St. Peter's Church in Geneva from 1545 until 1557. For the new French psalm versions he composed and adapted tunes and edited the music for Calvin's psalters that were published in Geneva. Bourgeois' most enduring tune is the one we use in singing the "Doxology" ("Praise God from Whom All Blessings Flow"). The tune is called "Old Hundredth" because of its association with Psalm 100.

Because of Queen Mary's persecution of Protestants in England in the middle sixteenth century, many Protestants fled to Europe and some settled in Geneva. Among this group was William Kethe. The French psalms Kethe heard there motivated him to make English poems of the psalms.

Kethe's version of Psalm 100 has been sung for more than four hundred years. Shakespeare mentions it in *Merry Wives of Windsor*, where he says of two characters, "They do no more adhere and keep peace together than the Hundredth Psalm to the tune of Greensleeves."

In *The Courtship of Miles Standish*, Henry Wadsworth Longfellow refers to Kethe's psalm version as "that grand old Puritan anthem." At the coronation of Queen Elizabeth II, June 2, 1953, this was the first congregational hymn.

The text has remained unchanged since 1561, with one exception. In stanza two, the word "flock" was originally "folck," and old spelling of "folk." Many years ago, apparently, some well-meaning editor thought this a misspelling and made the substitution. "Folk," however, is more appropriate to indicate that we are God's people.

A HYMN INSPIRED BY THE GENEROUS GIFT OF TEN DOLLARS

All the way my Savior leads me;
What have I to ask beside?
Can I doubt his tender mercy,

Who through life has been my guide?
Heavenly peace, divinest comfort,
Here by faith in him to dwell!
For I know whate'er befall me
Jesus doeth all things well.

Fanny Crosby and her husband, Alexander Van Alstyne, lived in small, meager apartments, called "flats," in tenement houses on the east side and west side of Lower Manhattan. Their many wealthy friends would have gladly provided better accommodations, but they declined their help. Bernard Ruffin, in his excellent biography *Fanny Crosby,* points out that Fanny gave away all she received above her basic needs. To live with the poor and be one of them was her desire, and ministering to the poor was part of her mission in life. Dressmakers, hackmen, grocery clerks, carpenters, shoemakers, and porters—even some freed slaves—were her neighbors. Frequently she invited neighbors into her flat and entertained them by playing the guitar and singing.

One day in the fall of 1874, Fanny did not have enough money to pay the rent. She prayed earnestly that the Lord would provide her need. Not long after, there was a knock at the door. When Fanny opened the door, someone pressed a folded paper into her hand and left without speaking a word. It was the ten dollars she needed for the rent. Later that day, out of gratitude for this blessing from the Lord, she wrote the hymn "All the Way My Savior Leads Me." What a blessing it is for us to read the words and sing the hymn knowing the event that prompted it.

Little is known about Fanny's husband except that he was a talented musician and that he and Fanny, both blind, taught at the New York Institute for the Blind in New York City. Fanny usually used her maiden name in her writing, though she apparently used more than two hundred pen names, among them variations of her married name: Fanny Van Alstyne, Mrs. Alexander Van Alstyne, Mrs. Van A. In her public appearances she was always introduced as Fanny Crosby.

VETERINARIAN BORROWS HYMN LINES FOR BOOK TITLES

All things bright and beautiful
All creatures great and small,
All things wise and wonderful,
The Lord God made them all.

An Irish woman's imaginative mind and her sincere love for children produced this hymn. Cecil Frances Alexander wrote these lines in 1848 to illustrate for children the opening sentence of the Apostles' Creed, "I believe in God, the Father Almighty, maker of heaven and earth."

All the aspects of nature that she mentions were well-known to the Irish children who first sang this joyful song. She refers to flowers, birds, mountains, rivers, sunsets, sunrises, winter wind, summer sun, and garden fruit as things God has made. Her concluding stanza reminds us:

He gave us eyes to see them,
And lips that we might tell
How great is God Almighty,
Who has made all things well.

Recently the opening lines of the hymn have become familiar to people who have never sung it. An English veterinarian, J. A. Wight, writing under the pen name James Herriot, has published four books, each using as a title a single line of Mrs. Alexander's opening stanza.

When he was searching for a title for his first book, published in 1972, his young daughter suggested *Ill Creatures Great and Small*. She was familiar with the hymn and also her father's practice of treating animals that were ill. Wight thought the play on the word "all" was very clear. His New York publisher, however, thought it "unnecessarily flippant" and decided the line should be used in its original form.

The second book, *All Things Bright and Beautiful,* followed in 1974; the third, *All Things Wise and Wonderful,* in 1977; and the fourth, *The Lord God Made Them All,* in 1981. All made the best-seller lists and have been very popular.

Mrs. Alexander wrote many hymns for children but never in a childish or condescending style. The high quality of her writing is evident in her *Hymns for Little Children,* published in 1848, in which this hymn first appeared.

Her husband, the Reverend William Alexander, became a distinguished clergyman in the Church of Ireland and was appointed Bishop of Ireland in 1867. Though she shared the prominence and lifestyle of her husband's position, Mrs. Alexander devoted much time to charitable work among the poor and ill. She was as much at home on the back streets of Londonderry as she was in the bishop's residence.

The suggestion of a veterinarian's daughter in the English village of Thirsk has brought new and extraordinary significance to an Irish woman's hymn.

ALLELUIA MEANS PRAISE YE THE LORD

Alleluia! Alleluia!
*   Hearts to heaven and voices raise;*
Sing to God a hymn of gladness,
*   Sing to God a hymn of praise.*
He who on the cross as Savior
*   For the world's salvation bled,*
Jesus Christ, the King of Glory,
*   Now is risen from the dead.*

Alleluia is an exciting word in Christian vocabulary. It has especially been associated with the celebration of the resurrection of Christ. Among the early Christians, it was an oft-repeated greeting. "Christ is risen!" one would say to another, and the reply would be "Alleluia!"

The word means "Praise Jehovah" or "Praise ye the Lord." "Alleluia" (or the Hebrew "hallelujah") is a common word in many languages. George F. Handel's chorus "Hallelujah," from his *Messiah,* uses the word forty-five times. The word is often found in our hymnals, and one of the interesting uses is in a hymn by Christopher Wordsworth, written during or before 1872. A double "alleluia" graces the first line of the hymn and also the seventh line of the final stanza.

An Anglican minister, Christopher Wordsworth served for eight years as headmaster of Harrow School, a school for boys near London, whose illustrious graduates include Robert Peel, Lord Byron, and Winston Churchill. When Wordsworth became headmaster of Harrow, discipline was almost nonexistent. His strict and inflexible methods failed to correct these problems, and in 1844 he was given other responsibilities.

In 1850 he was assigned to a quiet parish in a small village called Stanford-in-the-Vale-cum-Goosey, where he served for nineteen years. Encouraged earlier by his uncle, poet William Wordsworth, he had discovered his poetic skills and written extensively. All of his 127 poems were written during these years, including "Alleluia! Alleluia!" based on 1 Corinthians 15:20, "But now is Christ risen from the dead, and become the firstfruits of them that slept."

The hymn is usually sung to "Hymn to Joy," a singable tune adapted from the final movement of Beethoven's *Ninth Symphony,* composed during the years 1817–23.

A HYMN ENTITLED
"HOLY FORTITUDE"

Am I a soldier of the cross,
A follower of the Lamb,
And shall I fear to own his cause,
Or blush to speak his name?

Isaac Watts was born in 1674 to parents who were Dissenters, people whose religious affiliation was outside the Church of England, the state church. His father, a deacon at the Above Bar Congregational Church in Southampton, was arrested several times and imprisoned in St. Michael's prison. When Isaac was an infant, his mother would sit on a stone opposite the jail and nurse her baby while visiting her husband.

Dissenters (such as Congregationalists, Presbyterians, Baptists, and Quakers) often experienced persecution in the seventeenth century. The Act of Uniformity in 1662 expelled all dissenting clergy from their pulpits. In 1664 another law forbade religious meetings not in accordance with the state church. In 1667 a law forbade dissenting clergymen from coming closer than five miles to places where they had preached.

The Toleration Act of 1689 granted freedom of worship for Dissenters. Isaac, at fifteen, was old enough to know what religious freedom meant. When he was twenty-five years old, Isaac became assistant pastor of the Mark Lane Independent Chapel, London, and three years later became its pastor.

As he prepared his weekly sermon, Isaac Watts would frequently write a hymn for the congregation to sing at the conclusion of the service. In Watts's collected sermons, the hymn "Am I a Soldier of the Cross" appears following a sermon on "Holy Fortitude" based on 1 Corinthians 16:13: "Stand fast in the faith, quit you like men, be strong."

Watts lived to see Dissenters tolerated in England, and Congregationalists, of which he was one, respected in English life. But the memories of the persecution his family and friends had known in his childhood lingered in his mind.

A SLAVE CAPTAIN WRITES OF GOD'S AMAZING GRACE

Amazing grace! how sweet the sound,
That saved a wretch like me!
I once was lost, but now am found,
Was blind, but now I see.

John Newton, an obscure minister in the Church of England, wrote this simple, unsophisticated hymn for the working people of Olney, a small village in the county of Buckinghamshire, where he served. His congregation consisted largely of lacemakers in the community where the world-famous Buckinghamshire bobbin lace was made.

Though Newton wrote it when he was in his early fifties, the hymn reflects the fascinating story of his life. His mother died when he was six, he went to sea with his sailor father when he was eleven, and he was in the British Royal Navy on a man-of-war when he was seventeen.

Abandoning his early religious training, he became an aggressive atheist and delighted in shocking people with his profanity. First a sailor on a slave ship, he later became a ship's captain engaged in transporting slaves from Africa to ports where they could be sold for the best prices.

Throughout his early turbulent life, the memory of his mother and his love for Mary Catlett, later his wife, served as strong and continuing influences. On a stormy night on a waterlogged ship in 1748, as he faced imminent death, Newton had an extraordinary and genuine spiritual experience. Six years later he abandoned the sea and became the tide surveyor in Liverpool. He was responsible for checking all ships that entered the harbor for contraband goods.

While John and Mary Newton were living in Liverpool, John developed a deeper interest in spiritual matters and felt the Lord's call to the ministry. Because of his lack of university training the bishops of the Church of England were unwilling to ordain him. Only the intervention of an influential patron secured for him his ordination and appointment to the parish church at Olney when he was forty years of age. Seventeen years later he went to London as minister of St. Mary Woolnoth Church, which was located in the heart of London's banking district. He remained there for twenty-seven years.

Never did he lose his bluff sailor ways, but his genial manner and straightforward preaching won him many friends and endeared him to the people to whom he ministered. Newton preached almost to the end of his eighty-two years. When he was no longer able to read and was advised by his friends to give up preaching, he replied, "What, shall the old African blasphemer stop while he can still speak!" Today his words about God's amazing grace are sung around the world.

ADORATION OF
THE NEWBORN KING

Angels from the realms of glory,
Wing your flight o'er all the earth;

Ye who sang creation's story,
  Now proclaim Messiah's birth:
  Come and worship,
  Worship Christ, the newborn King!

James Montgomery was the son of Moravian missionaries. Although associated with the Wesleyans for a while, he became a communicant of the Church of England in his later years. A man of genuine integrity and devotion, he possessed extraordinary writing ability, which he applied to producing more than 360 hymns. None has been more widely used than this one about the birth of Jesus, first published in *The Iris,* on Christmas Eve, 1816. This newspaper, published in Sheffield, England, was edited by Montgomery.

The central focus of the hymn is the worship and adoration of Christ. It is addressed to those who witnessed the nativity and whose lives were touched by this event. The first stanza invites the angels who sang at the creation of the world "to proclaim Messiah's birth." The invitation to "come and worship . . . Christ, the newborn King" is extended to the shepherds in stanza two, and to the sages (wise men) in stanza three. The word "saints" in stanza four refers to Simeon and Anna, who saw the child Jesus in the temple (Luke 2:22–39).

Most frequently this Christmas hymn is sung to the tune "Regent Square," composed by Henry Smart in 1867. The tune was named for the Regent Square Presbyterian Church, known then as the "cathedral of Presbyterianism in London." Largely self-taught in music, Smart became one of the finest organists of his day. Troubled with poor eyesight for many years, he became totally blind about 1865, but his memory and skill enabled him to continue playing and composing.

JOIN THE HEAVENLY HOST

Angels we have heard on high,
  Sweetly singing o'er the plains:
  And the mountains in reply,
  Echoing their joyous strains.
  Gloria in excelsis Deo!

Although many of our Christmas carols originated in England, English translations of carols from other countries have greatly enriched our Christmastime singing. Finland gave us "Unto Us a Boy Is Born"; Germany, "Silent Night, Holy Night"; Poland, "Infant Holy, Infant Lowly"; Czechoslovakia, "Little Jesus, Sweetly Sleep"; and other countries, many more.

One of the best-known French carols is "Angels We Have Heard on High." Some believe it dates from the eighteenth century, but the earliest documented appearance is in an 1855 French collection of Christmas songs. Numerous English versions have appeared with this tune, but all evidently stem from the same source. Some of the more familiar are "Bright Angels We Have Heard on High," "Hearken All! What Holy Singing," and "Shepherds in the Fields Abiding."

The tune is characteristic of many French carol melodies. With two exceptions in the refrain, the melody stays within the range of six tones of the scale. The melodic phrases of the stanzas are almost monotonous, but this is offset by the childlike mirth and unsophisticated grace of the refrain. The sequential "gloria," an expression of sheer joy and delight, stretches over four measures twice in the refrain. The sonority of the "o" vowel in the first syllable of the word heightens the beauty of the sound. The part-singing in the refrain is great fun.

A HYMN OF THE MAGI

> As with gladness men of old
> Did the guiding star behold;
> As with joy they hailed its light,
> Leading onward, beaming bright;
> So, most gracious Lord, may we
> Evermore be led to thee.

Epiphany commemorates the first manifestation of Jesus Christ to the Gentiles. "There came wise men from the east to Jerusalem, saying, 'Where is he that is born King of the Jews? For we have seen his star in the east and are come to worship him'" (Matt. 2:1–2). Other than that they were "from the east," there is no specific information as to the wise men's origins. No other gospel writer mentions them.

In the Latin version of Matthew's gospel, the original word *magi* refers to Persian astrologers. Later, this meaning broadened to include men of great wisdom—teachers, philosophers, doctors. In the second century Tertullian, one of the greatest of the early Christian writers at Rome, helped the "magi" to become "kings" by pointing out that these men were the fulfillment of the Old Testament prophecy that kings bearing gifts would come to Israel (Isa. 60:3).

Slowly across the years we have come to accept the legend that there were three wise men, each with a name and personality. Melchior was an old man; Balthazar, a middle-aged man from Ethiopia; and Caspar, a young man. On Epiphany Sunday in 1858, William Chatterton Dix, twenty-one years old, was at home recovering from a serious illness. Reading the Bible passage for the day, Matthew 2:1–12, inspired him to write the hymn.

The manger and the manger bed mentioned by Dix in two stanzas have brought criticism of the hymn. Scripture does not say how old Jesus was when the wise men followed the star to Bethlehem. Matthew simply states that they came "into the house," and "saw the young child with Mary his mother." But this deviation from the scriptural account has not been a major problem, for congregations continue to sing that the wise men, these "men of old," came to the manger.

A HYMN OF JESUS CHRIST,
THE CRUCIFIED

Ask ye what great thing I know
That delights and stirs me so?
What the high reward I win?
Whose the name I glory in?
Jesus Christ, the crucified.

From 1701 until his death in 1730, Johann Schwedler was pastor at Niederwiese, a city about fifty miles northeast of Berlin, in what is now East Germany. A powerful preacher, he was especially effective in prayer. His Sunday church services lasted from six in the morning until two or three in the afternoon. Relays of people came from far and near to hear his messages. God's grace through Jesus Christ was the major theme of his sermons and hymns. Of his more than five hundred hymns, one alone remains in our hymnals.

While he served as headmaster at England's Shrewsbury School, Benjamin Kennedy published a collection of 1,500 hymns for Anglican services in 1863. He included his own translation of Schwedler's German hymn that had appeared more than a century earlier. The dialogue structure of the hymn is obvious with the questions in each stanza answered with the resounding "Jesus Christ, the crucified." The final stanza is an affirmation for the singer, "faith in him who died to save."

"Hendon," named for a suburb of London, is the tune usually associated with this hymn. It was composed about 1827 by Henri Malan, who lived in Geneva, Switzerland. An extraordinary man, Malan wrote many hymns, both words and tunes. Skilled as a blacksmith, carpenter, and mechanic, he was also a gifted artist. Malan was ordained in the National Church of Geneva but lost his appointment because of an unorthodox sermon he had preached. Then, in his own garden, he built a chapel and preached there for forty-three years. As a fervent evangelist, his visits to France, Belgium, Scotland, and England made him well-known in those countries.

A HYMN WRITTEN FOR THE SICK AND LONELY

At the name of Jesus
Every knee shall bow,
Every tongue confess him
King of glory now;
'Tis the Father's pleasure
We should call him Lord,
Who from the beginning
Was the mighty Word.

Women hymnwriters have added a rich dimension to the songs we sing. Their hymns frequently reflect a spirit of sensitivity and understanding not always found in masculine writing. Charlotte Elliott, who wrote "Just As I Am, Without One Plea"; Sarah Adams, "Nearer My God to Thee"; Cecil Frances Alexander, "All Things Bright and Beautiful"; Elizabeth Clephane, "Beneath the Cross of Jesus"; Katherine Hankey, "I Love to Tell the Story"; and Fanny Crosby, "To God Be the Glory," stand tall in this company of female writers.

A lesser known writer is Caroline Noel, daughter of an Anglican clergyman. Born in 1817, she was reared in London and was well educated. In her late teens she displayed a gift of poetic expression and wrote a dozen poems. Other interests claimed her attention, however, and it was not until the age of forty that she was inspired to resume writing. By this time she had been an invalid for five years, but in her suffering her faith burned brightly. Through her writings she sought to encourage and comfort others similarly afflicted.

"At the Name of Jesus," written in 1870, was included in her collection of poems entitled *The Name of Jesus, and Other Verses for the Sick and Lonely*. The hymn is based on Philippians 2:5–11. The four stanzas provide a magnificent description of Jesus—his presence at creation, his coming into the world in human flesh, his suffering and death, his resurrection and ascension, his desire that our lives be submissive to his will, and the certainty of his return.

WOODBINE WILLIE'S HYMN

Awake, awake to love and work,
The lark is in the sky,
The fields are wet with diamond dew,
The worlds awake to cry
Their blessings on the Lord of life,
As he goes meekly by.

In the bitter cold of December 1915, a new British chaplain landed in France to minister to the British troops. Geoffrey A. Studdert Kennedy, ordained in the Church of England seven years earlier, had served two churches. Now he was in the midst of the war. He preached and ministered to the soldiers, comforted the wounded on the battlefield, and conducted burial services for the dead. To parents, wives, and children back home, he wrote comforting letters.

He was at home among the soldiers, who nicknamed him "Woodbine Willie" for his practice of passing out free copies of the New Testament and packets of Woodbines, an English brand of cigarette. His unselfish service, his thoughtful ministry to military personnel, and reckless courage in rescuing wounded men in the midst of battle won for him the British Military Cross. Of all the British chaplains in World War I, Studdert Kennedy was the most dearly loved and best known.

After the war he was appointed chaplain to the king. His eloquent preaching brought him fame in both England and America. His persuasive manner and creative style were unique, and he had many opportunities to preach on both sides of the Atlantic Ocean. In a small book of poems that he published in 1921 was a poem of six stanzas entitled "At a Harvest Festival." The last three verses have been made into a hymn beginning "Awake, awake to love and work."

Studdert Kennedy's concern that the gospel speak to people's social as well as spiritual needs kept him writing and speaking on this subject. In the closing years of his life, he chafed at the world's continued indifference to Christ and to humankind's needs. Perhaps his best-known poem most eloquently expresses his feelings, making reference to the city of Birmingham in his native England:

> *When Jesus came to Birmingham they*
> *simply passed him by,*
> *They never hurt a hair of him, they*
> *simply let him die.*

A HYMN ERRONEOUSLY CREDITED TO MARTIN LUTHER

Away in a manger, no crib for a bed,
The little Lord Jesus laid down his sweet head;

The stars in the sky looked down where he lay,
The little Lord Jesus asleep on the hay.

Whether accidentally or intentionally, James R. Murray almost succeeded in crediting this carol to Martin Luther. For almost sixty years from its first appearance in 1887, and for forty years after Murray's death, the association of Martin Luther with this carol was commonly accepted.

It seems that Murray found these stanzas in a Lutheran collection published in 1885 in Philadelphia. He wrote a new tune for them and included it in a collection of songs two years later with his initials "J.R.M." He added the inscription "Luther's Cradle Hymn, composed by Martin Luther for his children and still sung by German mothers to their little ones."

For decades, every subsequent collection of Christmas carols included both words and music with the heading "Luther's Cradle Hymn." No one ever questioned the validity of the title and inscription, and the song became immensely popular. Somewhere along the line an editor credited the tune to "Carl Mueller," an unknown composer. Again innocent compilers copied the error, and Carl Mueller became another facet of the growing legend. With the passing years the association of the carol with Martin Luther became more deeply etched in the lore of the Christmas season.

In the early 1940s, an American musician, Richard S. Hill, became curious about the song's origin. His persistent probing revealed that the words of the carol were of American origin and the author was unknown. The music was composed by James R. Murray, who died in 1905. The carol was unknown in Germany until someone made a German translation of the American carol, and then German mothers could sing it "to their little ones."

For sheer beauty and childlike simplicity the carol claims special attention. It is a gentle lullaby, tender and warm, especially loved by children; and when adults of any age sing it, they become children again.

A HUSBAND-WIFE COLLABORATION

Be not dismayed whate'er betide,
God will take care of you;

Beneath his wings of love abide,
God will take care of you.

A minister and his wife were in Lestershire, New York, for a few weeks teaching at the Practical Bible Training School. During these weeks the minister, W. Stillman Martin, received many invitations to preach in churches of that area. Usually his wife, Civilla, accompanied him, but not on a particular Sunday. She was ill and remained at home. In the quietness of the lonely day, Mrs. Martin found inspiration and strength in writing a hymn. She wrote of the assurance of God's care and providence to the Christian in times of adversity. In her hymn is the repeated affirmation that God will provide sustenance "through days of toil when heart doth fail," when "dangers fierce your path assail," and "no matter what may be the test."

When her husband returned from the preaching appointment, she showed him the poem she had written in his absence. Immediately he sat down at a small reed organ and composed the tune as it now stands. The hymn was published in 1905 in a collection compiled by John A. Davis, popular evangelist and founder of the Practical Bible Training School.

W. Stillman Martin, a native of Massachusetts, was educated at Harvard University. He was ordained to the Baptist ministry and began his evangelistic work among Baptist churches. After a few years, however, he joined the Christian Church (Disciples of Christ).

In 1916 Dr. and Mrs. Martin moved to Wilson, North Carolina, where he became professor of Bible at Atlantic Christian College. Three years later they moved to Atlanta, Georgia, and spent the following years conducting Bible conferences and evangelistic meetings throughout many states.

Civilla Martin collaborated with her husband in writing many gospel songs. She also wrote texts for other composers. One well-known song which bears her name is "His Eye Is On the Sparrow."

THE LILTING RHYTHM OF ANCIENT IRISH PHRASES

Be thou my vision, O Lord of my heart;
Naught be all else to me, save that thou art:

Thou my best thought, by day or by night,
Waking or sleeping, thy presence my light.

This hymn is as Irish as the family names of O'Driscoll, O'Sullivan, O'Reilly, Murphy, McGrath, O'Donahue, and O'Shea. It comes from the land where the grass grows green on the hillside and the peat smoke hangs low in the valley. In these lines there is a hint of the soft, sometimes throaty sound of Gaelic speech, with its lilting rhythm of expressive ancient Irish phrases.

The ancient Irish poem on which the hymn is based probably dates from the eighth century. Mary Byrne translated these lines from the Gaelic into English prose in 1905. Seven years later Eleanor Henrietta Hull, noted Irish author and researcher, made the poetic version, "Be Thou My Vision."

Wedded to the Irish text is a traditional Irish melody known as "Slane." A lilting, singable tune, it has a rather wide range. Each musical phrase is different, but the appropriateness for the text is obvious.

Slane is a hill some ten miles from Tara in County Meath in Ireland. King Loigaire, in the fifth century, sent out word that no one should light the paschal fire on Easter eve until he had kindled the fire on Tara's hill signaling the return of spring. Either intentionally or accidentally, Patrick, Ireland's patron saint, lit the paschal fire at Slane first. Patrick's challenge to the king was successful, and he was permitted to preach throughout Ireland. Because of this, one of the many legends surrounding Patrick credits him with the establishment of Christianity in Ireland.

A SHERIFF'S DAUGHTER WRITES A HYMN

Beneath the cross of Jesus
I fain would take my stand,
The shadow of a mighty rock
Within a weary land;
A home within the wilderness,
A rest upon the way,

From the burning of the noontide heat
And the burden of the day.

Elizabeth Clephane, daughter of the sheriff of Fife County in Scotland, is the author of the hymn. She was born in Edinburgh in 1830, and after her father's death she lived the rest of her life in the village of Melrose, about thirty miles southeast of Edinburgh. Her radiant personality and her concern and love for the poor earned for her the nickname "Sunbeam of Melrose." In spite of ill health, which she experienced most of her life, she devoted her energies and most of her money to humanitarian causes. She and her sister even sold their horses and carriages to give more to the poor.

Clephane wrote eight hymns. After her death in 1869 they were published in *The Family Treasury*, a monthly magazine popular in Scottish homes at that time. One of her hymns, "The Ninety and Nine," became popular during the revivals of Moody and Sankey in Great Britain during the period of 1873–74.

The tune we sing with "Beneath the Cross of Jesus" was written for these words by Frederick Maker in 1881. A college music teacher and church organist, Maker was loved and respected in Bristol, England, where he lived his life.

Maker gave no explanation for naming the tune "St. Christopher," the name of the patron saint of travelers who lived in the third century. Many legends have been passed along which describe Christopher as a giant, who after his conversion to Christianity, spent the rest of his life carrying travelers across a river. One of the legends tells of a small child who asked to be carried across. In the middle of the river the child became so heavy that Christopher staggered and said, "Child, you seem to weigh as much as the world." The child replied, "I created the world, bore the sins of the world, and redeemed the world." The allegory of this legend has been pictured in Christian art with Christopher (which means "Christ-bearing") bearing the Christ child on his back.

A JOYFUL HYMN OF ASSURANCE

Blessed assurance, Jesus is mine!
O what a foretaste of glory divine!

Heir of salvation, purchase of God,
Born of his spirit, washed in his blood.
This is my story, this is my song,
Praising my Savior all the day long.

Fanny Crosby was visiting in the home of her good friend Phoebe Knapp one afternoon in 1873. Phoebe shared with her a new melody she had written and asked, "Fanny, what does that melody say to you?"

Without a moment's hesitation, Fanny replied, "Blessed assurance, Jesus is mine!" Fanny Crosby's poetic mind quickly pursued this thought and soon the three stanzas and refrain were completed.

Blind from birth, Fanny was a prolific poet. Her total output of gospel song texts numbered more than 8,000. In spite of her blindness she lived a vigorous life. She died in 1915, at the age of ninety-five. She had learned to read braille at an early age, but callouses on her fingertips from playing the harp and guitar made braille reading difficult.

Many distinguished leaders on the national scene were her friends. Grover Cleveland, as a young man, worked as a bookkeeper at the New York Institute for the Blind where Fanny Crosby taught. They remained good friends in later years.

She was a frequent visitor to the nation's Capitol. When she read a poem to the United States Senate in session, having been invited to do so, hers was the first woman's voice to be heard publicly in the Senate chamber.

Phoebe Knapp, the daughter of Methodist evangelist Walter Palmer, married Joseph Fairchild Knapp at age sixteen. Knapp, a successful business and political leader, founded the Metropolitan Life Insurance Company. Mrs. Knapp was a talented musician, composer, and singer. She entertained graciously in her elegant apartment in New York City's Hotel Savoy, in which was a large pipe organ.

A HYMN WRITTEN IN THE VILLAGE OF FAIRFORD

Blest are the pure in heart,
For they shall see our God;

The secret of the Lord is theirs,
Their soul is Christ's abode.

John Keble, a young Anglican minister, is the author of the hymn. A high-ranking scholar at Oxford University, he possessed unusual poetic gifts. In 1823, following the death of his mother, Keble returned home to assist his father, vicar of the parish church at Fairford, a small village about twenty miles west of Oxford, England. Father and son shared a close relationship both personally and with regard to their church activities. The father's high ideals concerning the church and its liturgy made a lasting impression on his son.

While at Fairford, Keble wrote a large number of poems that he published in 1827 under the title *The Christian Year.* The subtitle, "Thoughts in Verse for the Sundays and Holy Days Throughout the Year," explains Keble's purpose. Poetic meditations were provided for Sundays, festivals, and special days (such as saints' days, Christmas, Holy Communion, Baptism, Confirmation, Matrimony, Burial).

Primarily designed as devotional material, Keble's poetic writing was marked by a simplicity of expression, a spirit of genuine piety, and a gentle, quiet faith. In the course of time, *The Christian Year* became a household book of sacred poetry. "Blest Are the Pure in Heart" is only one of a number of Keble's poems that became hymns. This was Keble's commentary on Matthew 5:8 and was written for the Feast of the Purification of the Blessed Virgin Mary.

In 1836 Keble was appointed vicar of Hursley, a small village near Winchester. The church building and vicarage were both in need of major restoration. Keble used the proceeds from *The Christian Year* for this work. Since ninety-six editions were published before Keble's death in 1866, the proceeds from the collection of poems made a substantial contribution to the village of Hursley.

A HYMN OF CHRISTIAN FELLOWSHIP

Blest be the tie that binds
Our hearts in Christian love;

The fellowship of kindred minds
Is like to that above.

For nine years, beginning in 1763, John Fawcett served as pastor of two small Baptist churches at Wainsgate and Hebden Bridge, near Halifax, in what is now West Yorkshire, England. In 1772, Fawcett was invited to preach in London in a large Baptist church as a prospective successor to the aged and ailing pastor, Dr. John Gill, who had ministered there for fifty-four years. Following Gill's death later that year, Fawcett was invited to succeed him, and after prayerful consideration, consented to do so. Some days later, however, even though he had already packed some of his possessions in anticipation of the move to London, he reconsidered his decision.

Fawcett decided to remain at Wainsgate and Hebden Bridge, even though his meager salary was inadequate for his growing family. He asked his small congregation of farmers and shepherds if they could raise his salary, but they declined. Fawcett pastored these two small churches for a total of fifty-four years.

A very dramatic story associates Fawcett's writing of "Blest Be the Tie That Binds" with this experience in the Yorkshire village more than two hundred years ago. The story may be true, but in his autobiography and other writings Fawcett makes no mention of this hymn or experience.

His effective ministry extended beyond his congregations. He established a boarding school, primarily to train young preachers. In 1782 he published a collection of hymns to which he contributed 166 original hymns, most of which were written to be sung at the conclusion of his sermons. "Blest Be the Tie That Binds" was one of these.

In 1788 he published "Essay on Anger," a favorite of King George III. The king offered to confer on Fawcett any benefit he desired, but this he graciously declined, saying that he loved his own people in Wainsgate and Hebden Bridge, and God had blest his ministry among them. Fawcett said he needed nothing that even a ruling monarch could supply.

THE YEAR OF JUBILEE

Blow ye the trumpet, blow!
The gladly solemn sound
Let all the nations know,
To earth's remotest bound.
The year of jubilee is come!
Return, ye ransomed sinners, home.

Charles Wesley wrote the hymn in 1750 as one of seven which appeared in a pamphlet entitled *Hymns for the New Year*. The year of jubilee, as described in Leviticus 25:8–17, was celebrated each fifty years—the year following seven sabbaticals. Israelites who were in bondage to any of their countrymen were set free. Ancestral possessions were returned to any who had been compelled through poverty to sell them. Other provisions for righting wrongs were provided in the law for this year. Using the year of jubilee as a backdrop, Wesley vividly pictures salvation through Christ as he joyfully sings

Jesus, our great High Priest
Hath full atonement made;
Ye weary spirits, rest;
Ye mournful souls, be glad:
The year of jubilee is come!
Return, ye ransomed sinners, home.

In the last two lines, repeated in each stanza, Wesley addresses individuals not as children of God, or believers, or Christians, but as sinners who have been ransomed by Jesus Christ.

Lewis Edson, a native of Massachusetts and a blacksmith by trade, conducted singing schools in Massachusetts, New York, and Connecticut after the Revolutionary War. His tune "Lenox," composed in 1782 and named for a Massachusetts village, became one of the most popular of the "fuguing tunes" that were so widely sung. Some of its vigor and vitality was lost when it was converted to a regular hymn tune by eliminating two measures and filling in the harmony of the parts, thus doing away with the imitation or delayed entrances of the voice parts, one of the basic characteristics of the fuguing tunes. But the tune has remained and its use with this text by Wesley has remained unchallenged for more than two centuries.

A HYMN SUNG AT LAKE CHAUTAUQUA

Break thou the bread of life,
Dear Lord, to me,
As thou didst break the loaves
Beside the sea;
Beyond the sacred page
I seek thee, Lord;
My spirit pants for thee,
O living Word.

Mary Lathbury wrote the hymn in the summer of 1877 at the request of John H. Vincent, founder of the Chatauqua Assembly. Originally a Methodist camp meeting site, this charming setting among the rolling hills along the shore of Lake Chautauqua in western New York provides a beautiful location for spiritual renewal and Bible study. Begun in 1874, Chautauqua was intended for the study of the Bible and Sunday school materials and methods. In passing years it enlarged to encompass a wider field of adult education, including music and drama. Many of America's finest teachers, lecturers, musicians, performers, artists, and dramatists have appeared at Chautauqua.

The daughter of a Methodist preacher, Mary Lathbury became a professional artist. She wrote excellent prose and poetry for children and young people and served as editor of publications for these age groups for the Methodist Sunday School Union. Each summer she assisted with the work of the Chautauqua Assembly. Vincent suggested that she write a study hymn for the Chautauqua Literary and Scientific Circle.

She wrote two stanzas based on the biblical account of Christ's feeding of the multitude as recorded in Matthew 14:13–21. Some hymnals include two additional stanzas written by Alexander Groves more than twenty-five years later. Appropriately, his stanzas maintain the spirit and the theme of Lathbury's stanzas.

The music indelibly associated with Lathbury's words was composed in 1877 by William F. Sherwin, distinguished music educator who served as music director for Chautauqua. He served on the faculty at the New England Conservatory of Music in Boston. He was respected for his extraordinary ability in organizing and directing amateur choruses.

A HYMN WRITTEN BY AN OXFORD DON

Breathe on me, breath of God,
Fill me with life anew,
That I may love what thou dost love,
And do what thou wouldst do.

On the evening of the day of Jesus' resurrection, as John 20:21 relates, Jesus appeared to his disciples and said, "Peace be unto you: as my Father hath sent me, even so send I you." John, a witness to this scene, then says, "When he had said this, he breathed on them, and saith unto them, 'Receive ye the Holy Ghost'" (v. 22). This is the basis of Edwin Hatch's hymn, written in 1878. The hymn also contains a reminder of Genesis 2:7, "And the Lord God formed man of the dust of the ground, and breathed into his nostrils the breath of life; and man became a living soul." Michelangelo, in his painting "The Creation of Adam" on the ceiling of the Sistine Chapel in Rome, suggests this same theme as the spirit of God was transmitted from the finger of God to the finger of man.

Edwin Hatch, a distinguished scholar, historian, and teacher, wrote the hymn while he was vice-principal of St. Mary's Hall, one of the colleges of Oxford University. A man of high character, Hatch possessed a creative mind. In spite of his profound scholarship, his Christian faith was lived each day with sincerity and devotion. He was aware of God's handiwork all about him, and his writings were simple and unaffected. Only this one of his several hymns survives in today's hymnals.

The music most frequently found with this hymn was

composed by Robert Jackson in 1888 and bears the name "Trentham" for a small village in Staffordshire, England. In 1868 Jackson succeeded his father as organist at St. Peter's Church, Oldham, England, a position his father had held for forty-eight years. He remained there until his death in 1914, serving for forty-six years. The tenure of service of father and son at St. Peter's Church, covering almost a century, seems to be an unequaled record in the annals of church music.

HOMER RODEHEAVER'S THEME SONG

Brighten the corner where you are!
Brighten the corner where you are!
Someone far from harbor you may guide across the bar,
Brighten the corner where you are!

The most popular gospel song of the first half of the twentieth century was written by Ina Duley Ogdon, who lived in Toledo, Ohio. She was a gifted speaker and dreamed of being a lecturer on the Chautauqua circuit. Her dreams were changed in 1912 when her father suffered a severe stroke. Along with her husband and an eleven-year-old son, she spent her days in providing loving, tender care for her father. She accepted these responsibilities with a gracious spirit, and out of the circumstances she wrote "Brighten the Corner Where You Are." The first stanza begins:

Do not wait until some deed of greatness you may do,
Do not wait to shed your light afar,
To the many duties ever near you now be true,
Brighten the corner where you are.

She no longer dreamed of Chautauqua glory, but was daily involved in dishwashing, dusting, sweeping, doing the laundry, and other household work. She sent her manuscript to Charles H. Gabriel, who completed the music and sent the song to a young evangelistic singer who had just become associated with the popular evangelist Billy Sunday.

In the large tabernacles where Sunday preached, Homer Rodeheaver was a masterful song leader, using old familiar hymns and interspersing them with new gospel songs. "Brighten the Corner" was first introduced in a crusade in Wilkes-Barre, Pennsylvania, in 1913. Rodeheaver used it in every service, and the singable, catchy tune spread like wildfire. By 1916 it had become so well known that Theodore Roosevelt used it to begin each of his political rallies across the nation. The United States armed forces sang the song in the trenches in France during World War I. In China in 1925, the Nanking baseball team chose "Brighten the Corner" as their official team song and it was sung before every game. During World War II, the United States forces invaded Tarawa Atoll in the southwest Pacific on November 20, 1943. All the Japanese soldiers there were killed, and the natives who had gone into hiding during the battle rejoiced over the United States victory. Some of the smiling natives greeted the conquering heroes with singing "Brighten the Corner," which they had learned from the missionaries decades before.

Mrs. Ogdon died in Toledo in 1964 at the age of ninety-two. Instead of speaking to thousands via Chautauqua, she touched millions through the words she wrote for this song. How strange that this song that reached such a pinnacle of popularity during the 1920s and 1930s should have diminished by the 1940s and 1950s. Today it is rarely found in the hymnals used in American churches. Word Music, Inc., which owned the copyright for the song, failed to include it in their *Hymnal for Worship and Celebration* published in 1986.

IN THE LANGUAGE OF THE SEAFARERS

Brightly beams our Father's mercy
From his lighthouse evermore;
But to us he gives the keeping
Of the lights along the shore.
Let the lower lights be burning!
Send a gleam across the wave!

Some poor fainting, struggling seaman
You may rescue, you may save.

Those who live by the sea or a large body of water understand better than the rest of us some of the biblical accounts that involve the Sea of Galilee or the Mediterranean Sea. Those who have had firsthand experiences on a ship or boat sing with more understanding the hymns that speak of the Christian experience in nautical terms.

Dwight L. Moody, noted nineteenth-century evangelist, told in a sermon the story of a ship nearing the Lake Erie harbor at Cleveland. It was a stormy night and the waves were high. Seeing only the light from the lighthouse, the captain asked the pilot, "Are you sure this is Cleveland?" "Quite sure," replied the pilot. "But," said the captain, "where are the lower lights—the lights along the shore?" The pilot replied calmly, "They've gone out, sir." He assured the captain that they could make the harbor and turned the wheel, but in the darkness he missed the channel and crashed upon the rocks. Many lives were lost. Moody concluded his sermon with the comment, "Beloved, the Master will take care of the great lighthouse; let us keep the lower lights burning."

Philip P. Bliss, a well-known music teacher, songwriter, and Christian leader, listened intently to Moody's sermon. Following the service, Bliss wrote both words and music of "Let the Lower Lights Be Burning." The hymn was published in a small collection in 1871, intended for Sunday school use. Bliss's hymn became exceedingly popular, even in those inland areas where "lower lights along the shore" had little meaning. Many older people fondly remember the hymn from earlier years, but its use seems to be declining in our church services.

A DANISH PASTOR WRITES A HYMN

Built on the Rock the church doth stand,
Even when steeples are falling;
Crumbled have spires in every land,
Bells still are chiming and calling;
Calling the young and old to rest,

Calling the souls of men distressed,
Longing for life everlasting.

Long a favorite hymn among Christians of Denmark, Sweden, and Norway, "Built on the Rock the Church Doth Stand," by Nicolai Grundtvig, has been increasingly accepted in the United States in recent decades. Educated at the University of Copenhagen, Grundtvig started out studying for the ministry in the Evangelical Lutheran Church of Denmark. But during his senior year he came under the influence of rationalistic theologians, and he graduated in 1803, as he later stated, "without spirit and without faith."

In a few years he went through a deep period of soul-searching, seeking to rediscover his faith. His spiritual awakening brought new understandings. He was ordained in 1811 and became his father's associate at Udby, Denmark. During the decade that followed, his criticism of rationalist tendencies in the Danish church kept him from being given his own parish but also brought him a following of those who shared his beliefs. His popularity grew because of a hymnal he published in 1837, which included his hymn "Kirken den er et gammelt Hus" (literally, "Church it is an old house").

His concern for raising the intellectual level of the Danish people led Grundtvig to stress the need for a thorough understanding of the Danish language and the teaching of national and biblical history through narrative and song. After 1844 these principles led him to establish residential folk high schools (folke høyskole) in which youth of every class were urged to grow and develop in their understanding. Similar action followed in Sweden, Norway, and Finland, and Grundtvig was recognized as the "father of folk high schools in Scandinavia." His political ideas involved him in the introduction of parliamentary government in Denmark in 1849, and he served as a member of the constitutional assembly.

Ludvig Lindeman, a Norwegian composer, wrote the tune we use for Grundtvig's hymn three years after the appearance of the text. It was first published in Oslo, Norway, in 1840. Christian music has been greatly enriched by this text and tune from Scandinavia. This great hymn of the church deserves to be sung with great vigor and vitality.

A GAELIC SONG

Child in the manger,
Infant of Mary;
Outcast and stranger,
Lord of all;
Child who inherits
All our transgressions,
All our demerits
On him fall.

The Scottish Gaelic language seems to date from the sixth century and developed into a distinct dialect in the thirteenth century. Today people along the northwest coast of Scotland and in the Hebrides Islands speak this distinctive language.

Mary Macdougall Macdonald wrote a Gaelic poem "The Child of Agh" (meaning child of happiness, good fortune, power, or wonder). She was born in 1789 near the village of Bunessan on the Isle of Mull, one of the Inner Hebrides islands. Her father and brother were Baptist ministers in Mull. With her husband, Neill Macdonald, she lived in the village of Cancan, where he was a crofter (a small land holder) who supplemented the produce of their small plot of land by fishing. Mary Macdonald composed Gaelic songs and hymns of genuine beauty. She had no English education but was well versed in the Scriptures. Her neighbors were familiar with her joyful singing as she worked at her spinning wheel. She was deeply religious and a member of the Baptist Church. She died on the Isle of Mull at the age of eighty-three.

Lachlan Macbean, editor of *The Fifeshire Advertiser* in Kirkcaldy, Scotland, was an authority on Gaelic language and literature. He discovered Mary Macdonald's Gaelic poem and translated it into English to fit the Gaelic tune that had been written down from the singing of a wandering singer in the Highlands of Scotland. Macbean included his translation with the tune named "Bunessan" in his *Songs and Hymns of the Gael,* published in Edinburgh in 1888.

A SWEDISH HYMN

Children of the heavenly Father,
Safely in his bosom gather;
Nestling bird nor star in heaven
Such a refuge e'er was given.

A young Swedish woman wrote the hymn in 1858, when she was twenty-six years old, after she witnessed the tragic death of her father (he fell over the rail of a ship on Lake Vattern and drowned.). Her father had been a pastor of the Lutheran church in Foderyd, Smaland, Sweden, where Lina grew up. An early advocate of the evangelical movement in Sweden, he had provided strong leadership for his congregation.

Lina Sandell's spiritual life deepened as a result of this tragic experience, and though she had written several hymns prior to this, her writing greatly increased. "Children of the Heavenly Father" reflects simple, childlike faith in God and her awareness of the abiding presence of God in her life.

In 1861, following the death of her mother, Lina Sandell married Carl O. Berg, a successful businessman in Stockholm. She wrote more than 650 hymns, which she signed "L.S.," and which captured the spirit and expression of the spiritual revival that was spreading across Northern Europe at that time. A significant factor of this revival was the emergence of new gospel songs. Lina Sandell was the most prolific writer of these songs.

Oscar Ahnfelt, the leading musician and song leader of the evangelical movement, greatly encouraged Lina Sandell's writing and published many of her songs. Jenny Lind, the world-famous Swedish singer of that era, helped make her songs famous.

A HYMN OF THE EARLY CHURCH

Christ is made the sure foundation,
Christ the head and cornerstone,
Chosen of the Lord and precious,
Binding all the church in one;

Holy Zion's help forever,
And her confidence alone.

What we know of Christian songs in the early centuries of the Christian era is at best sketchy. But we know more about the early hymns of the Roman Catholic Church for two reasons. First, Latin was the language of the church, resulting in uniformity throughout the regions where the church existed. Second, the monasteries preserved the manuscripts of Latin hymns, some of which may be seen today in beautiful illuminated pages.

"Urbs beata Jerusalem," one of the Latin hymns preserved in manuscript, is of unknown origin and has been dated from the sixth to the eighth centuries. It is based on Ephesians 2:20, 1 Peter 2:5, and Revelation 21. "Christ Is Made the Sure Foundation" is a translation made by John Mason Neale in 1851, using the second division of the Latin hymn which began "Angularius fundamentum lapis Christus missus est." Neale was one of the many nineteenth century clergymen in the Church of England who were fascinated by Latin hymns. He was one of the most successful translators because of his great knowledge of Latin, his love for these early hymns, and his graphic English vocabulary.

"Regent Square" is the tune most frequently found with the hymn. Henry Smart composed it in 1877 and named it for Regent Square Presbyterian Church in London.

In addition to "Regent Square," Smart composed an equally famous tune, "Lancashire," indelibly associated with the hymn "Lead on, O King Eternal."

RETIRED TO HYMN WRITING

Christ is the world's Light, he and none other:
Born in our darkness, he became our Brother.
If we have seen him, we have seen the Father:
*Glory to God on high!**

About the time of his retirement from the Methodist ministry in 1969, Fred Pratt Green was invited to serve on a committee that was preparing a supplement for the *Methodist Hymn Book.* Though he had written a few poems and hymns, none were widely known. The committee urged him to write some hymns, specifically in some areas where hymns were lacking. This challenged him and at the age of sixty-six and facing retirement, he began a new career.

He began writing "Christ is the World's Light," using the suggestion of the committee that the text fit a specific tune, "Christe Sanctorum," a seventeenth-century French tune. The completed hymn fit the tune perfectly, and words and music greatly enhanced each other. An unusual feature of Green's hymn is that the final words of the first, second, and third lines of each stanza—"other," "brother," and "Father"—are the same. Also repeated is the final line of each stanza—"Glory to God on high!" It was apparent to those who first saw it that this was to be a significant hymn.

In a short time the hymn was used on several special occasions that gave it wide exposure. At Westminster Abbey it was sung at two special services, and it was sung by six combined choirs on BBC's popular television program *Songs of Praise.* Translated into French and German, it became known on the Continent. Erik Routley, the eminent hymnologist, wrote that this hymn is "perhaps the most immediately successful hymn of the recent wave of modern hymn writing in Britain."

Born in 1903 in the village of Roby, near Liverpool, England, Fred Pratt Green grew up in a Christian home. His father, who had a successful leather manufacturing business, was a devout Wesleyan Methodist. After he finished school, Fred worked for his father for four years. During this time, and while he was involved in the Claremont Road Wesleyan Church at Wallasey, Fred felt the call to the ministry. He completed his studies at Didsbury Theological College in Manchester in 1928 and became chaplain for Hunmanby Hall, a Methodist boarding school for girls. For the next four decades he served a number of Methodist churches, including the Dome Mission at Brighton, one of the largest congregations in England. He lives in retirement at Norwich, England.

IN PRAISE OF CHRIST

Christ is the world's true light,
Its captain of salvation,
The daystar clear and bright
Of every man and nation;
New life, new hope awakes
Where'er men own his sway:
Freedom her bondage breaks,
And night is turned to day.*

George W. Briggs wrote the hymn to be sung to the tune "Rinkart" by Johann Sebastian Bach. The hymn with that tune was published in *Songs of Praise* in London in 1931. Many hymnals have included Briggs's text since then, but not with Bach's tune. The tune most frequently found with this hymn today is "Darmstadt" by Ahasuerus Fritsch.

Briggs was educated at Emmanuel College, Cambridge, and was ordained in the Church of England. After serving as a chaplain in the Royal Navy, he held several distinctive appointments in the Church of England. From 1934 until his retirement in 1959, he was canon of Worcester Cathedral.

The hymns and prayers that he has written and published have been widely used. At the historic meeting of Franklin D. Roosevelt and Winston Churchill in the North Atlantic aboard HMS *Prince of Wales,* August 10, 1941, when the Atlantic Charter was developed, a prayer that Briggs had written for the occasion was read in the religious service.

Ahasuerus Fritsch composed the hymn tune "Darmstadt" in 1679. It was first published in a collection of tunes in Jena, a city in the southwestern section of what is now East Germany. He graduated from the University of Jena in 1661 and later became chancellor of the university. A prolific writer on antiquarian, legal, and sacred subjects, he wrote a number of hymns and composed several hymn tunes. The best-known harmonization of Fritsch's melody is the work of Bach, who used it in his Cantata No. 94.

*Words from *Enlarged Songs of Praise* by permission of Oxford University Press.

A SONG OF THE RESURRECTION

Christ the Lord is risen today,
    Alleluia!
Sons of men and angels say,
    Alleluia!
Raise your joys and triumphs high,
    Alleluia!
Sing, ye heavens, and earth, reply,
    Alleluia!

The celebration of the resurrection of Christ is a joyful experience for the Christian. On Easter Sunday church congregations are larger, hymn singing is stronger, choral singing is more enthusiastic, and preaching is more vibrant. No hymn is sung more frequently than this one.

The lines above capture the joy of the Lord's resurrection and the ecstasy and jubilance it brings to the believer. The repetition of "alleluia" following each line of each stanza heightens the excitement. Alleluia means "Praise the Lord." It occurs often in Old Testament psalms; in the New Testament it is only found four times in Revelation 19.

Charles Wesley wrote the hymn in eleven four-line stanzas. The "alleluias" were not in the original hymn. Today's hymnals usually group four of Wesley's original stanzas.

Wesley wrote this hymn in 1739, only a couple of years after he had returned to England from the American colony of Georgia. His brother John had been sent to be a chaplain to the colonists, and Charles was personal secretary to Governor James E. Oglethorpe.

Year after year, Charles Wesley's poetic skills greatly increased, and during his lifetime he wrote more than 6,500 hymns. He wrote with great ease and extraordinary facility on the slightest provocation—at home, at church, in the fields, on horseback, and while walking in the street. Of his rare talent, Robert McCutchan wrote: "Like Schubert with his melodic instinct, every thought that came into the mind of Charles Wesley seemed to shape itself in poetic form."

AT THE TRANSFIGURATION

Christ, upon the mountain peak
Stands alone in glory blazing;
Let us, if we dare to speak,
With the saints and angels praise him.
*Alleluia!**

The transfiguration of Jesus on a mountain near Caesarea Philippi is recorded in Mark 9:2–8, Matthew 17:1–8, and Luke 9:28–36. With Jesus were Peter, James, and John. In their midst on the mountaintop he was transfigured, "his raiment became shining, exceeding white as snow; so as no fuller on earth can white them" (Mark 9:3); "his face did shine as the sun, and his raiment was white as the light" (Matt. 17:2); and "the fashion of his countenance was altered, and his raiment was white and glistering" (Luke 9:29).

On the basis of this extraordinary New Testament incident, in 1962 Brian Wren wrote this hymn, which pictures Jesus as standing alone "in glory blazing." Wren does not mention the three disciples, but identifies Moses and Elijah, representatives of the Old Testament law and the prophets. As we sing the hymn, we have a strong sense of being there on the mountain peak, witnessing this significant event and joining in praising Christ.

This is God's beloved Son,
Law and Prophets fade before him,
First and last and only ONE.
Let creation now adore him—
Alleluia!

Wren completed this hymn during his student days at Mansfield College, Oxford. He shared it with Peter Cutts, a fellow student, and in a short time Cutts had composed a striking tune for the hymn and named it "Shillingford."

SINGING THE GLORY OF CHRIST

Christ, whose glory fills the skies,
Christ, the true, the only light,
Sun of Righteousness, arise,
Triumphant o'er the shades of night;
Dayspring from on high, be near;
Daystar, in my heart appear.

Charles Wesley, who wrote the hymn in 1740, uses three unusual terms in the first stanza that seem to have had great interest to him. All three are found in Scripture and are used as names for Christ. "Sun of Righteousness" occurs once, in Malachi 4:2, "But unto you that fear my name shall the Sun of Righteousness arise with healing in his wings." The prophet Malachi concludes his book by boldly speaking of the promised Messiah.

The second word, "dayspring," is found in Luke 1:78–79, "Whereby the dayspring from on high hath visited us, to give light to them that sit in darkness and in the shadow of death, to guide our feet into the way of peace." This is from the song of Zacharias, the "benedictus"; "dayspring" refers to the Messiah. The third word, "daystar," is from 2 Peter 1:19, "We have also a more sure word of prophecy; whereunto ye do well that ye take heed, as unto a light that shineth in a dark place, until the day dawn, and the day star arise in your hearts."

Wesley weaves these three words into the fabric of a hymn of adoration of Christ and also a prayer for spiritual fulfillment—that our lives may be conformable to the mystery of the gospel.

In her novel *Adam Bede,* published in 1859, George Eliot, famous English writer who concealed her own name, Mary Ann Evans, with a masculine pseudonym, mentions Wesley's hymn. She describes one of her characters, the village Methodist, as driving away all his griefs and worries as he walked across the lonely Derbyshire moors on a bright Sunday morning singing "Christ, Whose Glory Fills the Skies."

RESTORED AFTER CONFLICT

Christian hearts, in love united,
Seek alone in Jesus rest,
Has he not your love excited?
Then let love inspire each breast;
Members on our Head depending
Lights reflecting him, our Sun,
Brethren his commands attending,
We in him, our Lord, are one.

An extraordinary personality of the eighteenth century was Nikolaus Ludwig von Zinzendorf, who was born of a noble and wealthy family in 1700 in the city of Dresden in Saxony (now East Germany). Following his law studies at the University of Wittenberg, he held a minor position in the Saxon Court.

Ordained to the Lutheran ministry in 1734, von Zinzendorf was consecrated Bishop of the Moravian Brethren in 1737. The influence of this man of noble birth, independent wealth, and high social standing reached far beyond his own country. He made many trips to England, Holland, and Switzerland establishing Moravian settlements. In 1741 and again in 1742, he visited the American colonies, especially the Moravian settlement at Bethlehem, Pennsylvania.

A prolific hymn writer, von Zinzendorf is credited with more than two thousand hymns. "Christian Hearts, in Love United" is a translation of his hymn "Herz und herz vereint zusammen" written in 1723 when he was working in the government office in Dresden. Later that year, he and his new bride moved into the manor house just completed at Berthelsdorf, where he would be closer to the growing flock at Herrnhut. (See "Jesus, still lead on," page 155, for additional information.) It is thought that some conflict among the Moravian Brethren occasioned the writing of the hymn, but no specifics are known. Frederick W. Foster, an English Moravian leader, made the English translation in 1789.

The very appropriate tune for this hymn is called "Cassell" and seems to have been a popular melody known as early as 1700. By the 1730s it was known at Herrnhut, was written down in the manuscript book of hymn tunes that was kept there, and was frequently sung by the Moravians.

SINGING "ALLELUIA! AMEN!"

Come, Christians, join to sing
 Alleluia! Amen!
Loud praise to Christ our King;
 Alleluia! Amen!
Let all, with heart and voice,
Before his throne rejoice;
Praise is his gracious choice:
 Alleluia! Amen!

Christian Henry Bateman was born in 1813 at Wyke, near Halifax, Scotland. He was ordained as a Moravian minister and served several churches. In 1843 he left the Moravian fellowship and became minister of the Richmond Place Congregational Church in Edinburgh. In 1869 he was ordained in the Church of England, where he served several appointments during the last twenty years of his life.

"Come, Christians, Join to Sing" was one of twenty-five hymns Bateman wrote and published in 1843, in *The Sacred Song Book,* a collection of hymns for children. This accounts for the original first line being "Come, children, join to sing." Bateman's collection became exceedingly popular and numerous editions were published. It was used in Scotland as the standard collection for Sunday school, and by 1881 more than six million copies had been published.

Benjamin Carr, a highly respected music publisher and dealer in Philadelphia, published an arrangement of this hymn tune for piano in 1825. The following year he published a choral arrangement, featuring solo, quartet, and full chorus. Carr indicated that the tune was an "ancient Spanish melody." Beyond this we know nothing. It is highly probable that Carr composed the melody himself and thought its appeal might be greater if he labeled it a "Spanish melody." Publishers had done this before and have done it since then.

Two versions of the tune appear in our hymnals. When used with "Come, Christians, join to sing" or any other eight-line hymn text, the tune is usually called "Madrid." When used for a six-line text, it is called "Spanish Hymn." (The two versions are not interchangeable.) Nevertheless, each version is a joyful tune appropriate for the text that fits it.

A HYMN WRITTEN ON THE WESTWARD TRAIL

Come, come, ye saints, no toil or labor fear:
But with joy wend your way.
Though hard to you this journey may appear,
Grace shall be as your day.
'Tis better far for us to strive
Our useless cares from us to drive;
Do this, and joy our hearts will swell—
All is well! All is well!

In the cold winter of 1846, Diantha Clayton gave birth to a son in Nauvoo, Illinois. Some weeks earlier her husband, William, had left with a group of hardy pioneers under the leadership of Brigham Young on a venturesome trek to Utah. She knew of her husband's concern for the birth of their first child. In her joy over the new son, she wrote a letter to her husband conveying the good news and closing with the assuring phrase, "All is well." William Clayton recorded these lines in his diary for April 15, 1846, fitting them to a tune both he and Diantha knew and ending with the words "All is well." The hardship of the journey as this determined group moved westward on the American frontier is reflected in the hymn.

A native of England, William Clayton joined the Church of Jesus Christ of Latter-day Saints when he was twenty-three, and for three years he engaged in missionary work in England. He emigrated to the United States and reached the Mormon settlement in Nauvoo, Illinois, on November 24, 1840. He was a close associate of Joseph Smith, serving as his private secretary until Smith's death in 1844.

Quite gifted musically, Clayton was a member of the Nauvoo Brass Band, and later in Utah he played second violin in the first Salt Lake Theatre Orchestra.

The Mormon Tabernacle Choir has made this hymn its trademark. Featured in every concert by popular demand, it is frequently heard on the choir's weekly broadcast from Salt Lake City. The music is not of Mormon origin, but has been traced to a tunebook published in Boston in 1842, credited to C. Dingley. Because it was in the Southern tunebook *The Sacred Harp* in 1844, it was thought to be a "Southern melody."

The words of the Mormon pioneer and the Yankee tune are indelibly wedded. The hymn has become so popular that in recent decades several non-Mormon hymnals have included it—with some alterations in the text for theological reasons.

AN AMERICAN GOSPEL SONG SUNG AT HER MAJESTY'S THEATRE

Come, every soul by sin oppressed,
There's mercy with the Lord,
And he will surely give you rest
By trusting in his word.
Only trust him,
Only trust him,
Only trust him now.

While on a voyage to England with Dwight L. Moody in 1873, Ira D. Sankey spent considerable time studying a scrapbook of unpublished songs he had accumulated before he left New York. One of these was a song with words and music by John H. Stockton. The original refrain was

Come to Jesus,
Come to Jesus,
Come to Jesus just now.

The song impressed Sankey, but he felt that the refrain was trite. Substituting the words "Only trust him," Sankey used it with great success at the meetings he and Moody conducted at Her Majesty's Theatre in Pall Mall, London.

John H. Stockton, born in Buck's County, Pennsylvania, in 1813, was converted at a Methodist camp meeting near Paulson, New Jersey, when he was twenty. Ordained to the Methodist ministry, his fervent evangelical preaching and his gift of sacred song made his ministry most effective. Uniting with the New Jersey Methodist Conference, he served in several appointments until poor health restricted his activities.

"Come, Every Soul by Sin Oppressed," sometimes referred to as "Only Trust Him," has been translated into many languages and sung around the world. When the Salvation Army began its work in Tanganyika in 1933 an officer reported, "Our first open-air was held on Sunday, October 29th. Taking our stand under a tree we sang, 'Come, Every Soul by Sin Oppressed,' using the Swahili songbook." Stockton wrote many hymns, and for some he wrote both words and music. The singability of his music is evident in the familiar tunes we sing for Elisha Hoffman's "Down at the Cross" and William Hunter's "The Great Physician Now Is Near."

A HYMN THAT SURPRISED
THE BRITISH SOLDIERS

Come, thou Almighty King,
Help us thy name to sing,
   Help us to praise:
Father! all-glorious,
O'er all victorious,
Come, and reign over us,
   Ancient of Days.

A detachment of British soldiers surprised worshipers in a church service on Long Island one Sunday morning during the American Revolution. A British officer ordered the startled congregation to stand and sing "God Save the King." The congregation obeyed by singing heartily the right tune but substituting the words of "Come, Thou Almighty King."

The tune, which in England is used for "God Save the King [Queen]" and in the United States for "My Country 'Tis of Thee," dates from about 1745. "Come, thou almighty King" had appeared in the 1730s in England, and was widely sung to this tune, and the colonial congregation on Long Island felt quite comfortable singing the hymn to this tune, to the chagrin of the British soliders.

The writer of "Come, Thou Almighty King" is unknown. The hymn appeared in some of the tracts and pamphlets published by John Wesley in the 1730s, and may have been the work of John's brother, Charles. The evidence does not support this position, however, and Charles Wesley never claimed it as his own.

In the form of a prayer, the hymn addresses the Holy Trinity, using in the four stanzas eight names for the Deity: Almighty King, Father All-Glorious, Ancient of Days, Incarnate Word, Spirit of Holiness, Holy Comforter, Spirit of Power, and the Great One in Three. It is a magnificent expression of praise.

The tune we sing to the hymn has been associated with it for more than two hundred years. Felice de Giardini, referred to in London's musical circles as "The Italian," was a gifted violinist, a distinguished teacher and conductor, and a successful impresario of the Italian opera group in London. By special request of a wealthy patron he wrote several hymn tunes, which were published in a collection in 1769. Only this one remains. It quickly replaced all other tunes for "Come, Thou Almighty King." It is known today by the name "Italian Hymn." This, no doubt, is a slight alteration of an earlier reference to it as "The Italian's Hymn."

CALL FOR SONGS OF LOUDEST PRAISE

Come, thou Fount of every blessing
*   Tune my heart to sing thy grace;*
Streams of mercy, never ceasing,
*   Call for songs of loudest praise:*
Teach me some melodious sonnet,
*   Sung by flaming tongues above;*

Praise the mount! I'm fixed upon it,
Mount of thy redeeming love.

Apprenticed to a London barber when he was fourteen, Robert Robinson preferred reading books to cutting hair. When he was seventeen he was converted through the influence of the preaching of George Whitefield. Soon after his conversion, he began to preach: first, with a Methodist congregation in Norfolk, then with an Independent congregation in Norwich. He was pastor of the Stone Yard Baptist Church, Cambridge, from 1761 until his retirement in 1790.

In addition to his pastoral work at Cambridge, Robinson farmed and worked as a coal and corn merchant to supplement his family's income. He possessed unusual oratorical gifts and spoke out loudly for the abolition of slavery. Before and during the revolutionary war, Robinson championed the independence of the American colonies.

Robinson wrote "Come, Thou Fount of Every Blessing" in 1758. Numerous scriptural allusions are evident in the hymn, most significantly the use of the word "Ebenezer" in the first line of stanza two. The word is found in 1 Samuel 7:12: "Then Samuel took a stone, and set it between Mizpeh and Shen, and called the name of it Ebenezer, saying, Hitherto hath the Lord helped us." Ebenezer is a Hebrew word meaning "stone of help."

The tune most frequently used in singing the hymn is of unknown origin. It appeared without a name in a collection published by John Wyeth in Harrisburg, Pennsylvania, in 1813. Wyeth, a successful businessman and an active Unitarian, made no claim to any musical skills or knowledge. He sensed the need for a compilation of the folk tunes so popular in the camp meetings and revivals of the Methodists and Baptists of Pennsylvania at that time. Wyeth was successful in publishing this collection, which was widely used and widely copied by compilers of subsequent tune books.

John Wyeth's popularity and political stature secured his appointment as postmaster of Harrisburg by President George Washington in 1793. He served in that position for five years.

AN ADVENT HYMN

Come, thou long-expected Jesus,
Born to set thy people free;
From our fears and sins release us;
Let us find our rest in thee.
Israel's strength and consolation,
Hope of all the earth thou art;
Dear desire of every nation,
Joy of every longing heart.

The Christian church's advent season is a time of preparation for the celebration of the birth of Christ. This practice seems to date back to as early as the sixth century. "Come, Thou Long-Expected Jesus" was one of eighteen hymns about the birth of Jesus written by Charles Wesley. Five years earlier, in 1739, he had written "Hark, the Herald Angels Sing."

Born in 1707 in Epworth, England, where his father was the minister of the Anglican parish church, Charles became a scholar at Christ Church College, Oxford, at the age of nineteen. In 1735 he went with his brother John to the colony of Georgia but after a few months returned to London, happy to be far from the primitive conditions in the American colony.

Through the influence of some Moravian friends in London, Charles experienced spiritual renewal and later became an eloquent preacher, ordained in the Church of England. The enthusiastic, evangelical preaching of both John and Charles Wesley met with opposition by Anglican church leaders, and they were forbidden to preach in their churches. Undeterred, the Wesleys preached anyplace that people would gather and listen.

Translating the gospel into singable hymns, Charles Wesley wrote more than 6,500 hymns under all kinds of conditions. Many of his hymns remain in our hymnals and bear witness to his gifts as a hymnwriter.

SINGING THE JOY OF
THE CHRISTIAN LIFE

Come, we that love the Lord,
And let our joys be known;
Join in a song with sweet accord,
And thus surround the throne.

Isaac Watts wrote these lines in 1707 while he was pastor of a Congregational church in London. The hymn of ten four-line stanzas was published as "Heavenly Joy on Earth." That Watts believed in the mirth and joy of the Christian life is evident in the hymn. His confidence shines forth in each stanza and provides an exuberant expression for those "who love the Lord." The original second stanza, no longer found in our hymnals, reflects a positive note.

The sorrow of the mind
Be banished from this place;
Religion never was designed
To make our pleasures less.

Thirty years later John Wesley included the hymn in one of his collections, changing the pronoun "we" to "ye" and the title to "Heaven Begun on Earth."

Some years ago a disagreement in a New England church caused the choir to become rebellious. The pastor was notified that the choir would express its protest by refusing to sing the next Sunday. At that service the resourceful pastor announced the hymn "Come, We That Love the Lord" and read it aloud. Then he turned to the choir and requested them kindly to lead in the singing of the second stanza:

Let those refuse to sing
Who never knew our God;
But children of the heavenly King
May speak their joys abroad.

With its four-line stanza, the hymn has been sung to a number of tunes that fit the short-meter metrical form.

Perhaps the most used is "St. Thomas," to which we sing "I love Thy Kingdom, Lord."

Robert Lowry, a Baptist preacher in Brooklyn, composed a tune for these words in 1867 that required repeating the third and fourth lines of each stanza. He also added a refrain for which he wrote original words. Lowry's version, titled "We're Marching to Zion," is a joyful song.

A HYMN BY
AN OUTSTANDING IRISH POET

Come, ye disconsolate, where'er ye languish,
Come to the mercy seat, fervently kneel;
Here bring your wounded hearts, here tell your anguish;
Earth has no sorrow that heav'n cannot heal,

These lines were written by an Irish Roman Catholic poet in 1818. Thomas Moore was born in Dublin, where his father was a grocer and wine merchant. Moore studied law in London and briefly held a government post in Bermuda. He championed the Irish in the highest levels of London society in the early nineteenth century. By his disarmingly pleasant personality and the beauty of his songs, he greatly aided the Irish cause and became a national hero as had no other poet in Irish history. "The Last Rose of Summer" and "Believe Me If All Those Endearing Young Charms" are examples of his poetic skills and imagination.

He was a friend of poets Byron and Shelley and was highly respected in the literary community of his day. His literary publications brought him fame and fortune. London's leading literary critic, Lord Jeffrey, so bitterly criticized Moore's "Odes and Epistles" in 1806 that Moore challenged him to a duel. Just as they were ready to fire, officers intervened and prevented bloodshed.

Moore's musical gifts, charming social graces, and sparkling wit made him welcome in the most exclusive gatherings. The imaginative lyric style so characteristic of Moore's writing is evident in this hymn. His poetic expression is of unusual quality—typical of the romantic poetry of his day.

The biblical imagery in the "mercy seat" is found in Exodus 25:17–22, where God gave specific instructions to Moses regarding the ark. The mercy seat, adorned with two cherubim of gold, was the elaborate gold covering of the ark of the covenant. It was regarded as the place of atonement; the high priest entered the most holy place once a year and sprinkled blood on the mercy seat to make atonement for his sins and the sins of Israel. Moore's hymn points to God's availability to forgive sins and bring salvation.

GREEK ORTHODOX "GOLDEN ORATOR" WRITES EASTER HYMN

Come, ye faithful, raise the strain
Of triumphant gladness;
God hath brought his Israel
Into joy from sadness;
Loosed from Pharaoh's bitter yoke
Jacob's sons and daughters;
Led them with unmoistened foot
Through the Red Sea waters.

The original Greek hymn was written by John of Damascus, one of the last of the early fathers of the Eastern Church (Greek Orthodox). John was born into a wealthy family. His father was financial adviser to Caliph Abd-el-Melik, who built the mosque called the "Dome of the Rock" on the site of Solomon's temple. John was named for the city where he was born. A staunch defender of the orthodox faith, John of Damascus urged the use of pictures and images in the church as devotional and worship aides at a time when this practice was strongly opposed by other church leaders.

The hymn dates from the eighth century and was written for St. Thomas's Sunday, the first Sunday after Easter. The biblical background is drawn from God's deliverance of the children of Israel from bondage in Egypt, across the Red Sea with "unmoistened foot" into the Promised Land. As Moses had led the children of Israel to the Promised Land, Christ, the victor over sin and death, now leads Christians to eternal life.

Against this picture the hymn declares Christ's resurrection and the deliverance from the bondage of the grave.

> 'Tis the spring of souls today;
>   Christ hath burst his prison,
> And from three days' sleep in death
>   As a sun hath risen.

John spent the last decades of his life as a monk at Mar Saba, near Jerusalem. Here, in the spartan life of the monastery, he studied, wrote, and preached. Because of his effective preaching, he was known as the "golden orator."

The hymns of the early Greek Orthodox Church caught the attention of translators in the Church of England in the mid-nineteenth century. Most significant of the translators was John Mason Neale, whose English version of this hymn by John of Damascus is "Come, Ye Faithful, Raise the Strain."

A CORDIAL INVITATION TO
COME TO JESUS

> Come, ye sinners, poor and needy,
>   Weak and wounded, sick and sore;
> Jesus ready stands to save you,
>   Full of pity, love and power;
>   He is able, he is able,
>   He is willing; doubt no more.

The hymn has been a favorite of evangelicals in the United States for two hundred years. The compilers of shape-note tunebooks of the early nineteenth century dared not omit this text, and gospel song compilers of the same period always included it. Numerous tunes are found in these collections for the hymn—even a tune by Jean Jacques Rousseau, mistaken for the folk song "Go Tell Aunt Rhody." How ironic that Rousseau's tune should be used for a hymn inviting unbelievers to faith in Jesus Christ, when this freethinker of eighteenth-century enlightenment, by his own account, seems never to have experienced a vibrant Christian faith. The hymn may be found in today's hymnals with one of several tunes of American folk origin—"Pleading Savior," "Arise," and "Beach Spring."

Joseph Hart, who wrote the words, was born in London and reared in a Christian home. He received an excellent education and, because of his knowledge of the classics and languages, became a highly esteemed teacher. For a number of years he drifted from the faith of his family and, by his own confession, became a "loose backslider, an audacious apostate, and a bold-faced rebel." In 1757, at the age of forty-five, he experienced a spiritual awakening as the result of a service at a Moravian chapel in London. Out of his experience Hart became a radiant Christian and found great joy in his new relationship with God. Writing verse had been a frequent pastime because of his classical education. Now, in his newfound joy, he turned his talents to writing Christian hymns. During the two years that followed his renewal he wrote many hymns marked by earnestness and love for Christ.

In the spring of 1759 Hart published a hymnal that included this hymn. The book became quite popular and was reprinted in many editions. Largely because of the reception this hymnal received, Hart was urged to enter the ministry. Friends procured for him an old wooden meetinghouse in London on Jewin Street, and he became pastor of an independent congregation. Hart was an ardent Calvinist and a powerful preacher and throngs attended his services. When he died in 1768, it was reported that more than twenty thousand people attended his funeral at Bunhill Fields, London.

A GRATEFUL SONG OF HARVEST

Come, ye thankful people, come,
Raise the song of harvest home!
All is safely gathered in,
Ere the winter storms begin;
God, our Maker, doth provide
For our wants to be supplied:
Come to God's own temple, come,
Raise the song of harvest home.

Thanksgiving is a favorite season of the year. Although those in rural communities are more aware of the activities of harvesting crops than those in urban areas, "Come, Ye Thankful People, Come," a hymn long associated with the season, is sung in many urban and rural churches throughout the land.

Henry Alford, the author of these lines, was an Anglican clergyman gifted in many areas. A noted scholar, theologian, poet, writer, and musician, he had a distinguished career in the Church of England. A little more than a dozen years after he wrote the hymn in 1844, he was appointed dean of Canterbury Cathedral, where he remained until his death in 1871. Living a full and productive life, Alford was involved in many activities. One of his friends commented that at the end of a demanding day, Alford would "stand up, as at the end of a meal, and thank God for what he had received."

The hymn is an invitation for us to express gratitude from thankful hearts for God's bounty. Stanzas two and three refer to the parable of the tares and Jesus' explanation of the parable as recorded in Matthew 13:24–30, 36–43.

The music we sing for Alford's hymn was composed in 1858 by George J. Elvey for the words of another hymn. Three years later, a London hymnal put Elvey's music with Alford's words, and they have been inseparable ever since. At the age of nineteen, Elvey became organist at St. George's Chapel, Windsor, the home church of England's royal family. During his forty-seven years of continuous service there, he played for many services involving the royal family. He was knighted by Queen Victoria in 1871.

SINGING ISAIAH'S PROPHECY

Comfort, comfort ye my people,
Speak ye peace, thus saith our God;
Comfort those who sit in darkness,
Mourning 'neath their sorrows' load.
Speak ye to Jerusalem
Of the peace that waits for them;
Tell her that her sins I cover,
And her warfare now is over.

Johannes Olearius, who wrote these lines, graduated from the University of Wittenberg with a doctor of divinity degree in 1643. The hymn, a paraphrase of Isaiah 40:1–8, was originally written for St. John the Baptist's Day which, in the church year, falls on June 24, the traditional date of his birth. In 1671, at Leipzig, Olearius published a hymnal that included it. This hymnal contained more than twelve hundred hymns (over three hundred by Olearius) and was the largest and most significant German hymnal of the seventeenth century.

Catherine Winkworth, a skillful translator of German hymns, made this English translation in 1863. It has found wide acceptance in English-speaking countries.

"Psalm 42," the tune used with this English text, is based on a French folk song dating from 1505. "Psalm 42" appeared in the 1551 edition of the Genevan Psalter. Louis Bourgeois served as music editor for this and the other psalters of John Calvin for fifteen years in Geneva, Switzerland. He adapted, arranged, and composed tunes to fit the poetic versions of the psalms made by Clement Marot and Theodore Beza. His wise judgment in choosing and shaping these tunes is evident in the fact that some of them have lasted more than four hundred years. The more familiar tune "Old Hundredth," which we use to sing "Praise God from whom all blessings flow," appeared along with Psalm 42 in the 1551 edition of the *Genevan Psalter.*

John Calvin, whose death occurred in the same year that William Shakespeare was born, was a contemporary of Martin Luther. John Calvin's Reformation activities took place in the French-speaking city of Geneva. A systematic theologian of strict conviction, Calvin allowed only Scripture—actually only Old Testament psalms—to be sung in his church. He enlisted some poets to cast the psalms into consistent metrical verses, which could be sung to the same tune. The poets were carefully instructed not to deviate from the original Hebrew in making the French lyrics, nor to interpret or inject any new ideas into their psalm versions.

Calvin wanted the congregation to sing pure Scripture to unison tunes without accompaniment of any kind. Bourgeois' psalm tunes, the musical vehicles of these psalm texts, laid the foundation for English hymn tunes, and the pages of our hymnals bear witness to this.

CROWNING THE KING OF KINGS

Crown him with many crowns,
The Lamb upon his throne;
Hark! how the heavenly anthem drowns
All music but its own:
Awake, my soul, and sing
Of him who died for thee,
And hail him as thy matchless King
Through all eternity.

When the British Bible Society celebrated its one-hundredth anniversary in London in November 1905, greetings were read from government leaders of many nations. The presiding officer, the Marquis of Northampton, said, "Now that we have read these addresses from earthly rulers, let us turn our minds to the King of Kings. We will sing, 'Crown Him with Many Crowns.'"

The hymn of six stanzas was written in 1851 by Matthew Bridges, three years after he had left the Church of England and joined the Roman Catholic Church. The idea of "many crowns" is suggested by the description in Revelation 19:12 of the one who sat upon the white horse: "His eyes were as a flame of fire, and on his head were many crowns." Each of the six stanzas deals with a different crown—crowning Christ as the Lamb upon his throne, the Virgin's Son, the Son of God, the Lord of love, the Lord of peace, and the Lord of years.

Twenty-three years after Bridges wrote the hymn, an Anglican minister, Godfrey Thring, wrote some additional stanzas that added more "crowns" to Bridges' format—crowning Christ as Lord of life and Lord of light. Our hymnals today generally include four stanzas—two or three by Bridges and one or two by Thring. Regardless of the selection of stanzas, the hymn is worthy of heartfelt singing and provides an extraordinary dimension of praise for the worshiper.

The tune we associate with the hymn was written in 1868 by Sir George Elvey. For forty-seven years he was organist and choirmaster at St. George's Chapel, Windsor, the home church of the English royal family. Elvey named the tune "Diademata," from the Greek word for crowns.

A QUIET HYMN BY A QUAKER POET

Dear Lord and Father of mankind,
Forgive our foolish ways;
Reclothe us in our rightful mind;
In purer lives thy service find,
In deeper reverence, praise.

In the busy, noisy world in which we live there is frequently the need for stillness, silence, the quiet spaces of time. With a concern for this dimension of life, John Greenleaf Whittier wrote these lines in 1872 as part of a larger poem entitled "The Brewing of Soma."

The first part of the poem describes some of the ways people have devised to get in touch with and please their gods. Soma, called the "drink of the gods," is brewed by Hindu priests from milk and honey. It produces a wild, frenzied drunkenness and makes the old feel young, the sick feel well, and the hungry forget their hunger. Eventually each falls in exhausted stupor and knows nothing. Similar rituals have been performed across the centuries using music, incense, vigils, trances, ascetic practices, beds of spikes, self-scourging, shakings, and other rites to appease and please humankind's gods.

This hymn that begins by asking forgiveness for our "foolish ways" is the conclusion of Whittier's poem. The third line refers to the man who was healed of unclean spirits as recorded in Mark 5:1–15. When he was healed the man was seen "clothed and in his right mind."

Other biblical references may be seen in the hymn as Whittier, the Quaker poet, draws picture after picture of the spirit and act of worship. The stanza that tells of the disciples following Jesus mentions the "Syrian Sea." This refers to the Sea of Galilee, where much of Jesus' ministry occurred and the disciples "left their nets" and followed him. Though this body of water is in Galilee and not Syria, poetic license allows Whittier to make the substitution. "Syrian Sea," with its alliteration, has a more poetic sound than "Galilean Sea," besides having one less syllable, enabling it to fit this iambic trimeter line.

WORDS BY A TEXTILE MILL WORKER

Draw thou my soul, O Christ,
Closer to thine;
Breathe into every wish
Thy will divine!
Raise my low self above,
Won by thy deathless love;
Ever, O Christ, through mine
Let thy life shine.

Lucy Larcom's father, a New England sea captain, died when Lucy was a child. With her mother she moved to Lowell, Massachusetts. After a brief grade-school education, Lucy worked for eight years in a textile mill. So diligent was her work that she advanced positions in the mill, working the last two years in the cloth room as a record keeper of the bales and pieces of cloth. Her articles about her experiences in the mills, published in *The Atlantic Monthly,* were well received.

For a time she was a rural schoolteacher in Looking Glass, Illinois. Then after attending Monticello Female Seminary at Alton, she returned to Massachusetts, taught school, and was a student at Wheaton Seminary at Norton. She became a prolific writer of verse, and her poems were widely circulated. "Draw Thou My Soul, O Christ" appeared in a collection of poems she published in 1892, a year before her death.

Usually the hymn is sung to a tune composed by Arthur S. Sullivan in 1872. He wrote it for another hymn, but it has become best identified with "Draw Thou My Soul, O Christ."

After receiving his education at the Royal Academy of Music, Sullivan studied in Europe. He returned to England at the age of twenty-four to become professor of composition at the Royal Academy. He wrote a considerable amount of church music, including "Onward, Christian Soldiers." He also composed "The Lost Chord," which enjoyed great popularity. His greatest fame came from the music he composed for the Savoy Operas, in which he was associated with Sir W. S. Gilbert. The Gilbert and Sullivan operettas became a part of English life and tradition. Sullivan was knighted in 1883.

NOT "EVERY HOUR" BUT "MOMENT BY MOMENT"

Dying with Jesus, by death reckoned mine;
Living with Jesus, a new life divine;
Looking to Jesus till glory doth shine,
Moment by moment, O Lord, I am thine.

Refrain:
Moment by moment I'm kept in his love,
Moment by moment I've life from above;
Looking to Jesus till glory doth shine;
Moment by moment, O Lord, I am thine.

A chance remark by a friend motivated Daniel W. Whittle to write the hymn. During the World's Columbian Exposition in Chicago in 1893, Henry Varley, an English lay preacher, said to Whittle, "I do not like the hymn 'I Need Thee Every Hour' very well, because I need the Lord every moment of the day." Varley's comment lingered in Whittle's mind and he wrote these words, opening the refrain with, "Moment by moment I'm kept in his love." For twenty-five years, Whittle was a successful evangelist throughout the United States.

The music was written in 1893 by Major Whittle's daughter, May, and named "Whittle" for her family. Her educational background included the Girls' School at Northfield, Massachusetts; Oberlin in Ohio; and for a couple of years, the Royal Academy of Music in London. In many of Major Whittle's meetings May soloed, for she was a gifted singer. In 1894 she married William R. Moody, son of evangelist D. L. Moody. She lived a long and fruitful life in Northfield, where she died in 1963 at age ninety-three.

TWO ENGLISHMEN WROTE THE "NAVY HYMN"

Eternal Father, strong to save,
Whose arm doth bind the restless wave,
Who bidd'st the mighty ocean deep

Its own appointed limits keep;
O hear us when we cry to thee
For those in peril on the sea.

Americans know this century-old hymn and tune of English origin as the "Navy Hymn." The favorite hymn of Franklin Delano Roosevelt, it was sung at his funeral on April 14, 1945, at Hyde Park, New York. On November 24, 1963, as the body of John Fitzgerald Kennedy was borne up the steps of the Capitol Building in Washington to lie in state in the rotunda, the hymn was played by the Navy band. The following day, at Arlington National Cemetery, it was played by the Marine band at the conclusion of the burial service.

For thirty-six years William Whiting was master of the Winchester College Choristers' School. He taught and directed the sixteen boys who sang regularly in the Anglican services in the school chapel. Whiting wrote the words of the hymn in 1860 for a student who was about to set sail for America. The school is located only twelve miles from Southampton, a port second in size only to London, and the boys of the school were familiar with the lore of the sea.

John B. Dykes composed the tune for this hymn shortly after the words were written. It was published in 1861 in *Hymns Ancient and Modern,* the most widely distributed nineteenth-century English hymnal. Dykes named the tune "Melita," the Roman name for the Mediterranean island of Malta where the apostle Paul was shipwrecked while traveling as a prisoner to Rome. "When they were escaped, then they knew that the island was called Melita" (Acts 28:1). How appropriate this name is for the tune used for a hymn that is a simple prayer for travelers at sea.

A SEVENTEENTH-CENTURY
JESUIT HYMN

Fairest Lord Jesus,
Ruler of all nature,
O thou of God and man the Son;
Thee will I cherish,

Thee will I honor,
Thou my soul's glory, joy and crown.

"A song sung by German knights on their way to Jerusalem," is a footnote that appeared with this hymn in several collections more than one hundred years ago. Franz Liszt used the melody in his oratorio *Saint Elizabeth* in 1862 and called it in the preface "the old pilgrim's song." From these and other comments, an imagined, romantic story evolved that associates the hymn with the Crusades of centuries ago. The name of the tune in many hymnals today is "Crusaders' Hymn."

Though none of this is true, little is known about the origin of the words and music. The German text, "Schönster Herr Jesus," has been traced to the Jesuits in Münster, Westphalia (now West Germany). A handwritten copy from 1662 and a published collection from 1677 seem to mark its earliest appearances.

The hymn reflects the simple faith of the ordinary country people around Münster in the seventeenth century. The teachings, practices, and rituals of the Roman Catholic Church had been rejected by these people, but they held to their strong faith in God. They believed that Jesus was both Son of God and Son of Man and, while he was ruler of all nature, he was fairer than all. This is the theme of the hymn.

Richard Storrs Willis, a young American musician studying in Frankfurt, Germany, discovered this tune in a collection of Silesian folk songs that had been published in Leipzig in 1842. He returned to America in 1848 and became music critic for the *New York Tribune*. In 1850 he published a book of church music in which he included "Fairest Lord Jesus" under the mistaken caption "Crusaders' Hymn."

So popular has this hymn become that it appears in all our hymnals today and is often sung in our churches. It reminds us that regardless of the beauty of the meadows, the woodlands, the flowers of spring, the sun and stars, Jesus is fairer and brighter, even "purer than all the angels heaven can boast."

SINGING OF OUR FATHERS' FAITH

Faith of our fathers! living still
In spite of dungeon, fire, and sword,

O how our hearts beat high with joy
Whene'er we hear that glorious word.
Faith of our fathers, holy faith!
We will be true to thee till death.

The hymn reflects the stalwart Christian faith described in Hebrews 11. That faith has caused the pages of Christian history to be peppered with the names of martyrs who refused to repudiate their beliefs. They were crucified, beheaded, drowned, burned at the stake, or otherwise brutally killed.

Frederick William Faber, who wrote these lines, was born into the home of a clergyman in the Church of England. He was reared in the church, educated at Oxford, and later ordained in the Anglican Church. The influence of John Henry Newman and others who sought to bring about a renewal in the Anglican Church touched Faber deeply. Because of this influence he followed Newman and others into the Roman Catholic Church in 1846. He was rebaptized, took the name Wilfred, and founded a religious community in Birmingham, England. Two years later the group moved to London and became part of what was later known as Brompton Oratory. It was this church that Joseph P. Kennedy and his family attended while he was United States Ambassador to Great Britain (1937–40), and Robert F. Kennedy, as a teenager, frequently assisted the priests at the altar.

Faber sought to produce for Roman Catholics hymns with the same popular appeal as the hymns by John Newton and William Cowper, whom he greatly admired. To this end he wrote 150 hymns to match the number of Old Testament psalms. Faber had a vibrant personality and a rich, resonant voice. He was a gifted preacher and was respected in England as an outstanding Catholic leader. When he published "Faith of Our Fathers" in 1849, he made two versions, one for England and one for Ireland. In the version for England, one stanza read:

Faith of our fathers! Mary's prayers
Shall win our country back to thee;
And through the truth that comes from God,
England shall then indeed be free.

To make the hymn acceptable to persons of all Christian faiths, hymnal editors, within a few years of its appearance, altered the text until they had the version commonly used today. The final stanza speaks of Jesus' teaching to "love your enemies and pray for them that persecute you." Faber admonishes us to "love both friend and foe in all our strife," and to proclaim our faith "by kindly words and virtuous life."

A HYMN BY A SCOTTISH PRESBYTERIAN MINISTER

Fill thou my life, O Lord my God,
In every part with praise,
That my whole being may proclaim
Thy being and thy ways.

Horatius Bonar, who wrote the hymn in 1866, was the outstanding Scottish Presbyterian minister of his day. Five years after he was ordained to the ministry in 1838, he was involved in a revolt against the established Church of Scotland. His evangelical preaching and strong leadership brought him much attention. In 1866 he became pastor of the Chalmers Memorial Free Church in Edinburgh.

Bonar was a student of the Bible and a prolific writer of evangelical material. For him, hymn writing was spontaneous, and ideas and poetic fragments were jotted down in his notebooks as they occurred. He wrote more than six hundred hymns, including some well-known ones: "I Heard the Voice of Jesus Say" and "Here, O My Lord, I See Thee Face to Face."

His zeal, devotion, and intense concern for witnessing to unbelievers marked his extraordinary life. "Fill Thou My Life, O Lord, My God" expresses his true commitment.

The hymn tune usually found with Bonar's hymn "Richmond" was composed in 1792 by Thomas Haweis. Born in Cornwall, England, he was first apprenticed to a surgeon but then decided to enter the ministry. He went to Christ Church College, Oxford, and was ordained two years later in 1757.

For fifty-six years, until his death in 1820, Haweis

ministered to the parish church in the village of Aldwicke in Northamptonshire. Though he remained faithful to the Church of England, he was sympathetic toward evangelicals. He was a friend of the Wesleys and corresponded frequently with John Newton, first at Olney and later in London. Haweis was interested in missionary enterprise and took an active part in the organization of the London Missionary Society in 1795.

A HYMN BASED ON PAUL'S ADVICE TO YOUNG TIMOTHY

Fight the good fight with all thy might;
Christ is thy strength, and Christ thy right;
Lay hold on life, and it shall be
Thy joy and crown eternally.

The apostle Paul admonished Timothy, the young preacher, to "fight the good fight of faith, lay hold on eternal life" (1 Tim. 6:12). Then about his own life Paul wrote to Timothy, "I have fought a good fight, I have finished my course, I have kept the faith" (2 Tim. 4:7). Basing it on these words, John Monsell wrote the hymn in 1863. Though it speaks of courage in discipleship, it centers on the need for Christ in the life of the disciple. The four stanzas point out that Christ is "strength," "right," "prize," "love," "life," and "all in all" to the Christian. Without Christ in one's life, there is little reason or power to fight the good fight.

Born in Londonderry, Ireland, Monsell was educated for the Anglican ministry at Trinity College, Dublin. Ordained in 1834, he held several appointments until he went to England in 1853 and served churches in Surrey and Guildford. In 1875, while he was watching workmen repair his church in Guildford, he was killed by a falling stone.

Congregational singing was a major concern for Monsell. He wrote almost three hundred hymns for his congregation and urged that singing be "more fervent and joyous. We are too distant and reserved in our praise."

Monsell's hymn is usually sung to the tune "Pentecost," composed in 1864 by William Boyd. He had written it for another hymn and was quite shocked about ten years later to find that his friend Arthur S. Sullivan had set his tune to the vigorous text, "Fight the Good Fight."

Born in Montego Bay, Jamaica, Boyd was educated in England and ordained in the Church of England in 1877. Although a skilled organist, Boyd spent his life as an Anglican minister, serving his appointments with distinction. He wrote many hymn tunes, but only "Pentecost" survives today.

SING OF THE SAINTS OF FAITH'S "HALL OF FAME"

For all the saints who from their labors rest,
Who thee by faith before the world confessed,
Thy name, O Jesus, be forever blest,
Alleluia!

When I sing William Walsham How's hymn, I think back to the small town where I grew up. My father would mention some dearly loved elderly person in the community and say, "If there is a saint on earth, he surely is one." I too have known persons whose lives seemed more radiant than others, whose faith shone brightly through joy and sorrow.

William W. How seems to gather from across all the ages these saintly persons and express his gratitude for them in these stanzas. Surely the line "who thee by faith before the world confessed" is a reference to the eleventh chapter of Hebrews. Here the writer to the Hebrews illustrates the essential quality of faith by a walk through faith's "hall of fame." Abel, Enoch, Noah, Abraham, Sara, Isaac, Jacob, Moses, Rahab, Gideon, Barak, Samson, Jepthae, David, and Samuel are mentioned by name. For these and all those whose faith has burned brightly down through the ages, the hymn writer wrote these stanzas of three rhyming poetic lines followed by a joyful Alleluia.

An Anglican clergyman, How was highly respected and dearly loved. He wrote fifty-four hymns during the years he was the minister at Whittington, an English farming village on the Welsh border. Written for the people of his village, his hymns show his personal belief that a good hymn should be like a good prayer—simple, real, earnest, and reverent.

The tune most used for singing the hymn was written by Ralph Vaughn Williams, one of England's greatest composers of this century. He was thirty-four years old and not well known for his gifts of composition when he wrote the tune. He included it in *The English Hymnal,* published in 1906, for which he was musical editor. His keen sense of humor shows in the name he gave the tune—"Sine Nomine," which means "without a name." Regardless of its name, the tune has come to be recognized as one of the truly great hymn tunes of our time. The words and music are well matched and move with the bold strides of a victorious Christian faith.

A HYMN ORIGINALLY WRITTEN AS A "SACRIFICE OF PRAISE"

For the beauty of the earth,
For the glory of the skies,
For the love which from our birth
Over and around us lies:
Christ, our God, to thee we raise
This our sacrifice of praise.

Folliot S. Pierpoint wrote the hymn in 1864 for the communion service in the Church of England. Hymnal editors later altered the final two lines to read

Christ our God, to thee we raise
This our hymn of grateful praise.

or

Lord of all, to thee we raise
This our hymn of grateful praise.

These alterations were perhaps meant to make the hymn more usable in general praise. Pierpoint's intent, however, was that since Christ was sacrificed for us, and the communion service reenacts this deed, then our praise is a return sacrifice unto God.

In the eight original stanzas of his hymn, Pierpoint lists many things that evoked his "sacrifice of praise"—objects of nature, family members and friends, the senses, emotions, the church, and others—but in no apparent sequence.

Born in Bath, England, Pierpoint was educated at Queen's College in Cambridge, graduating in 1857. He taught classical literature at Somerset College for a while, then spent the latter part of his life (by virtue of the family inheritance he received) traveling and writing as he pleased. He published several volumes of poetry and a number of hymns, but only this one remains in today's hymnals.

"Dix," the tune most frequently used for singing Pierpoint's hymn, is based on a German chorale tune from a collection of tunes published in Stuttgart, Germany, in 1838. It was made into a hymn tune in 1861 for William C. Dix's hymn "As with Gladness Men of Old" and given his name.

A HYMN BY A GERMAN LUTHERAN PASTOR

Give to the winds thy fears;
Hope and be undismayed.
God hears thy sighs and counts thy tears,
God shall lift up thy head.

Life was not kind to Paul Gerhardt. He grew up in a small village near Wittenberg, Germany, where his father was mayor. Paul was only eleven years old when the tragic Thirty Years' War (1618–1648) began and ravaged the country. When he was twenty-one he entered Wittenberg University, but after a short while he discontinued his studies because of the war. Finally, at the age of forty-five, he was ordained to the Lutheran ministry and became pastor in Mittenwalde, a small village near Berlin. Now he was able to marry the woman with whom he had shared a romance for many years. The blessings of his ministry and his marriage caused an outpouring of joy that resulted in his writing a number of hymns. After six years at Mittenwalde he joined the ministerial staff of St. Nicholas' Church, Berlin, but this proved to be an unhappy experience. He refused to sign a Calvinistic statement and was removed from his position there.

Sorrow colored his personal life also. Four of the five children born to Gerhardt and his wife died, and his wife passed away after a long illness. After his dismissal at St. Nicholas, he accepted a position at the Lutheran Church at Lubben, where he remained until his death. Today in the Lubben church there stands a life-sized portrait of Gerhardt with an inscription in German, "A theologian sifted in Satan's sieve," a reference to his many trials and tribulations.

Confident faith warmed the heart of this Lutheran pastor. In spite of hardship and conflict, his inner strength revealed him to be firmly grounded in the Lord. The depth of his spiritual resources is reflected in his hymns, many of them written in situations that would have made most persons cry rather than sing. Numerous translations of Gerhardt's hymn have been made, but John Wesley's in 1739 has been more widely used than any other English version. The hymn is as appropriate today as ever before, for in every age there is the need to place our trust in God and give our fears to the winds.

THE "LESSER DOXOLOGY"

Glory be to the Father,
And to the Son,
And to the Holy Ghost;
As it was in the beginning,
Is now and ever shall be,
World without end. Amen.

Known as the "Lesser Doxology" (to distinguish it from the "Gloria in Excelsis," the "Greater Doxology"), this ancient song is a joyful expression of praise to the Holy Trinity. The first part, "Glory be to the Father, and to the Son, and to the Holy Ghost," is found in the Great Commission given by Christ as recorded in Matthew 28:19: "Go ye therefore, and teach all nations, baptizing them in the name of the Father, and of the Son, and of the Holy Ghost." In the Eastern church in the Greek language, and in the Western church in Latin, the first part dates from the second century.

The second part, "As it was in the beginning, is now and ever shall be," was added during the fourth century to affirm equal praise to the three persons of the Trinity. This was done to counteract the belief that Christ was a created being and not divine, not coequal with God the Father. The early Christians sang these lines heartily to etch in their minds and hearts the truth of the Christian doctrine of the Trinity.

In his collection of hymns published in the early eighteenth century, Isaac Watts, an English Congregational preacher, wrote: "Though the Latin name of it 'Gloria Patri' be retained in the English nation from the Roman Church; and though there may be some excesses of superstitious honor paid to the words of it, which may have wrought some unhappy prejudices in weaker Christians, yet I believe it still to be one of the noblest parts of Christian worship."

Two tunes are used for this text in most of our churches. These were composed by Charles Meineke and Henry W. Greatorex in the mid-nineteenth century for use in Episcopal churches in the United States. Wherever it is sung in the service, and whatever tune is used, it should be sung heartily in praise to Father, Son, and Holy Ghost.

A CHRISTMAS SPIRITUAL

Go, tell it on the mountain,
Over the hills and everywhere;
Go tell it on the mountain
That Jesus Christ is born!

Songs of Christmas reflect the many facets of the Christmas story: Mary's baby, the manger scene, the heavenly host, the shepherds, the wise men, and the star. Some are quiet songs, some rousing, some slow, and some spirited. "Go, Tell It on the Mountain" is a joyful clarion call to proclaim from the mountain that a Savior is born. Messiah is come! It is an expression of joy and ecstasy for the poor, the downtrodden, the lonely, the insignificant. It is a fresh declaration each

Christmas that Jesus is in the world—he was born in Bethlehem.

Shortly after the turn of the twentieth century, John Wesley Work II, who taught Latin and history at Fisk University in Nashville, Tennessee, heard someone sing this refrain. He shaped the melody, harmonized the tune, and added some original stanzas. In 1907 he published it in a small booklet, *Folk Songs of the American Negro.* This song and well-known versions of "New Born Again," "Lord, I Want to Be a Christian," "Somebody's Knocking at Your Door," and "Were You There" were also included. Because no copyright was registered, Work lost all claim to his writing.

John W. Work III recalled his Christmas experiences at Fisk when he was a child. Early each Christmas morning, around five o'clock, the Fisk Jubilee Singers, directed by his father, walked around the campus singing Christmas songs. Their favorites were "Go, Tell It on the Mountain" and "Glory to That Newborn King." After the early morning singing, the students and faculty gathered in the dining hall for a brief Christmas service and breakfast amid glowing candles and decorated tables.

Those gathering on chilly Christmas mornings in Nashville before sunrise and filling the sky with this song little knew that years later this spiritual would sound in many lands and in many tongues during the celebration of the Lord's birth.

A BENEDICTORY HYMN

God be with you till we meet again!
By his counsels guide, uphold you,
With his sheep securely fold you;
God be with you till we meet again!

The farewell remark "good-bye," so much a part of our daily conversation, is a contraction of the phrase "God be with you." In 1880 Jeremiah E. Rankin was the pastor of the First Congregational Church in Washington, D.C. People thronged to his church on Sundays to hear his effective preaching, to experience the warm, friendly spirit of the congregation, and to join in the hearty congregational singing.

Rankin wrote the hymn to conclude the church services and requested two friends to compose music for it. By Rankin's own account, one of the composers was well known and the other quite unknown. However, the latter wrote the better tune. He was William G. Tomer, a government employee in Washington. He served as the part-time music director for the Grace Methodist Episcopal Church there.

Rankin was ordained to the Congregational ministry in 1855, and served prominent churches in New York, Vermont, and Massachusetts. For fifteen years he had a successful ministry in Washington and later was elected president of Howard University.

Though first sung only in Rankin's church, the hymn was soon being used by other churches and groups as knowledge of it spread by word of mouth. Visitors who heard it carried to their churches the words and tune for their congregations to sing. In a short time the hymn was being sung in summer assemblies, camp meetings, and evangelistic crusades.

Evangelist Dwight L. Moody and his music director, Ira D. Sankey, discovered the hymn and used it often in services both in America and abroad. Singing the hymn at partings of Christians became an accepted custom. Today the hymn is often sung in our churches by the entire congregation or by the choir as a choral benediction or blessing.

AN AWARENESS OF
THE PRESENCE OF GOD

> *God himself is with us: let us now adore him,*
> *And with awe appear before him.*
> *God is in his temple, all within keep silence,*
> *And before him bow with reverence.*
> *Him alone,*
> *God we own;*
> *To our Lord and Savior*
> *Praises sing forever.*

Gerhard Tersteegen, author of the original German hymn in 1729, was one of the important hymn writers of the Reformed

Church in Germany. His father died when Gerhard was six years old, and the family financial situation would not afford him a university education. Following his conversion at the age of sixteen, he spent whole days and nights in fasting and prayer. He permitted himself only one meager meal a day and gave what he saved to the poor. Very much the introvert, he was repelled by the world with its noise and commercial activity. He provided for his physical needs by making and selling silk ribbons. He worked ten hours each day at his loom, then prayed for two hours. The next two hours he spent writing and discussing spiritual matters with friends.

Through Tersteegen lived apart from the Reformed Church in Germany, he made no effort to set up a new sect; he simply lived the quiet life of a celibate and ascetic. He published a collection of hymns in 1729 that included this hymn. "God Himself Is with Us," the German original, was written to fit an existing tune, "Arnsberg," composed by Joachim Neander almost fifty years earlier.

The English version of Tersteegen's hymn is largely the work of two Moravians, Frederick W. Foster and John Miller, but the hymn has received a number of alterations at the hands of well-intentioned editors. The hymn with the tune "Arnsberg" appears in many hymnals today and is a reminder of a devout German Christian who expressed earnestly his worship and awareness of God in these stanzas. He and the friends who joined him at his humble cottage in spirit and practice were called by their neighbors "Die Stillen im Lande" (the quiet folk of the land).

A HYMN BY
A DISTINGUISHED LINGUIST

God is love; his mercy brightens
All the path in which we rove;
Bliss he wakes and woe he lightens:
God is wisdom, God is love.

The major emphasis of this hymn by John Bowring is the fourth line, "God is wisdom, God is love," which concludes each stanza of the hymn. The repetition is a reminder that God who provides light for daily living, who brings happiness and helps bear our burdens, is the source of wisdom and love.

John Bowring had a remarkable interest in languages. He claimed to understand two hundred languages and to speak fluently in one hundred. For over forty years he published English translations of poetry from the Russian, Polish, Serbian, Batavian, Magyar, Hungarian, and Czech languages. He became an ardent advocate of social reform in the 1820s and 1830s—vigorously supporting popular education, urging prison reform, championing free trade, advocating parliamentary reform, and speaking out against slavery and other such controversial concerns. These interests brought him into active participation in the political life of England.

John Bowring wrote quite a number of hymns. Today most hymnals include two by which he is remembered: "God Is Love, His Mercy Brightens" and "In the Cross of Christ I Glory." These continue to be sung in our churches.

A PARAPHRASE OF PSALM 27

God is my strong salvation:
*   What foe have I to fear?*
In darkness and temptation,
*   My light, my help is near.*
Though hosts encamp around me,
*   Firm in the fight I stand;*
What terror can confound me,
*   With God at my right hand?*

James Montgomery wrote the hymn, based on Psalm 27:1–3, in 1822. For thirty-one years he was editor of the *Sheffield Iris* in Sheffield, England. He was twice imprisoned for expressing his opinions in his newspaper: once for printing a song to celebrate the fall of the Bastille in France, and once for his account of a riot in Sheffield. A public-spirited man and a champion of humanitarian causes, Montgomery was a strong voice for the abolition of slavery, and in support of foreign missions and the British Bible Society.

He became involved in a controversy over a hymnal compiled by Thomas Cotterill, vicar of St. Paul's Church, Sheffield. The archbishop of York finally approved Cotterill's hymnal and it was published in 1820. For the first time the singing of hymns was permitted in the Church of England. Montgomery's interest in hymn singing and hymn writing greatly increased through his involvement in the activity surrounding the approval and publication of Cotterill's hymnal, and in 1822 Montgomery wrote "God Is My Strong Salvation." It was published with other original hymns written on Old Testament psalms.

The tune most frequently found with this hymn in our hymnals is called "Wedlock." Of unknown origin, the music is a sturdy Appalachian folk tune discovered in North Carolina about 1918. It is an appropriate setting for Montgomery's hymn.

AN ETON MASTER WRITES A HYMN

> God is working his purpose out
> As year succeeds to year;
> God is working his purpose out,
> And the time is drawing near;
> Nearer and nearer draws the time,
> The time that shall surely be,
> When the earth shall be filled with the glory of God
> As the waters cover the sea.

Arthur Campbell Ainger, son of an Anglican minister, wrote the hymn at Eton College in 1894. The scriptural basis is Habakkuk 2:14. The hymn expresses great confidence in the coming of God's kingdom in all its fullness. Christians are urged to share the gospel and help those who are captive to sin to find freedom and liberty in Christ. The final stanza reflects that the coming of the kingdom is dependent upon God.

> All we can do is nothing worth
> Unless God blesses the deed;
> Vainly we hope for the harvest-tide
> Till God gives life to the seed;

> *Yet nearer and nearer draws the time,*
> *The time that shall surely be,*
> *When the earth shall be filled with the glory of God*
> *As the waters cover the sea.*

Ainger was educated at Eton College and Trinity College and graduated with honors. Eton, established in 1440 by King Henry VI, has had a long and distinguished history in public school education in England. For thirty-seven years Ainger taught at Eton and was one of the most beloved and respected masters there. He has been described as "a fine scholar with a remarkable memory, an incisive critic, a good speaker, fertile in suggestions, and completed in execution." His unruffled good humor won the praise and admiration of the boys.

"God Is Working His Purpose Out" was written seven years before Ainger's retirement. Martin Shaw composed the tune "Purpose" for Ainger's text in 1931, and the two are still together.

SINGING THE GREATNESS OF GOD

> *God moves in a mysterious way*
> *His wonders to perform;*
> *He plants his footsteps in the sea*
> *And rides upon the storm.*

William Cowper wrote these lines in the spring of 1773. The legendary story that he wrote it after experiencing great depression and attempting to take his own life is unfounded. The vivid pictures Cowper used in describing God as one who "plants his footsteps in the sea and rides upon the storm" are from the Old Testament (2 Sam. 22:8–20). God is portrayed as working in the world in all his majesty and power, yet having a fatherly concern and love for his children.

> *Judge not the Lord by feeble sense,*
> *But trust him for his grace;*
> *Behind a frowning providence*
> *He hides a smiling face.*

Cowper's father was an Anglican clergyman who was chaplain to King George II, and his mother was a descendant of John Donne. At Westminster School, Cowper excelled at cricket and soccer, but his interest in literature and literary people shaped his life's direction and pursuits. A series of unfortunate experiences resulted in periods of melancholy that occurred throughout his life. In 1767 he moved to Olney, in Buckinghamshire, and began his long friendship with John Newton, then Anglican minister for the village.

The people of Olney, in their dismal, cold, poorly lit homes, made beautiful bobbin lace by hand. They were poor and illiterate and endured great hardship. Newton loved them and ministered to them, in spite of some wealthy parishioners who did not want noisy, uncouth villagers in their church.

Writing hymns was an activity that fascinated both Cowper and Newton, and a collection of their hymns entitled *Olney Hymns* was published in 1779. To this collection Cowper contributed 68 hymns and Newton 280 hymns. These hymns were sung during weeknight services conducted by Newton. At that time the Church of England allowed only the singing of metrical versions of the Old Testament psalms, not hymns of "human composure." But at these weeknight Bible classes, the villagers heartily sang Cowper's hymn about God who "moves in a mysterious way his wonders to perform."

A HYMN WRITTEN FOR
A CHURCH DEDICATION

God of grace and God of glory
On thy people pour thy power;
Crown thine ancient church's story,
Bring her bud to glorious flower.
Grant us wisdom,
Grant us courage
For the facing of this hour.

When Harry Emerson Fosdick was called as pastor of a church in New York City, a new building was to be erected through the generosity of John D. Rockefeller, Jr., a member of the congregation. It was to be a magnificent structure near the George Washington Bridge, overlooking the Hudson River. In the summer of 1930, Fosdick was vacationing at his home on Mouse Island in Boothbay Harbor, Maine. As he thought about the new building then being built and his beginning ministry there, the lines of the hymn took shape in his mind.

One of Fosdick's favorite hymn tunes was "Regent Square," usually associated with the Christmas hymn "Angels, from the Realms of Glory." He wrote the lines of the new hymn so they could be sung to it and published it that way. At the opening services of The Riverside Church on October 5, 1930, and again at the dedication service on February 9, 1931, it was sung with great enthusiasm.

Born in Buffalo, New York, Fosdick was educated at Colgate University and Union Theological Seminary. Ordained to the Baptist ministry in 1903, he became pastor of the First Baptist Church, Montclair, New Jersey. After serving as a chaplain during World War I, he was pastor of New York City's First Presbyterian Church, then Park Avenue Baptist Church, which became The Riverside Church. During his twenty years at The Riverside Church his preaching, writings, and radio broadcasts from the church brought him worldwide acclaim. He died in 1969 at the age of ninety-one.

Today this text is sung almost always to "Cwm Rhondda" (literally "low valley of Rhondda"). Composed by John Hughes in 1907 for the annual Baptist Cymanfa Ganu (singing festival) at Chapel Rhondda, Pontypridd, Wales, it has been immensely popular. The joining of Fosdick's hymn and Hughes' tune was the work of Robert G. McCutchan in the 1935 *Methodist Hymnal*. Later Fosdick expressed his displeasure with what he called "my hymn's divorce from 'Regent Square' and remarriage to 'Cwm Rhondda.' The Methodists did it! And both here and abroad they are being followed!" McCutchan's judgment has been more than validated by this enduring "marriage," for the Welshman's tune and the Manhattan minister's text will be sung together by generations yet to come.

A CENTENNIAL CELEBRATION

God of our fathers, whose almighty hand
Leads forth in beauty all the starry band
Of shining worlds in splendor through the skies,
Our grateful songs before thy throne arise.

Opening with an expression of gratitude that acknowledges God's guidance and help in the past, the hymn appeals to God for his presence and blessing in the present and also in the future. The final stanza voices a plea for God's people.

Refresh thy people on their toilsome way,
Lead us from night to never-ending day;
Fill all our lives with love and grace divine,
And glory, laud, and praise be ever thine.

Daniel Crane Roberts wrote the hymn in 1876 for the July Fourth centennial celebration at St. Thomas Episcopal Church, Brandon, Vermont, where he was pastor. It was sung to the hymn tune "Russian Hymn" (usually used for "God the Omnipotent"). In the late 1880s, Roberts submitted the hymn to the committee for the 1892 Episcopal *Hymnal,* and it was accepted. Before the hymnal was printed, George W. Warren, organist at St. Thomas's Church in New York City, and J. Ireland Tucker were appointed to choose a hymn for the centennial celebration of the United States Constitution in 1889. They selected "God of Our Fathers" and put it to the tune Warren composed for the occasion and named it "National Hymn." In Tucker's musical edition of the 1892 *Hymnal,* it made its first appearance.

Roberts, a graduate of Kenyon College in Gambier, Ohio, served with the 84th Ohio Volunteers during the Civil War. Ordained a deacon in 1865 and a priest the following year, he served Episcopal appointments in Vermont and Massachusetts. He became vicar of St. Paul's Church in Concord, New Hampshire, and served there almost thirty years.

George W. Warren, educated at Racine College in Wisconsin, was a self-taught organist who became highly successful. After several distinguished appointments, Warren served as organist at St. Thomas's Church for twenty years. While there he edited *Hymns and Tunes as Sung at St. Thomas' Church* (1888). He composed a considerable amount of organ and choral music, but only this tune remains in common usage.

A HYMN WRITTEN FOR A NEWBORN BABY

God sent his Son, they called him Jesus;
He came to love, heal, and forgive;
He lived and died to buy my pardon,
An empty grave is there to prove my Savior lives.
Because He lives I can face tomorrow;
Because He lives all fear is gone;
Because I know He holds the future,
And life is worth the living just because He lives.*

Bill and Gloria Gaither have become the best-known gospel songwriters of our time. "There's Something About That Name," "The King Is Coming," "Let's Just Praise the Lord," "He Touched Me," and "Because He Lives" are only a few of the many songs they have jointly written. "Because He Lives" was written in 1971, shortly after the birth of their son, Benjy. Bill and Gloria were greatly concerned about the condition of the world into which Benjy had been born. Yet in the midst of political, economic, and moral uncertainty, they both felt assurance and affirmation. The resurrection is more than a historical fact but a daily reality of life. Because Jesus lives, we all can face the unknown future without fear.

The second stanza, which begins "How sweet to hold a newborn baby," was written first, and the rest of the song took shape quickly. The first stanza tells of Jesus, who came to earth in human flesh to be the Savior, the second stanza is about their new baby boy, and the third stanza is about the glorious hope of eternal life in Jesus Christ. The song quickly received wide acceptance. In 1974 the Gospel Music Association named it the Song of the Year, and the Gaithers received the Dove Award for this popular song.

Bill and Gloria Gaither live in Alexandria, Indiana, in the heart of farm country. Both are graduates of Anderson College (now Anderson University) in Anderson, Indiana. After completing college, they were both teachers until their music activities demanded their full time. In recent years their concerts have filled the largest auditoriums throughout the nation. Their record albums have been the most popular in the contemporary Christian music field. In spite of their extraordinary success as songwriters, concert artists, recording artists, and publishers, Bill and Gloria share their musical and lyrical gifts generously, carefully maintain their family lifestyle, remain committed to the local church fellowship, and continue to express their Christian faith in writing and song.

ONE HYMN COMBINES
THE WRITINGS OF TWO AUTHORS

God the Omnipotent! King, who ordainest
Thunder thy clarion, the lightning thy sword;
Show forth thy pity on high where thou reignest;
Give to us peace in our time, O Lord.

Two hymns written twenty-eight years apart have been combined to make this hymn. The earlier hymn was written by Henry F. Chorley in 1842, and the later one by John Ellerton in 1870. Chorley was fond of the hymn tune known as "Russian Hymn" and thought it should have a text that spoke of the greatness of God. So he wrote one. A music critic and writer, Chorley moved in London's literary circles. In his writings he was very positive regarding Felix Mendelssohn and Louis Spohr but quite critical of Frèdèric Chopin, Robert Schumann, and Richard Wagner, all contemporaries.

John Ellerton wrote a hymn, "God, the Almighty One, Wisely Ordaining," imitating Chorley's hymn. In the years that followed, hymnal editors combined the two hymns and made other alterations that resulted in the four-stanza version that appears in many hymnals today. Ordained in the Church of England in 1850, Ellerton served faithfully in a number of appointments. He was interested in various welfare movements, but devoted a great deal of time to literary endeavor. The poetic structures of hymnody intrigued him and he wrote more than fifty hymns, compiled several collections of hymns, and wrote helpful articles about hymns and hymnwriters.

The tune "Russian Hymn," which fascinated both Chorley and Ellerton, was written by Alexis F. Lvov in 1833 by order of Czar Nicholas I. Set to a text beginning "God save the Czar," the music was first performed before the czar in the court chapel on November 23, 1833, by a large choir accompanied by two orchestras.

With words by Chorley and Ellerton and music by Lvov, this magnificent hymn tells of the greatness of God and reflects Old Testament writings about God. One such reference is David's psalm of thanksgiving as recorded in 2 Samuel 22. The climax of the hymn is the repeated final line appealing to an omnipotent God: "Give to us peace in our time, O Lord." What an appropriate line in our day!

A PARAPHRASE OF A FOURTEENTH-CENTURY CAROL

Good Christian men, rejoice
With heart and soul and voice!
Give ye heed to what we say:
Jesus Christ is born today.
Man and beast before him bow,
And he is in the manger now:
Christ is born today.

John Mason Neale's free rendering of a fourteenth-century carol made up of Latin and German lines appeared in 1853. According to a legendary story, Heinrich Suso, a Dominican monk, heard angels sing this song. In his excitement, he joined the angels in a heavenly dance. This type of carol came out of an era when the practice of using the language of the people in sacred song was just beginning to happen. Adding lines in the local language to the Latin texts of the church was a device used by early reformers of Christian song and paved the way for Martin Luther's German hymns.

Leonard Ellinwood, eminent American hymnologist, tells of a gathering at the Moravian Mission in Bethlehem, Pennsylvania, on September 14, 1745. The mission diary records the singing of "Good Christian Men, Rejoice" simultaneously in thirteen European and Indian languages.

This carol and text have been together from the beginning. Its name "In Dulci Jubilo" means "in sweet shouting" and indicates that the carol should be sung joyfully.

To replace exclusive language, recent hymnals have used "friends" or "folk" in the first line of each stanza to replace "men." This is in keeping with Neale's paraphrase pointing out that Jesus Christ brings salvation to all people. Here is the climactic thrust of the final stanza with the first line altered.

> *Good Christian folk, rejoice*
> *With heart and soul and voice!*
> *Now ye need not fear the grave:*
> *Jesus Christ was born to save;*
> *Calls you one and calls you all,*
> *To gain his everlasting hall.*
> *Christ was born to save!*

A SONG OF PRAISE TO GOD

> *Great is the Lord,*
>   *He is holy and just;*
>   *By his power we trust*
> *In his love.*
> *Great is the Lord,*
>   *He is faithful and true;*
>   *By his mercy he proves*
> *He is love.**

Michael W. Smith is a native of Kenova, a suburb of Huntington, on the western edge of West Virginia. After finishing high school there, he attended Marshall University in

Huntington, majoring in music. In 1978 he moved to Nashville to be closer to a center of musical activities. During the early months there he planted shrubs for a landscape company, wrote music in his spare time, and played in club bands. Although already a Christian, Michael experienced a spiritual awakening and recommitted his life to the Lord. For several months after this he toured with a Christian band called "Higher Power."

Michael then settled down to devote his full time to writing and singing. In 1981 he signed a writer's contract with the Benson Company, a Christian record company in Nashville. Deborah Davis, born and reared in Nashville, was working in the Benson office. Michael and Debbie soon discovered their love for each other and were married. They make their home in Franklin, a suburb of Nashville, and God has blessed them with three children—two boys and a girl.

One day in 1982, Debbie brought to Michael some lyrics she had written which began "Great is the Lord." They sat down together and in less than twenty minutes completed the song. It reflects the words of the psalmist "For as the heaven is high above the earth, so great is his mercy toward them that fear him" (Ps. 103:11) and the words of our Lord spoken to the one that had been possessed with the devil: "Go home to thy friends, and tell them how great things the Lord hath had done for thee, and hath had compassion on thee" (Mark 5:19).

INSPIRED BY A VERSE IN LAMENTATIONS

Great is thy faithfulness, O God my Father,
There is no shadow of turning with thee;
Thou changest not, thy compassions, they fail not;
*As thou hast been thou forever wilt be.**

Thomas O. Chisholm was reared near Franklin, Kentucky. At the age of sixteen he taught in the country school where he had received his education. At twenty-one he became associate editor of his hometown weekly newspaper, *The Franklin Favorite.* At thirty-six he was ordained to the Methodist ministry and joined the Louisville Methodist Conference. After a one-year pastorate his health failed, and he moved to Vineland, New Jersey, and opened an insurance office. Always interested in poetry, he began writing hymn texts. In 1923 he mailed a number of poems to a longtime friend, William M. Runyan, then living in Baldwin, Kansas. Among the poems he sent was the one beginning "Great is thy faithfulness," for which Runyan composed the music.

Runyan, also a Methodist minister, had grown up in Kansas. He was ordained to the ministry when he was twenty-one and pastored several churches for a period of twelve years. In 1903 he was appointed evangelist for the Central Kansas Methodist Conference. He was associated with John Brown University in Arkansas and later with Moody Bible Institute in Chicago. For a number of years he served in an editorial capacity with Hope Publishing Company. He died in 1957 at the age of eighty-seven.

Chisholm's text is based on Lamentations 3:22–23: "It is of the Lord's mercies that we are not consumed, because his compassions fail not. They are new every morning: great is thy faithfulness." In the initial stanza there is also a phrase from James 1:17: "Every good gift and every perfect gift is from above, and cometh down from the Father of lights, with whom is no variableness, neither shadow of turning."

WELSH HYMNWRITER RELIES ON BIBLICAL IMAGERY

Guide me, O thou great Jehovah,
Pilgrim through this barren land;
I am weak, but thou art mighty;
Hold me with thy powerful hand;
Bread of heaven,
Feed me till I want no more.

William Williams was born in Pantycelyn, Wales, the son of a well-to-do farmer. His plans to be a physician were suddenly changed by the fervent preaching of Welsh evangelist Howell Harris. He was ordained in the Church of England, but his strong evangelical views brought him opposition from church leaders. For this reason he withdrew from the Anglican church and joined the Calvinistic Methodists.

Not interested in settling down to a local congregation, Williams became an itinerant evangelist and was assisted by his wife, a gifted singer. His fame as a preacher spread throughout Wales, and for almost a half century, by his own records, he traveled more than 95,000 miles preaching the gospel.

On foot, horseback, or by carriage, he traveled in all kinds of weather. Pouring rain, freezing snow, chilling wind, and blistering sun all became part of his daily experiences. Sometimes he was physically attacked by local gangs, once almost beaten to death for his preaching.

Even more distinctive than his preaching are the hymns he wrote—over eight hundred in the Welsh language and more than one hundred in English. Several editions of his hymns have been exceedingly popular in Wales.

A significant factor of his hymns was the motivation they provided to illiterate Welsh people to learn to read. So popular were his hymns that people who could not read used them in learning to read and subsequently memorized a great many of Williams' hymns.

"Guide Me, O Thou Great Jehovah," written in Welsh in 1744, is full of word pictures from the Scriptures. "Bread of heaven," "fiery, cloudy pillar," "verge of Jordan," "Land me safe on Canaan's side," all bring reminders of the trek of the children of Israel from bondage in Egypt to the Promised Land. Many other biblical references may be identified.

Several different tunes are sung with this hymn. But the tune that seems to be increasingly popular is "Cwm Rhondda," composed by John Hughes in 1907. (See "God of Grace and God of Glory" on page 90 for details.)

A HYMN OF RECONCILIATION BETWEEN GOD AND HUMANKIND

Hark! the herald angels sing,
"Glory to the newborn King;

Peace on earth and mercy mild;
God and sinners reconciled."
Joyful, all ye nations rise,
Join the triumph of the skies;
With angelic hosts proclaim,
"Christ is born in Bethlehem."

Written less than a year after his spiritual renewal at Aldersgate in 1738, these lines reflect Charles Wesley's joy in his new relationship with God. Wesley wrote more than 6,500 hymns, but this hymn, sung around the world at Christmastime, may be the best of all. The opening line of the original poem did not mention angels, but used the Old English word "welkin," which means the vault of heaven, or the sky.

Hark! how all the welkin rings
Glory to the King of Kings.

No one surpasses Charles Wesley when it comes to filling a short hymn with an extraordinary amount of scriptural truth. Because of our familiarity with the text and its frequent use at Christmastime, the theological substance may be overlooked. Wesley intended for all who sang this song to understand more fully the redemptive and reconciling mission of Christ. He adds line to line, truth to truth, doctrine to doctrine to impress upon the singer that Christ came to redeem all humankind. The dominant theme of the hymn is found in the fourth line of the first stanza: "God and sinner reconciled."

The tune that has become inseparable from this text has a fascinating story. In 1840 Felix Mendelssohn wrote a festive choral work for men's voices and brass instruments to commemorate the four-hundredth anniversary of the invention of printing. Fifteen years later, English musician William H. Cummings was struck by the fact that the melody from the second chorus of Mendelssohn's work was perfect for Wesley's text. He made the adaptation and it has been a perennial favorite since that time. Unfortunately, Mendelssohn never knew of the use of his melody for this Christmas hymn because he died in 1847.

A HYMN INSPIRED BY
A PRAYER MEETING

Have thine own way, Lord!
Have thine own way!
Thou art the potter,
I am the clay!
Mold me and make me,
After thy will,
While I am waiting,
Yielded and still.

An old lady entered a Christian bookstore in Philadelphia seeking some study material. The young clerk who helped her mentioned her own conversion experience. The clerk told of the minister's message, which spoke so directly to her, and the singing of "Have Thine Own Way, Lord," which led her to accept Christ. At the mention of the hymn the old lady's face brightened, and she told how the hymn came into being.

The woman who had written it was in great difficulty. Though she prayed earnestly for the Lord's guidance, she was rebelling against the obvious decision she should make. With some friends she attended a prayer meeting. The devotional message and prayers provided little help until someone leading in prayer said, "Lord, it doesn't matter what you bring into our lives, just have your own way with us." The words stuck in the woman's mind, and she found herself saying again and again, "Have thine own way, Lord." That evening at home she wrote the four stanzas of the hymn.

After the old lady finished telling the story to the salesclerk, her eyes filled with tears as she said, "I wrote that hymn many years ago, never dreaming how much God would use it for a blessing in other lives."

Adelaide Pollard was born and reared in Iowa. A skillful teacher of the art of public speaking, she taught in several schools in Chicago and the northeast. She wanted to be a missionary, but ill health prevented this. Finally, just before World War I, she became a visiting missionary in South Africa. During the war she and other missionaries of her group were transferred to Scotland. After the war they returned to New

York and she continued her ministries in New England. She died in New York City in 1934, just before Christmas.

INSPIRED BY WORDS OF SCHWEITZER

He comes to us as one unknown,
A breath unseen, unheard;
As though within a heart of stone,
Or shriveled seed in darkness sown,
*A pulse of being stirred.**

Albert Schweitzer, in *The Quest of the Historical Jesus,* says of Christ: "He comes to us as One unknown, without a name, as of old, by the lakeside, He came to those first men who knew him not."

Timothy Dudley-Smith heard these words quoted in a lecture on the Gospels by the dean of Norwich, David Edwards, in 1982. They lingered in his mind and he wrote them down in his notebook.

In August of that year Dudley-Smith and his family were in their summer home on the southern coast of Cornwall in England. During the days of quiet relaxation, he thumbed through his notebook, reading the ideas, words, phrases, and Scriptures he had written down in the previous months. His eyes fell on the notes he made during David Edwards' lecture. He quickly completed two stanzas reminding us of the way we perceive God as "He comes to us." He later added three stanzas, the final stanza reflecting the maturity of the Christian pilgrimage.

He comes in truth when faith is grown;
Believed, obeyed, adored:
The Christ in all the Scriptures shown,
As yet unseen, but not unknown,
Our Savior and our Lord.

Since the mid-seventies, Timothy Dudley-Smith and his family have enjoyed summer vacations in their cottage at Ruan Minor in Cornwall. There they swim, surf, and sunbathe on nearby beaches. At the cottage there is abundant time for leisure reading, writing, and rest. Since the demands of his work schedule as Bishop of Thetford in Norwich leave Dudley-Smith little opportunity for creative writing, most of his hymn writing has been done during summer holidays at Ruan Minor. What a wealth of hymnic excellence has emerged from this Anglican as he has provided new songs for Christians everywhere.

A HYMN WRITTEN AFTER
A PRAYER MEETING

He leadeth me! O blessed thought!
O words with heavenly comfort fraught!
Whate'er I do, where'er I be,
Still 'tis God's hand that leadeth me.

A young ministerial student was invited to preach for a couple of weeks in the First Baptist Church of Philadelphia. His discourse at the midweek service on Wednesday evening, March 26, 1861, was based on the familiar Twenty-third Psalm, a message he had brought on several previous occasions. This time, however, because of his grave concern for the conflict between the states of the union, and for other reasons, the words "he leadeth me" seemed to have unusual significance. He was staying in the home of Deacon Wattson, who lived next door to the church. Following the service he discussed his message with his host family, then went to his room and penciled on the back of his notes the stanzas of the hymn "He Leadeth Me."

The young minister was Joseph H. Gilmore, who was ordained to the Baptist ministry the following year. His father was elected governor of New Hampshire in 1863, and during his term in office young Gilmore served as his private secretary and also as editor of the Concord *Daily Monitor*. In addition to his pastoral work, Gilmore was professor of logic, rhetoric, and English literature at the University of Rochester for forty-three years.

When Gilmore returned home after his days in Philadelphia, he gave the hymn to his wife and forgot about it. Mrs. Gilmore kept the poem safely for some months, then sent it anonymously to the *Watchman and Reflector,* a weekly paper, which published it on December 4, 1862.

The poem fell into the hands of William B. Bradbury, who was already well known for composing "Jesus Loves Me, This I Know," "Sweet Hour of Prayer," and "Savior, Like a Shepherd Lead Us." Bradbury made some alterations in Gilmore's text, wrote the tune that we know today, and published it in his collection *The Golden Censer* in 1864.

For more than fifty years, until the building was demolished, a bronze tablet commemorating the writing of the hymn was mounted on a building on the northwest corner of Broad and Arch Streets in Philadelphia.

A HYMN WRITTEN IN JAIL

> *He who would valiant be*
> *'Gainst all disaster,*
> *Let him in constancy*
> *Follow the Master.*
> > *There's no discouragement*
> > *Shall make him once relent*
> > *His first avowed intent*
> > *To be a pilgrim.*

John Bunyan wrote these lines while in a jail in Bedford, England. Born in 1628, Bunyan learned to read and write in the local grammar school. From his father he learned the trade of a tinker—mending kettles and pots. His preaching in the Baptist church brought him into conflict with the local authorities because his services did not conform to those of the Church of England. He was imprisoned for twelve years and during this time wrote many pamphlets. He was released from prison in 1672, but in less than six months he was arrested again for illegal preaching.

During his second imprisonment Bunyan wrote *Pilgrim's Progress,* a fictional story drawing on the common life and culture of the countryside. The story involves a man named Christian whose pilgrimage took him through danger and distraction to the Celestial City.

Virtues and weaknesses became the names of persons or places Christian encountered, such as Simple, Sloth, Presumption, Mistrust, Watchful, Hopeful, Ignorance, Vanity Fair, Delectable Mountain, Faith.

To the 1684 edition of *Pilgrim's Progress,* Bunyan added a second part that included the poem "Who Would True Valor See." For Bunyan bravery was the basic virtue of Christian character, and this is reflected in these lines.

While Bunyan was not opposed to hymn singing in his Baptist church in Bedford, he did not intend for any of the poems in *Pilgrim's Progress* to be so used. So, for two centuries, until the beginning of the present century, "Who would true valor see" remained an unsung text.

For the 1906 *English Hymnal,* Percy Dearmer altered the original text to make it suitable for congregational singing. He changed the opening line to "He who would valiant be" and removed such words as "hobgoblins," "foul fiends," "lion," and "giant" lest they shock some worshipers.

A HYMN FOR TRINITY SUNDAY

Holy, holy, holy! Lord God Almighty!
Early in the morning our song shall rise to thee;
Holy, holy, holy, merciful and mighty!
God in three Persons, blessed Trinity.

Reginal Heber, who wrote these lines, was born into a family of wealth and culture. Following his graduation from Oxford University in 1807, he took holy orders in the Church of England and became rector of his father's church in the small village of Hodnet in western England.

The hymn singing was poor at Hodnet, and Heber obtained some copies of John Newton's and William Cowper's *Olney Hymns* to bring new enthusiasm to the singing. This 1779 book included "Amazing Grace."

For his weekly services Heber followed the Anglican Prayer Book and the ecclesiastical year, but he could not find appropriate hymns for all the Sundays of the year. So he solicited new hymns from friends and wrote some himself. "Holy, Holy, Holy" is Heber's hymn for Trinity Sunday, which occurs in the Church Year eight weeks after Easter.

After 16 years at Hodnet, Heber was appointed Bishop of Calcutta. His diocese included most of India; the distances he had to travel and the climate of the country drained his strength. He died in India at the age of 43 after three short but effective years of service for the Church of England.

The tune we sing to these words was written by John B. Dykes, noted English hymn composer. It is one of the most frequently used tunes in hymnals around the world.

When Dykes published the tune in 1861 he named it "Nicaea" in recognition of the Council of Nicaea, which met in A.D. 325. The meeting in Nicaea, an ancient town in Asia Minor, produced a summary of Christian doctrine that included an important affirmation of the doctrine of the Trinity. The belief in the Trinity—that God is three persons in one: God the Father, God the Son, and God the Holy Spirit—was clearly set forth in this document and is reflected today in the Nicene Creed.

EXCEEDING GREAT AND PRECIOUS PROMISES

How firm a foundation, ye saints of the Lord,
Is laid for your faith in his excellent Word!
What more can he say than to you he hath said,
To you who for refuge to Jesus have fled?

Strangely, the names of the persons who wrote these words and composed the tune we sing to them are unknown. There is, however, a tantalizing clue as to the author of the words. This hymn first appeared in John Rippon's hymnal published in London in 1787. Below it was one initial: "K." Scholars have searched for almost two hundred years in an effort to identify the mysterious person represented by this initial.

Robert Keen, George Keith, and some Kirkhams have been proposed as the anonymous writer, but none with valid proof.

The 1787 version of the hymn had seven stanzas and was entitled "Exceeding Great and Precious Promises." Today's hymnals use four, sometimes five, of the original. The first stanza reminds us that the Bible is the foundation of the Christian faith. The stanzas that follow are printed in quotation marks in most hymnals, "I am with thee," "I am thy God," "I'll strengthen thee," "I will not desert to his foes," "I'll never ... forsake." These are sayings from God, selected from Scripture and carefully pieced together in poetic form. There are from two to five scriptural references obviously identifiable in each stanza, more than in most other hymns we sing. The unknown author was certainly familiar with the Bible.

The tune most frequently used today for this text is called "Foundation." It first appeared in a shape-note book published in the Shenandoah Valley of Virginia. Joseph Funk, the compiler of the book, was a devout Mennonite. He was a farmer, school teacher, printer, and singing-school teacher in Rockingham County. "Foundation" was one of the six new tunes that he included in *Genuine Church Music* in 1832, but he gave no composer or source for it.

The tune "Foundation" has a simple, folklike quality, but also a sturdiness that makes it appropriate for the text. The melody fits each stanza in a unique way, the accents of the music and the words coinciding. What a thrilling emphatic climax occurs in the hammering repetition of the last line of the final stanza, "I'll never, no never, no never, forsake."

This was the favorite hymn of Theodore Roosevelt, and Andrew Jackson requested that it be sung at his bedside shortly before he died at the Hermitage near Nashville, Tennessee. By his own request, the hymn was sung at the funeral of Robert E. Lee "as an expression of his full trust in the ways of the Heavenly Father."

FOR SINGING IN A
BIBLE STUDY CLASS

How sweet the name of Jesus sounds
In a believer's ear!

It soothes his sorrows, heals his wounds,
And drives away his fear.

John Newton was the tide surveyor in Liverpool, England. He kept the records of all ships entering the harbor and the cargo they carried. At the age of thirty, he had settled down in Liverpool after a rather tumultuous life as a seafaring man. His wife, Mary, was a woman of strong Christian faith, and had been in love with John Newton for many years. She had prayed that he would leave his life at sea and find a calmer, quieter life. After two or three years in Liverpool, John Newton became concerned about spiritual matters and felt the Lord's call to the ministry. He began to read all the theological books and Bible commentaries he could find.

Because of Newton's lack of university training, the bishops of the Church of England were unwilling to ordain him. Only the intervention of an influential patron secured for him his ordination and appointment to the parish church in Olney, a small village in Buckinghamshire famed for its bobbin lace. John and Mary Newton were very happy in Olney.

A wealthy patron had willed to the Olney church a large house on adjacent property. To make good use of the Great House, as it was called in the village, and to provide opportunities for Bible study, Newton began Thursday evening classes in it. For these Bible classes for adults and children, Newton decided to add some new hymns to those the people knew. He enlisted the help of his friend William Cowper, and together in 1779 they published their hymns under the title *Olney Hymns*. "How Sweet the Name of Jesus Sounds" was one of Newton's hymns in this collection. It is based on a phrase in Song of Solomon 1:3, "Thy name is as ointment poured forth." Uncomplicated and clear in meaning, the hymn expresses a simple, personal devotion to Christ.

A BETTER TEXT FOR
A SINGABLE TUNE

I am resolved no longer to linger,
Charmed by the world's delight;

Things that are higher,
Things that are nobler,
    These have allured my sight.
I will hasten to him,
    Hasten so glad and free,
Jesus, greatest, highest,
    I will come to thee.

The hymn had its beginning as a song written for a worldwide convention in San Francisco. Christian Endeavor, a religious organization founded by Frances E. Clarke, held a convention in 1896 for members from around the world. Fourteen trainloads of people made the trip from Ohio to San Francisco. For the occasion James H. Fillmore, a composer and music publisher who lived in Cincinnati, wrote a delegation song—words and music. All the way to San Francisco and back to Ohio, the song was sung joyfully on all the trains.

So popular was the music that some suggested that a more permanent text be written. Palmer Hartsough, one of Fillmore's staff writers, was assigned the task, and wrote the present text. An itinerant singing-school teacher, Hartsough settled in Rock Island, Illinois, about 1877, where he opened a music studio. He taught vocal and instrumental music and directed music at the Baptist church. About 1893 he moved to Cincinnati and began work at the Fillmore Music Company.

James H. Fillmore and his brothers had established a successful music publishing firm in Cincinnati. Many popular publications for churches and Sunday schools were distributed throughout the nation by this firm. Choral music, sheet music, hymnals and songbooks, and band and orchestral music filled the Fillmore catalogs. A devout member of the Christian Church, Fillmore composed much sacred music. He was a highly respected leader in his church's denomination.

Henry Fillmore, James H. Fillmore's son, became famous as a band director and composer of band marches. For a number of years before his death in 1956, Henry Fillmore was the distinguished conductor of the massed band that played annually for the Orange Bowl in Miami, Florida.

INSPIRED IN CINCINNATI

I am thine, O Lord, I have heard thy voice,
And it told thy love to me;
But I long to rise in the arms of faith,
And be closer drawn to thee.
Draw me nearer, nearer blessed Lord,
To the cross where thou hast died;
Draw me nearer, nearer, blessed Lord,
To thy precious, bleeding side.

The blind poet Fanny Crosby composed many poems on the spur of the moment. A chance remark or an unexpected experience would provide the inspiration for her poetic expressions. In 1874 she left New York for a speaking tour that took her as far west as Cincinnati. During her brief visit there she spoke to crowds of people in churches and missions. She was an extremely popular speaker.

In Cincinnati she was a guest in the home of William Howard Doane, a wealthy manufacturer of woodworking machinery and an amateur composer. Crosby and Doane had met six years earlier and had already collaborated in writing hymns. Crosby enjoyed the fellowship with the Doane family. One evening she and Doane talked at length about the nearness of God in their lives. When Fanny went to her room, her mind and heart were flooded with ideas from their conversation. Before she went to sleep, the lines of "I Am Thine, O Lord" were in her mind.

The next morning she recited the words to Doane, who wrote down the stanzas and composed the tune. The next year, in a Sunday school songbook entitled *Brightest and Best,* he included this hymn along with "All the Way My Savior Leads Me," "Savior, More Than Life to Me," and "To God Be the Glory," all written by Crosby and Doane.

"I Am Thine, O Lord," one of Fanny Crosby's most popular hymns, is based on Hebrews 10:22, "Let us draw near with a true heart in full assurance of faith." After more than a century, the popularity of the hymn has not waned.

REFLECTIONS IN
A PHOTOGRAPHY LAB

I come to the garden alone,
While the dew is still on the roses;
And the voice I hear, falling on my ear,
The Son of God discloses.
And he walks with me, and he talks with me,
And he tells me I am his own,
And the joy we share as we tarry there,
None other has ever known.

At thirty, C. Austin Miles became editor and manager of a music publishing firm in Philadelphia in 1898. His hobby was photography, and he had converted a room in his home into a combination darkroom and study. One day Miles was sitting in his study, reading his Bible about the arrival of Mary, Peter, and John at the tomb where Christ had been buried (John 20). They were still in shock from his crucifixion and death. They loved him and believed him to be the Son of God and could not understand the tragic events of recent days.

When she arrived at the tomb, Mary was surprised to find the stone rolled away. She hastened to tell Peter and John that the body of Jesus had been removed. As Mary stood weeping by the tomb, she looked in and saw two angels sitting where the body of Jesus had lain. In her grief and frustration Mary then turned and saw someone she thought to be the gardener and asked if he had taken Jesus' body and where he had put it. When he called her name, she realized it was Jesus.

In Miles's vivid imagination he saw these events and heard the voices, watching as a silent observer to the scene. From the inspiration of this experience, he wrote the words and music of the hymn. For more than three-quarters of a century Miles' words and music have been a lasting part of evangelical hymnody. The hymn ranks high in most polls of favorite hymns throughout the country.

In addition to editorial positions with Hall-Mack Music Publishers in Philadelphia and the Rodeheaver Company in Winona Lake, Indiana, Miles served as a music director in churches, camp meetings, and conventions. He died at age seventy-eight in Pitman, New Jersey, in 1946.

SAVED FROM A FIREPLACE

I gave my life for thee,
My precious blood I shed,
That thou might'st ransomed be,
And quickened from the dead.
I gave, I gave my life for thee;
What hast thou given for me?

Frances Havergal, daughter of an Anglican minister, wrote the hymn in 1858. An intelligent and sensitive child, she was nicknamed "Little Quicksilver" by her father, for she learned quickly and enjoyed to the fullest every new discovery. Her bright, cheerful disposition endeared her to all who knew her. She was educated in England and Germany and was interested in many subjects, especially languages. She became proficient in Italian, French, German, Latin, Greek, and Hebrew.

As a teenager Frances began memorizing portions of the Bible, and she eventually knew the Gospels (Matthew, Mark, Luke, and John) the Epistles, Revelation, Psalms, and Isaiah.

On one of her travels, Frances Havergal visited the study of a German pastor. On the wall was a large picture of Christ with the words underneath, "I did this for thee; what has thou done for me?" She jotted down the motto in her notebook. Later, at her home in England, she read again the motto and recalled the experience in the pastor's study. In a few minutes she wrote the lines of the poem on a scrap of paper. Rereading the completed poem, she judged it insignificant and tossed the paper into the fireplace. It was strangely untouched by the flame, however, and she retrieved it. Some months later she shared the poem with her father, who urged her to preserve it. It was printed in a leaflet in 1859 and the following year was included in an issue of a religious periodical, *Good Words*.

Philip P. Bliss composed the tune for Havergal's hymn in 1873. The tune, known as "Kenosis," was published with these words in Cincinnati in a Sunday school songbook, *Sunshine for Sunday Schools*.

A SONG FROM INDIA

I have decided to follow Jesus,
I have decided to follow Jesus,
I have decided to follow Jesus,
No turning back, no turning back.

"I Have Decided to Follow Jesus" was first heard in the United States in the 1950s. Its source and circumstances are unknown other than that it seems to have originated in Assam, one of the twenty-one states of India. This interesting province is located in northeast India, almost isolated from the other Indian states by Bangladesh. Geographically it is comprised of more than thirty thousand square miles, and its population is about fifteen million people.

The northern part of Assam borders on the Himalayan Mountain range and the Brahmaputra and Barak rivers. About two-thirds of the Assamese are Hindus, and about a fourth are Muslims. Many of the hill tribes, such as the Garos, have been converted to Christianity by missionaries, but the majority of the people still practice their traditional region.

"I Have Decided to Follow Jesus" seems to have originated with the Garo tribe. To become a Christian is a significant decision for the Garos. In some families it means separation and possible disinheritance. It may also involve the loss of recognition in the community, of means of livelihood, and of friends. To sing "I have decided to follow Jesus" and not turn back is no simple matter for them.

In a conversation with a Baptist minister from Assam at the Baptist World Alliance meeting in Rio de Janeiro in the summer of 1960, this song was mentioned. When the song was sung, Longri Ao smiled in recognition. He confirmed that the song was used with new believers as a statement of their decision to accept Christ and to encourage them in their determination to follow Christ so that there will be "no turning back."

WRITTEN DURING
A CHURCH SERVICE

I hear the Savior say,
  "Thy strength indeed is small,
Child of weakness, watch and pray,
  Find in me thine all in all."
Jesus paid it all,
  All to him I owe;
Sin had left a crimson stain,
  He washed it white as snow.

During a Sunday morning service in the spring of 1865 in Baltimore's Monument Street Methodist Church, Elvina Hall was sitting in her accustomed place in the choir. Some comments and suggestions filled her mind during the service and the lines of a poem began to take shape. To keep from distracting the attention of the congregation, she waited until the minister prayed to quickly open the hymnal in her lap and write the words on the flyleaf. Later she told her minister about the experience and gave him a copy of the poem.

John T. Grape, a skilled amateur musician, was a successful coal merchant in Baltimore who played the organ each Sunday at the Monument Street Methodist Church. Occasionally Grape enjoyed composing hymn tunes. He wrote the tune we associate with "Jesus Paid It All" for another poem he found in a hymnal.

Rev. George W. Schrick, the minister of Monument Street Methodist Church, shared Mrs. Hall's poem with Grape, and they discovered that her words and his new tune fit together perfectly. In the weeks that followed Grape shared the words and tune with friends in other Baltimore churches, where it was sung and well received. With this response, and the encouragement of friends, Grape sent a manuscript of the hymn to Theodore Perkins, a well-known New York publisher of religious music, and it appeared in one of his collections in 1868. The Moody-Sankey songbooks included the hymn, which contributed greatly to its popularity.

SPAWNED BY AN IOWA REVIVAL

I hear thy welcome voice,
That calls me, Lord, to thee,
For cleansing in thy precious blood
That flowed on Calvary.
I am coming, Lord!
Coming now to thee!
Wash me, cleanse me in the blood
That flowed on Calvary.

A Methodist minister who preached on the western frontier in Wyoming and Utah after the Civil War wrote these lines. At a time when mountain men of Wyoming guided pioneering parties across the Oregon Trail and cattlemen and sheepherders engaged in open warfare, Lewis Hartsough went West as the first superintendent of the Methodist Churches of the Utah Mission and was presiding elder of the Wyoming District.

Born in Ithaca, New York, Hartsough completed his theological studies at Cazenovia Seminary in 1852, was ordained, and joined the Oneida Conference in New York. For fifteen years he served churches in the conference and then, because of some health problems, requested a transfer to the West. Hartsough came to Iowa in 1871 and for two years was pastor of the Methodist church at Epworth. Under his leadership the church experienced two great revivals that had tremendous impact on the community. It was at Epworth that he wrote "I Hear Thy Welcome Voice." Of his several hymns, this is the only one that remains in our hymnals today.

Hartsough kept careful records of his ministerial labors throughout the years. According to his own account, he served fifteen pastoral charges and five districts as presiding elder; traveled about four-hundred thousand miles; made nine thousand pastoral visits; led seven thousand prayer meetings, quarterly conferences, and love feasts and preached fifteen hundred sermons. In every circuit and assignment where he preached, the revival fires burned brightly. Most districts doubled their number of pastoral churches and membership during his tenure of service. Settlers poured into the various regions he served, and he was vigilant in ministering and witnessing to them. The hardships and dangers of the West did not shorten his life, for he was ninety years old when he died in Mount Vernon, Iowa, on January 1, 1919.

A HYMN OF VICTORY IN JESUS

I heard an old, old story, how a Savior came from glory,
*   How he gave his life on Calvary to save a wretch*
*   like me:*
I heard about his groaning, of his precious blood's atoning,
*   Then I repented of my sin and won the victory.*
O victory in Jesus, my Savior, forever,
*   He sought me and bought me with his redeeming blood;*
He loved me ere I knew him, and all my love is due him,
*   He plunged me to victory beneath the cleansing flood.**

Eugene M. Bartlett, who wrote both words and music to this song, was born in Missouri. He graduated from Hall-Moody Institute in Martin, Tennessee, and began to teach singing schools and to write songs. His unusual musical talents made young Bartlett a much-sought-after music teacher. His songs were increasingly popular with each succeeding year.

He established the Hartford Music Company of Hartford, Arkansas, in 1918. A large number of songbooks featuring Bartlett's songs and those of contemporary writers known to him were issued by the firm. Among his more popular songs were "I Heard My Mother Call My Name in Prayer," "He Will Remember Me," "Everybody Will Be Happy Over There." His humorous song "Take an Old, Cold Tater and Wait" recalled his experience as a boy when the preacher and other visitors came for Sunday dinner to the Bartlett home. He and the other children had to eat at the "second table" after the others were finished. Frequently they had to be satisfied with an "old cold tater."

For more than twenty years Bartlett conducted singing

116

schools throughout Arkansas, Oklahoma, Texas, Alabama, and Tennessee. For a number of years he edited a monthly music magazine, *Herald of Song,* which promoted the singing schools, carried news of local personalities and activities, and advertised the newest songbooks.

"Victory in Jesus" was written in 1939, two years before Bartlett's death. Bartlett speaks of the joy of salvation in a personal testimony: "then I repented of my sins and won the victory." The song first appeared that year in *Gospel Choruses,* a paperback songbook published by James D. Vaughn in Lawrenceburg, Tennessee. The song has become popular in evangelical congregations in recent years, and the newer hymnals compiled for these churches have included it.

THE BELLS REMIND US OF PEACE AND GOOD WILL

I heard the bells on Christmas day
Their old familiar carols play,
And wild and sweet
The words repeat
Of peace on earth, good will to men.

Henry Wadsworth Longfellow left no written account of the immediate circumstances surrounding the writing of this carol. He wrote it in 1864, when the Civil War was nearing an end. The irony and the importance of using the phrase "peace on earth, good will to men" at a time when the North and South were at war must have gripped his mind: in this context these lines poured from his pen.

The peace and good will about which the angels sang is the sole message of the carol. No other elements of the Christmas story are mentioned directly or implied. There is no reference to Christ's birth, to Mary, Joseph, the manger, Bethlehem, shepherds, wise men, angels, or heavenly host. Furthermore, there is no historical reference here, only the implication of the historical event of Christ's birth.

Longfellow writes in the first person singular throughout the stanzas, and in a very personal way, making known his feelings, thoughts, and responses. He projects the Christmas event into the present time. Peace and good will are not dealt with as something heard by frightened shepherds long ago on Judean hills, but as something strangely missing now. The reality of war denies the presence of peace, and human hatred "mocks the song" of good will to humankind. Yet, there is evidence of the poet's faith and hope in the strong affirmation expressed in the final stanza.

> Then pealed the bells more loud and deep:
> "God is not dead, nor doth he sleep;
>   The wrong shall fail,
>   The right prevail,
>   With peace on earth, good will to men."

THE QUAKER POET'S TRUST IN GOD

> I know not what the future hath
>   Of marvel or surprise,
> Assured alone that life and death
>   His mercy underlies.

John Greenleaf Whittier was a country boy, born in the Merrimac Valley in Massachusetts. His early education lasted only through the middle grades of the district school, but later he attended Haverhill Academy for two terms. His early enthusiasm for the works of poets Robert Burns, Lord Byron, and Sir Walter Scott later widened to include the writings of William Shakespeare and John Milton. His father persuaded him that writing poetry was an unprofitable vocation, and he became a journalist, editing newspapers in Boston and Haverhill.

An ardent abolitionist, Whittier championed the antislavery movement and eagerly supported political candidates, including Abraham Lincoln, who spoke out positively for this cause. Following the freeing of the slaves at the end of the Civil War, Whittier turned his energies to writing poetry. He was known as the "Quaker poet" because of his family's Quaker background and his deep religious sensitivity.

"I Know Not What the Future Hath" is a selection of

stanzas from a longer poem, "The Eternal Goodness," written in 1865. Whittier never intended it to be used as a hymn, but hymnal editors have shaped its present form and placed it in many hymnals today. In these stanzas Whittier claims the goodness of God, though he feels unworthy of God's mercy. The hymn reveals his unswerving faith and trust in God for both the present and the unknown future.

In 1866 Whittier published his most famous poem, "Snowbound," and the popularity that it achieved brought him financial security. He considered his success as a writer the result of a consecrated and disciplined life. In his old age, his words of admonition to a teenage boy were, "My lad, if thou wouldst win success, join thyself to some unpopular but noble cause." He died in 1892 at the age of eighty-five.

CONVERSION IN
A CONFEDERATE PRISON

I know not why God's wondrous grace
To me he hath made known,
Nor why, unworthy, Christ in love
Redeemed me for his own.
But "I know whom I have believed,
And am persuaded that he is able
To keep that which I've committed
Unto him against that day."

Based on 2 Timothy 1:12, the hymn was written by Daniel W. Whittle, a native of Massachusetts. When he was a teenager his family moved to Chicago, and he became a cashier at the Wells Fargo Bank. The Civil War began in 1861 when Whittle was twenty-one. He enlisted in the 72nd Illinois Infantry and fought in the Battle of Vicksburg, where he was wounded in the arm. He also was with General William T. Sherman on his march through Georgia late in 1864, was captured by the Confederate troops, and imprisoned. During this time he was converted through the reading of the New Testament his mother had given him when he left home for the army.

At the end of the war, Whittle was promoted to the rank of major for meritorious service during the campaigns against the city of Mobile, and from then on was known as Major Whittle. After a decade as treasurer of the Elgin Watch Company in Chicago, Whittle became an effective evangelist beginning in 1873. During the next twenty-five years he conducted revival meetings in many states. A close friend of D. L. Moody, Whittle became a highly respected leader in the evangelistic efforts of that era.

A significant aspect of Major Whittle's revivals was the music that he encouraged. Among those who served as music directors for his meetings were Philip P. Bliss, James McGranahan, and George C. Stebbins. Whittle is credited with writing about two hundred hymns, and for most of these he used the pseudonym "El Nathan." Among his hymns that are still found in our hymnals are "Dying with Jesus, by Death Reckoned Mine," "There Shall Be Showers of Blessing," and "There's a Royal Banner Given for Display."

"I Know Not Why God's Wondrous Grace" was written in 1883, with the tune composed by James McGranahan. This may have been Whittle's most popular gospel song.

THE PRESIDENT OF YALE
LOVED THE CHURCH

I love thy kingdom, Lord,
The house of thine abode,
The church our blest Redeemer saved
With his own precious blood.

Timothy Dwight was an extraordinary man. A grandson of the New England preacher Jonathan Edwards, he was born in Massachusetts in 1752. At the age of four he could read the Bible, at six he was enrolled in grammar school, and at thirteen he entered Yale College. Intense study in his youth permanently injured his eyesight, and in his later years he endured constant pain. At times he was able to read for only fifteen minutes a day.

Ordained to the Congregational ministry, he served as a chaplain in the Continental Army. A close friend of George Washington, Dwight became one of the most influential intellectual leaders during the first decades of the new republic of the United States. For seventeen years he served as president of Yale College. The extent of his scholarship may be seen in that in addition to his administrative duties he taught ethics, metaphysics, logic, theology, literature, and oratory. When he took office there were only five Christians among the student body. His preaching in chapel resulted in a remarkable spiritual awakening that changed the school and spread to other educational institutions in New England.

"I Love Thy Kingdom, Lord" was written in 1801. It is the oldest American hymn sung in our churches today. Dwight uses the words "kingdom," "house," "church," and "Zion" to mean the same thing—God's people, the church. Stanza two borrows phrases from David's prayer, "Keep me as the apple of the eye" (Ps. 17:8), and from Isaiah, "I have graven thee upon the palms of my hands" (Isa. 49:16). In stanza four, Dwight expresses his joy in the church's "heavenly ways"—communion, the solemn vows of confirmation at baptism, and the hymns—the simple rites of the church that Dwight served. The hymn speaks unashamedly of love and adoration for the church and can be a valued expression for any congregation.

A HYMN WRITTEN BY A BANKER'S DAUGHTER

I love to tell the story
  Of unseen things above,
Of Jesus and his glory,
  Of Jesus and his love;
I love to tell the story
  Because I know 'tis true;
It satisfies my longing
  As nothing else can do.

The author of these lines was christened Arabella Catherine Hankey, but she was known to her friends as Kate. Her father, a prominent banker in Clapham, a suburb south of London, was one of a group of evangelical Christians known as the Clapham Sect. They worked for the abolition of slavery in England and were active in promoting missionary endeavors.

All these activities influenced the Hankey family, and Kate became interested in religious and social activities. As a teenager she taught Sunday school, and later organized a large Bible class for girls who clerked in the shops of London. Later she began a class for friends in her social circle. She was quite successful and influential in these projects.

A trip to South Africa to care for her invalid brother proved enlightening, especially traveling "up country" by oxcart. The trip whetted her interest in foreign missions, and she devoted the income from her writing to this cause.

In 1866 Kate Hankey wrote the story of Jesus in poetic verse and titled it "The Old, Old Story." In simple language she articulated the beliefs of the evangelicals. "I Love to Tell the Story" is made up of verses from the poem.

The music we associate with these words was composed by William G. Fischer in 1869, three years after the poem first appeared. He had taught for ten years at Girard College and resigned that year to open a retail piano store in Philadelphia.

Fisher was a well-known and highly respected music teacher and choral conductor. He conducted the combined Welsh singing societies for the bicentennial celebration of the landing of William Penn, the founder of Pennsylvania. At the Moody-Sankey meetings in Philadelphia in 1876, he led a great chorus of one thousand voices.

Fischer composed the music for more than two hundred gospel songs, but those that survive today are "Whiter Than Snow," "I Am Coming to the Cross," "The Rock That Is Higher Than I," and "I Love to Tell the Story."

A HYMN OF COMFORT
IN TIMES OF DISTRESS

I must tell Jesus all of my trials;
I cannot bear my burdens alone;
In my distress he kindly will help me;

He ever loves and cares for his own.
I must tell Jesus! I must tell Jesus!
I cannot bear my burdens alone;
I must tell Jesus! I must tell Jesus!
Jesus can help me, Jesus alone.

In 1894 Elisha Hoffman, pastor of the Presbyterian church in Vassar, Michigan, visited an elderly lady who was experiencing great difficulties in her life. Distressed and troubled, she shared her problems with her pastor and asked for his counsel. Hoffman sought to comfort and console her, recalling several familiar passages from the Bible, such as, "come unto me all ye that labor and are heavy laden and I will give you rest." He urged her to pray and to tell her problems to Jesus. This suggestion struck a responsive note in her mind, and she smiled and exclaimed, "Yes, I must tell Jesus."

On his way home, Hoffman repeated to himself the line "I must tell Jesus," and shortly other lines seemed to fall into place. At home he completed the words and soon had written a singable melody for them.

Across the years Hoffman maintained an effective ministry. In his early ministry he was active in mission work in Ohio and Pennsylvania; later he was pastor of Congregational and Presbyterian churches in Michigan and Illinois.

In 1911, when he was 72, he accepted the pastorate of the Presbyterian church in Cabery, Illinois, and preached there for eleven years. At the age of 83 he retired from pastoral work, and he died in Chicago in 1929.

Many people were blessed by Hoffman's pastoral ministry, but vast multitudes have sung his songs and shared the joy of the experiences he described in "Down at the Cross Where My Savior Died," "Are You Washed in the Blood of the Lamb," and "What a Fellowship, What a Joy Divine."

A BROOKLYN WOMAN'S DEPENDENCE ON THE LORD

I need thee every hour,
Most gracious Lord;

No tender voice like thine
  Can peace afford.
I need thee, O I need thee;
Every hour I need thee!
  O bless me now, my Savior,
I come to thee.

Annie Hawks wrote these words in the summer of 1872. A Brooklyn homemaker, she enjoyed good health and was cherished by her husband and children. In the busy routine of her work in the home one day, she felt a "sense of nearness to the Master, and these words, 'I need thee every hour,' were ushered into my mind." She shared the poem with Robert Lowry, a former pastor of her church. Lowry, editor and composer as well as minister, had encouraged her in her poetic writing and provided music for her poems.

Robert Lowry wrote the music for "I Need Thee Every Hour" and introduced the song at the National Baptist Sunday School Convention in Cincinnati in November of 1872. The immediate response encouraged Lowry to include the song in a collection of Sunday school songs that he published in 1873. The following year it was sung in the meetings conducted in the east end of London by D. L. Moody and Ira D. Sankey.

The church building in Brooklyn where Mrs. Hawks and her family worshiped, Hansen Place Baptist Church, still stands today. In the early 1960s the Baptist congregation merged with the Emmanuel Baptist Church in Brooklyn and sold their church property to a congregation of another denomination. The building has been beautifully restored to its original design and now proudly bears the name—Hansen Place Seventh Day Adventist Church.

Mrs. Hawks lived to be almost eighty-two. She wrote more than four hundred hymns, but is remembered today for only this one.

A JOYFUL HYMN OF CREATION

I sing th'almighty power of God,
  That made the mountains rise,
That spread the flowing seas abroad,

And built the lofty skies.
I sing the wisdom that ordained
The sun to rule the day;
The moon shines full at his command,
And all the stars obey.

Isaac Watts wrote these lines at the request of a friend who worked with children. They were published with other writings in his *Divine Songs Attempted in Easy Language for the Use of Children,* 1715. Watts wrote these songs and said in the preface, "I have endeavored to sink the language to the level of a child's understanding."

The hymn presents a marvelous view of God's world in a panorama seen through the eyes of a believer, and with ideas from the first chapter of Genesis. After mentioning God's power, wisdom, and greatness, the last half of stanza two declares:

Lord, how thy wonders are displayed,
Where'er I turn my eye,
If I survey the ground I tread,
Or gaze upon the sky!

Sometimes referred to as the "father of English hymnody," Watts wrote more than six hundred hymns that consistently reflect a spirit of awe and reverence for the majesty and greatness of God. Watts is also the author of the familiar "When I Survey the Wondrous Cross," one of the many hymns he wrote for his congregation. Little did the people of this chapel on Mark Lane in London know when they sang the hymns for the first time that they would be known around the world in the last decades of the twentieth century.

In many hymnals today, "I Sing th'almighty Power of God" is sung to a tune called "Forest Green." Ralph Vaughan Williams, distinguished English composer, discovered this melody in 1903. He was in Surrey, England, in the village of Forest Green, listening to some elderly people sing some almost forgotten folk songs. He wrote this one down, harmonized it, made it into a hymn tune, and named it "Forest Green" for the village. What an excellent tune to complement an excellent text!

THE SAVING POWER OF JESUS' LOVE

I was sinking deep in sin,
Far from the peaceful shore,
Very deeply stained within,
Sinking to rise no more;
But the master of the sea
Heard my despairing cry,
From the waters lifted me,
Now safe am I.
Love lifted me! Love lifted me!
When nothing else could help,
Love lifted me.

When James Rowe finished writing these lines in Saugatuck, Connecticut, in 1912, he thought the poem might be singable as a gospel song. He invited his friend Howard E. Smith, a local church organist, to drop by his house. They read the poem together as they visited, then Smith sat down at the piano and began to play. Louise, Rowe's daughter, recounted that Smith was a small man whose hands were so misshapen with arthritis that she was surprised he could play the piano. For some time the two men worked at fitting words to music and music to words. With Smith at the piano and Rowe walking around and around the room humming and singing a phrase at a time, the song took shape.

Rowe came to the United States from England when he was twenty-five. First working for the railroad, then for a humane society, Rowe eventually became engrossed in literary work. Through writing song texts and editing music journals, he was successively associated with the Trio Music Company in Waco, Texas, A. J. Showalter Music Company in Chattanooga, Tennessee, and James D. Vaughn Music Company in Lawrenceburg, Tennessee, major publishers in the South. In his later years Rowe lived in Wells, Vermont, and devoted his time to writing serious and humorous verse for greeting-card publishers. He wrote poetic verse with the greatest of ease. In his lectures he delighted in composing extemporaneously a poem of some length as he spoke to the assembled audience. By his own record, he wrote more than nineteen thousand song texts. He died in 1933. The hymn entitled "Love Lifted Me" remains his most popular song.

A TREASURE IN A TRUNK

I will sing of my Redeemer
    And his wondrous love to me;
On the cruel cross he suffered
    From the curse to set me free.
Sing, oh, sing of my Redeemer,
    With his blood he purchased me;
On the cross he sealed my pardon,
    Paid the debt and made me free.

Philip P. Bliss and his wife were among the victims of the fire that ensued after a tragic train wreck. (See "Sing them over again to me," page 250 for more details). Bliss's trunk was not damaged in the train wreck, and among his personal papers was the poem "I Will Sing of My Redeemer."

Early in 1877 Major Whittle invited James McGranahan, a gifted young musician, to come to Chicago for an interview as a possible successor to Bliss. During their conversations Whittle showed McGranahan the poem that had survived the wreck, and McGranahan composed a tune for it. The song was first sung by a men's quartet at a great tabernacle meeting in Chicago that spring. Singing in the quartet were McGranahan, George C. Stebbins, and two singers from Chicago.

Some months later Stebbins attended an exhibition of the new Edison phonograph in New York City. In a demonstration recording he sang "I Will Sing of My Redeemer," giving it the distinction of being one of the first songs recorded on Thomas A. Edison's new invention. The recording was made on a cylinder wrapped in tinfoil and turned by hand. Stebbins later wrote that "the hearing of my own voice, and every word with striking distinctness enunciated, and even my characteristic manner of singing, modulation of voice and phrasing, produced a unique sensation."

A FRUITFUL COLLABORATION

I will sing the wondrous story
Of the Christ who died for me,
How he left his home in glory
For the cross of Calvary.

A young Swiss musician named Peter Bilhorn was leading the music in a revival meeting in the First Baptist Church in North Adams, Massachusetts, in 1886. He asked the church's minister, Francis H. Rowley, to write a hymn text for him. Rowley completed the words and Bilhorn composed the tune now know as "Wondrous Story." The following year the hymn was included in Ira D. Sankey's published collections, which were widely used in America and England.

Francis H. Rowley, a native of Hilton, New York, was educated at the University of Rochester and Rochester Theological Seminary and ordained to the Baptist ministry in 1878. After more than thirty years of pastoring churches in several states, he became president of the Massachusetts Society for the Prevention of Cruelty to Animals, and served until his retirement in 1945 at the age of ninety-one. Rowley's intense interest in humanitarian activities prompted the naming of the Rowley School of Humanities at Oglethorpe University in Atlanta, Georgia, in his honor.

Peter Bilhorn possessed a fine singing voice and became a popular singer in the German concert halls and beer gardens of Chicago. He became a Christian in 1883 during a revival in Chicago and later traveled extensively in evangelistic work. In need of a small, portable musical instrument for his revivals, he invented a small reed organ weighing less than seventy pounds. It was carried in a folding case. Portable organs, manufactured by the Bilhorn Folding Organ Company in Chicago, were very useful for evangelistic and missionary work. During World War I the American forces in France used the organs for religious services on the battlefront.

At the World's Christian Endeavor Convention in London's Crystal Palace in 1900, Bilhorn conducted a choir of four thousand singers. At the invitation of Queen Victoria, he sang several of his hymns in the chapel of Buckingham Palace.

Bilhorn wrote more than two thousand songs and became a successful publisher of gospel songbooks in Chicago.

Rowley's hymn is also sung to the Welsh hymn tune "Hyfrydol," composed by Rowland H. Prichard in 1830. This tune and text first appeared together in a songbook prepared for the evangelist Gipsy Smith in 1909. In all probability Prichard's tune will outlast Bilhorn's for Rowley's text.

A POSITIVE VIEW OF GOD'S PROVIDENCE

If thou but suffer God to guide thee,
And hope in him through all thy ways,
He'll give thee strength, whate'er betide thee,
And bear thee through the evil days;
Who trusts in God's unchanging love
Builds on the rock that none can move.

Georg Neumark left home in 1641 to enroll in the university at Konigsberg in East Prussia, the only school in the country that had not closed because of the Thirty Years' War. Frequently people traveling alone or in small groups were attacked by mercenary bands of robbers, so to make the journey safely from his hometown of Langensalya, Neumark attached himself to a caravan of merchants. The caravan was attacked and robbers took everything Neumark had except his prayerbook and a small amount of money he had sewn into his clothing. With his money and possessions gone, the possibility of his entering the university was gone. In vain he searched for work in several cities and eventually became destitute.

In Kiel, Neumark was befriended by a Lutheran pastor who got for him a position as tutor to the family of a judge. The job and the security it provided, after months of frustration and privation, brought Neumark indescribable joy. Later he wrote that his good fortune "coming suddenly, as if it had fallen from heaven, greatly rejoiced me, and on that very day I composed to the honor of my beloved Lord the hymn 'If Thou but Suffer God to Guide Thee.'" During his two years as a tutor he saved enough money to enroll in the university to study law and poetry. He became court poet, librarian, and registrar to Duke Wilhelm II at Thuringia, and was later responsible for the Ducal Archives. Neumark wrote thirty-four hymns, but only this one has survived.

The English translation of Neumark's hymn that we sing was made by Catherine Winkworth in 1863. Other translations have been made, but Winkworth's has been most widely accepted. In recent years her translation has been altered to update some of the expressions. "If you will only let God guide you" and "If you but trust in God to guide you" are two altered versions of the opening line.

The essence of Neumark's unquestioned confidence in God is captured in the final couplet of the final stanza:

God never yet forsook at need
The soul that trusted him indeed.

BORN IN A MARYLAND CAMP MEETING

If you are tired of the load of your sin,
Let Jesus come into your heart;
If you desire a new life to begin,
Let Jesus come into your heart.
Just now, your doubtings give o'er
Just now, reject him no more;
Just now, throw open the door;
Let Jesus come into your heart.

On a Sunday morning in 1898, a Methodist camp meeting was in progress at Mountain Lake Park in Maryland. In the morning sermon, the Reverend L. H. Baker preached with unusual power on "Repentance." At the conclusion of the service many came forward to the altar. One woman, by appearance and attire a person of culture and refinement, came to the altar obviously possessed by an inner struggle. Mrs. Leila Morris, who was standing near, knelt with the woman to pray and counsel with her. Dr. Henry L. Gilmour, the music director for the camp meeting, was also nearby. Mrs.

Morris whispered to the woman, "Just now your doubtings give o'er," and Dr. Gilmour added, "Just now reject him no more." Mrs. Morris concluded, "Let Jesus come into your heart." The woman accepted Christ and there was great rejoicing. Out of this experience Mrs. Morris wrote the hymn, and it was sung the last days of the camp meeting and in other meetings she attended that summer. Leila Morris made her home in McConnelsville, Ohio, and was active in the Methodist Episcopal Church. In the late 1890s, she began writing hymns—words and music—and over a period of thirty-seven years she wrote about fifteen hundred. Among her most popular hymns are "What If It Were Today?" "Nearer, Still Nearer," "Sweeter as the Years Go By," and "The Stranger of Galilee." In 1913 her eyesight began to fail, and to help her continue her song writing her son erected a large blackboard, twenty-eight feet long, with music staff lines on it. Within a year her sight was gone, but she continued to write music with the help of devoted friends. She died in 1929 at the age of sixty-seven in Auburn, New York.

The person instrumental in publishing "Let Jesus Come Into Your Heart" was Dr. Henry L. Gilmour. A dentist in Wenonah, New Jersey, and a devout Methodist layman, Dr. Gilmour practiced dentistry for eight months each year, and spent the four summer months leading music in camp meetings. Together with William J. Kirkpatrick, he compiled several collections and held the copyrights of quite a number of new gospel songs. He wrote the words for "The Haven of Rest."

A HYMN THAT SOLD FOR
FIVE DOLLARS

I'm pressing on the upward way,
New heights I'm gaining every day;
Still praying as I'm onward bound,
Lord, plant my feet on higher ground.
Lord, lift me up and let me stand,
By faith on heaven's tableland,

A higher plane than I have found;
Lord, plant my feet on higher ground.

Johnson Oatman was born and educated in New Jersey. At the age of eighteen he joined the Methodist Episcopal Church and was ordained to the ministry. Rather than accepting a church appointment, he remained a "local preacher," preaching in any church that invited him. He preached at every opportunity but continued working in his father's mercantile business. After his father's death he opened an insurance office in Mount Holly, New Jersey, which was quite successful.

In the early 1890s Oatman discovered his gift for poetic expression and began writing hymn poems at a tremendous rate. Several of the well-known gospel-song composers of his day eagerly purchased his lyrics. Charles H. Gabriel purchased several poems from Oatman for a price that is believed to have been $1.00 per poem. One of these was this hymn, "Higher Ground." Gabriel wrote the tune that we associate with these words and sold the hymn—words and music—to a Philadelphia publisher for $5.00. It was published in a songbook in 1898.

In the ensuing summers "Higher Ground" became a favorite song in camp meetings in New York, New Jersey, and Pennsylvania. One of the observers at these camp meetings wrote, "Nothing can bring forth more shouts at camp meeting of 'Glory' and 'Hallelujah' than the singing of 'Higher Ground.'"

A CHURCH FAMILY'S RESPONSE
TO TRAGEDY

I'm so glad I'm a part of the family of God,
I've been washed in the fountain, cleansed by his blood!
Joint heirs with Jesus as we travel this sod,
*For I'm a part of the family, the family of God.**

Bill and Gloria Gaither have been involved in the life of their church in the small town of Anderson, Indiana, for many years. The love and concern of this congregation was suddenly brought into focus when one of their members was involved in an accident. A young father was severely burned over most of his body as the result of an explosion that ripped through a garage where he was working. The first report from the hospital indicated that he would not live through the night.

Within an hour the whole church had been alerted Unwilling to accept the first reports, the church family prayed earnestly for his recovery. Early the next morning the doctors said that if he could make it through twenty-four hours, he might have a chance.

The next day was Easter Sunday. Early that morning those who had prayed all night learned that their friend was still alive. The church family gathered for worship, heavy-hearted and tired from a sleepless night. At the beginning of the service the minister announced to the congregation that he had just talked with the doctor, and the young man had just passed the first crisis and had a good chance of survival.

The congregation was jubilant. The weariness disappeared, faces were radiant, joy filled every heart. Prayers had been answered, and the body of Christ in that place celebrated the resurrection of our Lord in a fresh, new way.

On their way home from church Bill and Gloria Gaither talked about the family of believers, the love and concern they had seen in action, and how that commitment could be counted on to embrace their own family without needing to be earned. They began to piece together the words and music of this song, their noon meal forgotten. By the time they finally sat down to eat, the song had been completed.

A SCOTTISH PREACHER AND THE CREATIVE POWER OF GOD

Immortal, invisible, God only wise,
In light inaccessible hid from our eyes,
Most blessed, most glorious, the Ancient of Days,
Almighty, victorious, thy great name we praise.

Walter Chalmers Smith, a Scottish preacher, wrote these remarkable lines in 1867. Ordained to the ministry in the Free Church of Scotland, he pastored a church in London, then preached for almost forty years in Edinburgh. His hymn is based on 1 Timothy 1:17, "Now unto the King eternal, immortal, invisible, the only wise God, be honor and glory for ever and ever. Amen." The overarching figure of speech is "light"—silent light that reveals objects it strikes, but at the same time keeps its source hidden.

In the first stanza God is referred to as "Ancient of Days," a term found only once in Scripture in Daniel 7:9. The second stanza refers to God's patience and longsuffering, likens his justice to "high-soaring mountains," and says his goodness and love come from the "fountains of clouds." The third stanza points out that God is a lifegiver and that while we "blossom and flourish as leaves on the tree," God changes not. The final stanza praises God as "Father of glory" and "Father of light" and concludes with the prayer that we may see that "only the splendor of light hideth thee!"

Since 1906, Smith's hymn has been sung almost exclusively to a nineteenth-century Welsh folk melody associated with secular texts. Gustav Holst, noted English composer, adapted the tune and harmonized it to fit "Immortal, Invisible God Only Wise" for *The English Hymnal,* published in London in 1906. Holst named the tune "St. Denio." In some hymnals it is called "Joanna."

THE UNINTENTIONAL HYMN

Immortal love, forever full,
Forever flowing free,
Forever shared, forever whole,
A never-ebbing sea.

In the Merrimac Valley of East Haverhill, Massachusetts, a large farmhouse, the birthplace of John Greenleaf Whittier, is a favorite tourist attraction. The meetinghouse where his family and their neighbors met regularly for worship is also still standing. The Quakers met and waited in silence for the Spirit to move in their midst. They never sang hymns. As a youth John worked on the family farm. A schoolteacher, who sensed something extraordinary in this young boy, gave him a copy of the poems of Robert Burns. The poetry fascinated him and he made his beginning efforts to write poetic verse. When a friend suggested to John's father that he should send the boy to college to be a writer, the father scornfully replied, "Sir, poetry will not give him bread."

But two years of schooling at Haverhill Academy fueled his imagination and sharpened his writing skill. He became editor of the *Pennsylvania Freeman,* an anti-slavery newspaper published in Philadelphia. Whittier employed his pen and influence without restraint against the evils of slavery.

He thought many of his poems would not survive the occasion for which they were written. In his own words they were "protests, alarm signals, trumpet calls to action, words wrung from the writer's heart, forged at white heat." Whittier wrote no hymns, but editors have selected lines and verses from his writings, fitted them to appropriate melodies, and included them in our hymnals.

"Immortal Love, Forever Full" is taken from Whittier's larger poem "Our Master," written in 1866. Its thirty-eight verses seek to show that Christ is found not in great cathedrals, nor in rituals or rites, nor in systems or symbols, but in the heart of an individual in faith, hope, and obedience. Other hymns that bear Whittier's name are "O Brother Man, Fold to Thy Heart Thy Brother," "Dear Lord and Father of Mankind," and "I Know Not What the Future Hath."

A HYMN WRITTEN FOR AN EXHIBITION

In Christ there is no east or west,
In him no south or north;
But one great fellowship of love
Throughout the whole wide earth.

The writer of these lines had two names. William Arthur Dunkerly was born in 1852 and educated in Manchester, England. The literary world knew him as John Oxenham, distinguished English novelist and poet. Early in his career, Dunkerly took his pen name from a character—a sea captain—in Charles Kingsley's novel *Westward Ho!* His success demanded that he continue his career with his borrowed name. A devout Christian and an active churchman, Oxenham was a deacon and Bible teacher in the Euling Congregational Church in London.

In 1908 the London Missionary Society sponsored an exhibition for which Oxenham wrote a script for a pageant featuring India. The hymn was written for the pageant. Winston Churchill spoke at the opening of the exhibition, pointing out the "civilizing and humanitarian work of missionaries."

"St. Peter," the tune most widely used for Oxenham's hymn, was composed in 1836 by Alexander Reinagle. It was named after St. Peter's-in-the-East, the church in Oxford, England, where Reinagle was organist.

Another tune for this hymn that is growing in popularity made its first appearance in the 1940 Episcopal *Hymnal.* Titled "McKee," it is an adaptation of the Negro spiritual, "I Know the Angel's Done Changed My Name," which dates from Fisk University's *Jubilee Songs* of 1894. The adaptation was made in 1939 by Harry T. Burleigh, music editor for a major New York music publisher. He was also a successful song composer and arranger of Negro spirituals and a charter member of the American Society of Composers, Authors, and Publishers (ASCAP). The tune was named for the Reverend Elmer M. McKee, rector of St. George's Protestant Episcopal Church on Stuyvesant Square in New York City, where Burleigh was baritone soloist for fifty-two years.

A PARAPHRASE OF A FAVORITE PSALM

In heavenly love abiding,
*   No change my heart shall fear;*
And safe is such confiding,
*   For nothing changes here:*
The storm may roar without me,

My heart may low be laid;
But God is round about me,
And can I be dismayed?

Anna Waring, a native of Wales, wrote the hymn when she was twenty-seven years old and published it that year in a small collection of nineteen hymns she had written. Leaving Wales, she came to England and lived at Bristol. She was baptized into the Church of England. Known as a gentle person, she possessed a quiet, yet sparkling sense of humor. She learned Hebrew in order to read and study the Old Testament poetry in the original language, thus establishing the lifelong habit of reading the Hebrew Psalter each day.

"In Heavenly Love Abiding" is written in the spirit of Psalm 23; the second and third stanzas reveal a fairly close paraphrase of the Shepherd Psalm.

Few hymnwriters have been so sensitive and shy of publicity as was Anna Waring. She poured her heart into her hymn writing, but little is known about the particulars of her life and education. Her later years were given to philanthropic work, and she spent a great deal of time visiting the prisons of Bristol. She was an ardent supporter of the Discharged Prisoners' Aid Society, an organization devoted to the rehabilitation of released prisoners.

The hymn tune commonly associated with Waring's hymn is a folk melody from Finland called "Nyland" for one of the Finnish provinces. It first appeared in a hymnal published in 1909 by the Evangelical Lutheran Church, the national church of Finland.

WRITTEN IN GENEVA, SWITZERLAND

In the beginning: God!
No earth or sea or skies.
In the beginning: God,
But nothing other-wise.
In the beginning: Word.
Unheard and still unseen;

> *Not even brooding bird,*
> *Nor space or time for scene.**

At the Ecumenical Center in Geneva, Switzerland, Fred Kaan assisted in the production of a radio program in 1974 in honor of Duke Ellington, who had died earlier that year. The program included an extract from Ellington's jazz cantata that began "In the beginning: God." Kaan had not heard this music before and was greatly moved by it. So inspired was he that he immediately wrote this hymn, borrowing the first line. In the first stanza Kaan incorporates the first words of Genesis 1:1 and John 1:1 tying together Old and New Testaments.

In the fourth and final stanza Kaan reminds us that "God is first and last and in between are we!"

> *The great between is now*
> *And time is ours to tell.*
> *God comes and shows us how*
> *To stand and walk and spell.*
> *So life becomes a feast,*
> *A round to set us free,*
> *For God is first and last*
> *And in between are we!**

Fred Kaan, who has written more than 150 hymns, writes with freshness and vibrancy. In many respects he is a world citizen and his hymns reveal his awareness of God's world, problems, concerns, people, and great opportunities. For ten years Kaan lived in Switzerland, serving the International Congregational Council and the World Alliance of Reformed Churches. He returned to England in 1978 to serve as moderator of the West Midland Province of the United Reformed Church. For two years he was on the staff of the Central Church, Swindon, England, a local ecumenical project of United Reformed, Baptist, and Church of England congregations.

A LEGENDARY BUT UNFOUNDED STORY

In the cross of Christ I glory,
Tow'ring o'er the wrecks of time,
All the light of sacred story
Gathers round its head sublime.

The Apostle Paul wrote to the churches at Galatia, "God forbid that I should glory, save in the cross of our Lord Jesus Christ, by whom the world is crucified unto me, and I unto the world" (Gal. 6:14). Reserved for the vilest of criminals, the cross was a cruel instrument of death, a symbol of shame, pain, and disgrace. Since the cross of Christ meant salvation and the pardon of sin, to Paul the cross was truly wonderful.

A fascinating and oft-told story relates that John Bowring was inspired to write the hymn when he visited the ruins of a once great cathedral on the island of Macao, near Hong Kong. The building had been destroyed, but the front wall, topped by a great metal cross, stood blackened with age. The story is dramatic and interesting but untrue. Bowring did not visit Hong Kong until 1849, when he was appointed British Consul at Canton, China, twenty-four years after the hymn was written and published. (For more about John Bowring, see "God is love; his mercy brightens," page 86.)

The hymn tune, known as "Rathbun," was composed in 1849 by Ithamar Conkey, organist at Central Baptist Church in Norwich, Connecticut. On a rainy Sunday, only one choir member appeared for the morning service. In spite of his disappointment in this, Conkey returned to his home and later that afternoon composed the tune to fit the hymn "In the Cross of Christ I Glory." Words and music were published together in 1851 and have proved to be appropriately coupled.

A HYMN FOR A CHRISTIAN FILM

In the stars his handiwork I see,
On the wind he speaks in majesty,

Though he ruleth over land and sea,
  What is that to me?
I will celebrate nativity,
For it has a place in history,
Sure, he came to set his people free,
  *What is that to me?**

In the early 1960s Ralph Carmichael met Jarrell McCracken, president of Word Inc., a religious record company in Waco, Texas. Because of some financial needs, Carmichael offered McCracken some tapes of his choir for a cash payment of $1,000. McCracken agreed. In 1963 Carmichael took seven newly written songs and flew to Waco. There he proposed to McCracken that they form a new music publishing company on a fifty/fifty basis. Carmichael would write the songs and McCracken would manufacture, promote, and market the music, and fill the orders in Waco, Texas. Lexicon Music was born.

The following year Carmichael was asked to do the music for the Billy Graham film *The Restless Ones*. When he first saw the film he was strangely impressed that it demanded something unusual. He later said, "I knew I had to do more than use violins for the good guy and oboe for the bad guy. The music had to be as relevant as the film and its message." He wrote "He's Everything to Me," and then went to a studio with a Fender bass, a set of drums, and some rhythm guitars. After some trial and error, some creative experimentation, the whole thing seemed to come together. Some people called it rock and roll, but now it is considered almost traditional.

Following the direction of the first youth choir musical, *Good News,* published in 1967, Carmichael and Kurt Kaiser published *Tell It Like It Is* in 1969. Its success encouraged Carmichael to write other musicals, *Natural High* and *I'm Here, God's Here, Now We Can Start.* Carmichael's more than two hundred songs, arrangements for an untold number of record albums, film scores, Lexicon publications, and Light record albums all add up to an incredible musical output from an ingenious and creative man.

"HE LIES IN THE CRADLE"

Infant holy,
Infant lowly,
For his bed a cattle stall,
Oxen lowing,
Little knowing
Christ the babe is Lord of all.
Swift are winging
Angels singing,
Noels ringing,
Tidings bringing:
Christ the babe is Lord of all.

This English translation of a Polish carol appeared in 1925, in *Music and Youth,* a music periodical for youth published in London. The translator, Edith Reed, edited this magazine and several other music publications for children and youth. Where she found the Polish carol is not known. The tune had appeared in England more than fifty years earlier, but the text had not surfaced in any previous publications.

Where the author's name would be expected, Edith Reed placed the notice "W. Zlobie Lezy." Erik Routley, in preparing the 1951 hymnal for Congregational churches in England, presumed that the Polish author was a Mr. Lezy. So he attributed the Polish text to a man with a very Polish-sounding name, 'W. Zlobie Lezy." Somewhat red-faced, Routley confessed that "some years later a distinguished man of science, who knew Polish, wrote and gently told us that 'w zlobie lezy' is Polish for 'He lies in the cradle.'"

Part of the charm of Reed's translation is the sound of the rhymes. If one reads the two stanzas aloud, the result is quite delightful. These rhyming sounds remind us of the Mother Goose nursery rhymes so loved by children. In the last half of the stanza, "winging," "singing," "ringing," and "bringing" pile one on the other giving us a thrilling cumulative effect of the sounds. The singing of this carol during the Christmas season puts a smile on the face and joy in the heart.

DISTINGUISHED BY OMISSIONS

It came upon the midnight clear,
That glorious song of old,
From angels bending near the earth,
To touch their harps of gold:
"Peace on the earth, good will to men,
From heaven's all gracious King."
The world in solemn stillness lay
To hear the angels sing.

Here is the first of the carol-like hymns from the pens of American poets. Hymns stressing the social message of Christmas—"peace on earth, good will toward men"—are distinctly American. Carols from England and Europe do not reflect this concern. Edmund H. Sears, minister of the Unitarian Church at Wayland, Massachusetts, wrote the hymn in 1849. The stormclouds of strife were gathering and would erupt fourteen years later in the Civil War.

The first stanza mentions appearance of the heavenly host and the song they sang, though there is no reference to the shepherds who heard the song as told in Luke 2. The second stanza suggests that the message of peace comes again and again at Christmastime. Here is the assurance that though this seems to be a "weary world" with "sad and lowly plains" and "Babel sounds," yet the angels sing with "peaceful wings unfurled." Other lines speak plainly of people's inhumanity to fellow human beings through the practice of slavery.

Beneath the angel-strain have rolled
Two thousand years of wrong.

How strange it is that this well-known Christmas carol contains no mention of Christ, the newborn King. Other than the song of the Heavenly host, "Peace on earth, good will to men," there are no elements of the scriptural account of Christ's birth from Matthew and Luke.

The tune for this carol was composed in 1850 by Richard S. Willis, American journalist and musician. He studied under and was a close friend of Felix Mendelssohn. Later Willis was a vestryman in the Church of the Transfiguration (The Little Church Around the Corner) in New York City.

WRITTEN BY A FIREPLACE

It only takes a spark to get a fire going,
And soon all those around can warm up to its glowing;
That's how it is with God's love, once you've experienced it:
*You spread his love to everyone, you want to pass it on.**

Kurt Kaiser and Ralph Carmichael were collaborating on a youth musical in 1968. Each contributed a number of songs to the work *Tell It Like It Is.* They met together to discuss the completion of the work and agreed that a song of commitment should conclude the musical. The end of the project was in sight and both were eager to pull the loose ends together. With great excitement they returned to their homes, Carmichael to Los Angeles and Kaiser to Waco, Texas.

The next Sunday evening after church, Kaiser was sitting by the fireplace with many thoughts passing through his mind. The house was quiet, the lights were low, and the fire had burned down. As he stared into the fireplace, the glowing embers popped and sparkled. Instantly there came the idea that a spark can get a fire going. Lines began to flow and stanzas took shape. The creative muse was alive and Kaiser shared the beginning lines with his wife, Pat. As he groped for the third stanza, Pat suggested the idea of shouting from the mountaintops in sharing God's love, and soon the third stanza was completed.

I'll shout it from the mountaintops, I want my world to know:
*The Lord of love has come to me, I want to pass it on.**

As Kurt and Pat Kaiser, aglow with the excitement of a newborn song, strolled down their street in the evening air, the words and music played over and over in their hearts. The next morning Kaiser sang the song to Carmichael over the telephone. Both were ecstatic over the promise of this song of commitment to bring the musical to a climactic end.

Within months the work was published, and youth choirs throughout the nation discovered the joy of singing "Pass It On." A number of hymnals have included it for congregational singing. The song that was intended for youth choirs is now in the repertoire of believers of all ages, who urge one another to share the joy of the gospel with others by passing it on.

A CONVERTED MINSTREL SONG

I've found a friend in Jesus, he's everything to me,
  He's the fairest of ten thousand to my soul;
The Lily of the Valley, in him alone I see
  All I need to cleanse and make me fully whole.

Will Hays left Georgetown College in Kentucky at the age of twenty to become a riverfront reporter for the *Louisville Democrat.* Though he worked as a newspaper reporter, his hobby was writing songs, which he did well. Some of his songs so strongly supported the Confederacy that the Union forces put him in prison for a while. In 1868 he joined the staff of the *Louisville Courier-Journal,* and for thirty years he wrote a daily column of river news, gossip, witticism, and light verse. Both as a journalist and as a songwriter, Hays was very popular in Louisville from Civil War days through the Gay Nineties.

He had great success writing minstrel songs, which were so popular during his lifetime. He was second only to Stephen Collins Foster in this area. One of Hays's songs, "The Little Log Cabin Down the Lane," written in 1871, strangely became the basis for "The Lily of the Valley."

Charles W. Fry was in the construction business in Salisbury, England. He loved to play the cornet and taught his three sons to play instruments at an early age. The four of them, known as the Fry Family Band, became the first Salvation Army Band.

One day in 1881 Fry heard the strains of Will Hays's tune being played in a dance hall in London. The music stuck with him and he wrote it down from memory. In the days that followed he wrote three stanzas to fit the music, each ending with the lines:

> *He's the Lily of the Valley, the Bright and Morning*
> *   Star,*
> *He's the fairest of ten thousand to my soul.*

The "Lily of the Valley" comes from Song of Solomon 2:1, and the "Bright and Morning Star" finds its source in Revelation 22:16.

Hays died in Louisville in 1907 and probably never knew that a cornet player in England had converted his minstrel song to a gospel song with a set of new words. He would have been quite surprised to know that his name appears in hymnals being used in many churches in his hometown of Louisville, as well as throughout Kentucky and the nation.

In 1982, in the cloister of England's Salisbury Cathedral, a plaque was erected which was inscribed:

> *To commemorate the centenary*
> *of the promotion to glory of*
> CHARLES WILLIAM FRY
> *first bandmaster of the Salvation Army*
> *Born Alderbury, 29 May 1837*
> *Died Polmont, Scotland, 24 August 1882*
> *The clarion call of his cornet*
> *sounded in the Market Place, Salisbury,*
> *in the autumn of 1878,*
> *now echoes around the world.*

AN OLD SONG ABOUT HEAVEN

> *Jerusalem, my happy home,*
> *   When shall I come to thee?*
> *When shall my sorrows have an end?*
> *   Thy joys, when shall I see?*

John's description of heaven in Revelation has fired the imagination of many writers and poets. The above lines are part of a hymn with a checkered career dating from the sixteenth century. Both the origin and original form are uncertain; at least five different versions of the hymn have been identified. Most have twenty or more stanzas that describe the beauties of heaven in picturesque language: "walls are made of precious stones," "gates of Orient pearl," "streets are paved with gold," "houses of ivory," and "tiles are made of beaten gold." Other lines refer to heaven as a place of physical comfort and rare beauty where earthly sorrows, suffering, and sadness are not known.

Biblical names and historical personalities are sprinkled throughout the stanzas. David is "master of the choir" with his "harp for a baton"; the Virgin Mary is the "Prima Donna"; Augustine and Ambrose sing the "Te Deum" as they did, according to tradition, at the baptism of Augustine. Simeon and Zacharias are mentioned, both of whom sang songs that are recorded in Luke 1 and 2.

Leonard Ellinwood, one of America's outstanding hymnologists, has noted, "Here is sacred folk-literature at its very finest, coming at a time [sixteenth century] when the singing of English congregations was limited to the use of metrical paraphrases of the Psalms."

Most of our hymnals contain four stanzas from one of the versions of this hymn with a tune of unknown origin called "Land of Rest." While several other tunes using this text are identified in the well-researched writings of George Pullen Jackson, this tune is not mentioned. In J. R. Graves' *Little Seraph*, published in 1873 in Memphis, Tennessee, this tune is titled "Sweet Land of Rest." The present version of the tune was published by Annabel Morris Buchanan of Kentucky in 1938. She recalled that when she was a child her grandmother sang this tune. What a joyful folk tune from the South!

AN INVITATION TO DISCIPLESHIP

Jesus calls us o'er the tumult
Of our life's wild, restless sea;
Day by day his sweet voice soundeth,
Saying, "Christian, follow me!"

Walking along the shore of the Sea of Galilee, Jesus saw two men fishing. The two brothers, Simon and Andrew, were fishermen by trade. Jesus talked with them and invited them to leave their nets and come with him. He promised to make them not just fishermen, but fishers of men. And they followed him. This story, recorded by the gospel writers Matthew, Mark, and Luke, is the basis for the hymn by Cecil Frances Alexander.

The Sea of Galilee can be beautiful and calm, but it can also be rough and fearsome. Alexander uses this imagery in describing "life's wild, restless sea." Like Andrew and Simon, we are urged to respond to Jesus' invitation.

> *Give our hearts to thine obedience,*
> *Serve and love thee best of all.*

Cecil Alexander was born in Ireland and as a young girl showed great concern for persons in unfortunate circumstances. With her sister, she began a school for the deaf. She walked many miles taking food to the hungry and caring for those who were ill. After her marriage to William Alexander, clergyman in the Irish church and later archbishop of all Ireland, she continued to write hymns for children. At least three of them have been appropriated by people of all ages.

William H. Jude, English lecturer, organist, and recitalist, composed the music for these words in 1887. Born in Suffolk, England, Jude had a musical career that took him throughout Great Britain and Australia giving recitals and lectures. His name appears in our hymnals because he wrote a hymn tune more than a century ago for Alexander's "Jesus Calls Us O'er the Tumult." The tune is appropriately named "Galilee."

A HYMN FOUR CENTURIES OLD

> *Jesus Christ is risen today,*
> *Alleluia!*
> *Our triumphant holy day,*
> *Alleluia!*
> *Who did once, upon the cross,*
> *Alleluia!*

> *Suffer to redeem our loss.*
> *Alleluia!*

For over four hundred years, this hymn has been sung in Latin and other languages to celebrate the resurrection of Christ. Apparently some of its popularity can be attributed to the alterations and additions it has experienced across the centuries. The anonymous Latin carol "Surrexit Christus hodie" has been found in fourteenth-century manuscripts in Engleburg, Munich, and Prague. Many hands have changed and reshaped the lines to improve and strengthen the content. Stanzas have been rearranged, added and deleted, and lines borrowed from other sources. The English version in our hymnals is an interesting composite from numerous—and largely unidentified—sources. We know that the stanza beginning "Sing we to our God above" was written by Charles Wesley in 1740 and added to this hymn more than seventy-five years later.

The tune "Llanfair," usually associated with this text, is quite unusual for two reasons—the person who wrote it and its extraordinary name. Robert Williams, who composed the tune in 1817, was a blind basketweaver who lived on the island of Anglesey in North Wales. Tunes that he composed were written down for him in a notebook by a friend or relative. Williams named this melody "Bethel."

"Llanfair," the name by which this tune is now known, is composed of the first two syllables of one of the longest words in any of the world's languages—Llanfairpwllgwyngyllgogery-chwyrndobwllllantysiliogogogoch. The name of a small Welsh village where Williams lived, it means "Church of St. Mary in the hollow of white hazel near the rapid whirlpool of the Church of St. Tysillio by the red cave." Local residents and postal authorities abbreviated the name to "Llanfair P.G.," and today the railway station in the village is simply labeled "Llanfair."

PUBLISHER OF HIS OWN SONGS

> *Jesus is all the world to me,*
> *My life, my joy, my all;*
> *He is my strength from day to day,*

Without him I would fall:
When I am sad, to him I go,
No other one can cheer me so;
When I am sad
He makes me glad,
He's my friend.

In 1875, a music publisher in Cleveland, Ohio, received an envelope containing four songs from a young man in East Liverpool, Ohio. In the accompanying letter, he offered to sell the songs for one hundred dollars. Thinking this offer rather unreasonable, the publisher made a counter offer of twenty-five dollars. The young man, Will Thompson, declined the offer and kept the songs.

With the encouragement of his father, an East Liverpool dry goods merchant, Will decided to become his own publisher, for he was confident of his ability. The venture was successful, and he wrote and published popular, patriotic, and sacred songs, as well as collections of hymns, anthems, and concert pieces. At East Liverpool his music store was also tremendously successful. People came from miles around to buy music, pianos, and organs. A branch store was opened in Chicago and it too flourished.

Thompson was a talented poet and composer who wrote many gospel songs. He carried a small pocket notebook with him because he said, "No matter where I am, at home or hotel, at the store or in the car, if an idea or theme comes to me that I deem worthy of a song, I jot it down in verse, and as I do so the music simply comes to me naturally. So I write words and music enough to call back the whole theme again any time I open to it. In this way I never lose it."

In addition to his musical interest, Thompson was successful in other business ventures. He was skillful in creative marketing. His real estate investments were wisely made. He had a palatial home in East Liverpool, and other homes in Savannah, Georgia, DeLand, Florida, and Los Angeles, California. In May of 1909 Thompson, his wife, and his son sailed for Europe for several months of travel. Early in September he became ill, and the family returned to the United States. Thompson died in New York on September 20, at the age of sixty-two.

Of his many songs, two have consistent and widespread usage—"Softly and Tenderly Jesus Is Calling," written in 1880, and "Jesus Is All the World to Me," in 1904.

SINGING SAVES CONFEDERATE SOLDIER'S LIFE

Jesus, lover of my soul,
Let me to thy bosom fly,
While the nearer waters roll,
While the tempest still is high:
Hide me, O my Savior, hide,
Till the storm of life is past;
Safe into the haven guide;
O receive my soul at last.

Charles Wesley wrote these lines in 1738, and while the hymn reflects the seriousness of sin, its greater emphasis is on God's grace that makes the sinner whole through Jesus Christ.

A true story from the Civil War involves Wesley's hymn. Levi Hefner, a Confederate courier, was sent one night by his commanding officer, Gen. Robert E. Lee, to take a message through an area partially occupied by Union troops. As he approached a bridge, his horse balked and reared nervously. Hefner dismounted and attempted to calm him. In the darkness Hefner began singing softly an old familiar hymn, "Jesus, Lover of My Soul." In a few minutes the horse became quiet. Hefner mounted him, crossed the bridge without incident, and completed his mission.

A number of years after the war, Hefner attended a reunion of soldiers from both sides. They gathered in small groups to share experiences they remembered from the war. A Union soldier from Ohio remembered standing guard one dark night at a bridge. He had been ordered to shoot anyone approaching from the other side. During the night only one rider came his way, and he raised his rifle to shoot as soon as he could see the form in the darkness. The horse balked, however, and the rider dismounted. To calm the horse, the rider began singing softly an old hymn, "Jesus, Lover of My

Soul." The Union soldier told the circle of old soldiers that the sound of the hymn so touched him that he lowered his rifle and quietly turned away. He said, "I could not shoot him."

Levi Hefner jumped up and embraced the Union soldier, saying "That was me!" He realized for the first time that his singing that dark night had saved his life. Levi Hefner's great grandson, Danny Starnes, shared this true experience.

FROM A NOW-FORGOTTEN NOVEL

Jesus loves me! this I know,
For the Bible tells me so;
Little ones to him belong;
They are weak, but he is strong.

Two sisters, Anna and Susan Warner, collaborated in writing a novel titled *Say and Seal* in 1860. The main characters in the novel were John Linden (a young man), Faith Derrick (his fiancée), and Johnny Fax, a young lad. Johnny was the victim of a lingering illness. Linden was Johnny's Sunday school teacher, and he and Faith spent a great deal of time with Johnny to provide for his needs. Toward the end of the novel, Johnny asked Linden to pick him up in his arms and hold him. Clutching the feverish boy, Linden walked back and forth. The swaying motion of the walking seemed to calm and relax the lad. Looking up into Linden's face, Johnny said quietly, "Sing." So as he walked around the room, Linden began to sing softly, "Jesus loves me! this I know." A few hours later Johnny died.

Rather than use a familiar hymn for this scene in the novel, Anna Warner wrote a hymn of four stanzas that has endured well over a century. Today the hymn is enthusiastically sung, especially by children.

The talented daughters of a New York lawyer, Anna and Susan Warner lived on Constitution Island in the Hudson River at West Point, New York. Their literary careers brought them fame and fortune. Between them they wrote more than seventy books, some of the best being the result of their collaboration. For years the sisters taught a Sunday school class for West Point cadets in their home. Each Sunday the boys would crowd into the family sitting room, sing heartily some familiar hymns accompanied by a small reed organ, then engage in the Bible study taught by one of the sisters.

William B. Bradbury, famous New York composer and publisher, composed in 1861 the music we use to sing these words. Words and music were published that year in a small book of Sunday school songs. The hymn has been translated into many languages and is sung around the world.

Karl Barth, the world-renowned theologian, was asked one day what he considered to be the greatest theological discovery of his life. He smiled and replied,

> Jesus loves me! this I know,
> For the Bible tells me so.

HIS PASTURES ARE DELICIOUS

> Jesus makes my heart rejoice,
> I'm his sheep, and know his voice;
> He's a Shepherd, kind and gracious,
> And his pastures are delicious;
> Constant love to me he shows,
> Yea, my very name he knows.

What a delightful hymn that sings of Jesus Christ who "makes my heart rejoice!" The use of the word "delicious," fourth line, first stanza, is unique in hymnody. Henrietta Louise von Hayn wrote this song for the birthday of a friend, Christian Petersen, in Herrnhut on August 1, 1772. She cast the hymn to fit the tune "Herrnhut," which was written in the manuscript book about 1740. Because of association with this text, the tune later became known as "Hayn."

Henrietta was born in Idstein in Nassau, Germany, in 1724. At the age of twenty-two she was received into the Moravian community of Herrnhaag, where she taught in the girls' school and later served as caretaker of the older girls and single sisters. She was dearly loved by the entire community. A gifted hymnwriter, she contributed more than forty hymns to the Moravian hymnal of 1778. Frederick W. Foster, an English Moravian, translated the hymn into English for a hymnal which he prepared in 1789.

In Moravian settlements, family loyalties were gradually replaced by allegiance to one's choir—communal groupings by age, sex, and marital status. The choirs usually provided members with communal living accommodations, food, clothing, and employment. They also were responsible for providing child care and education. All aspects of daily life were subordinate to attaining a joyous fellowship with Christ. These ideals, expressed in the Brotherly Agreement of Herrnhut drawn up in 1727, reflected the ideas of Nikolaus Ludwig von Zinzendorf, the leader of the Moravians.

A SAILOR'S SONG

Jesus, Savior, pilot me
O'er life's tempestuous sea;
Unknown waves before me roll,
Hiding rock and treacherous shoal;
Chart and compass come from thee:
Jesus, Savior, pilot me.

Because New York City is a major world port with ships of every national registry in its harbor, many seagoing men walk the streets of the city. Men who work on the decks and in the engine rooms of oceangoing vessels often wander aimlessly on the streets when they have days ashore. Numerous agencies or institutions seek to minister spiritually as well as physically and psychologically to these men. One such place in the last decades of the nineteenth century was the Church of the Sea and Land.

Edward Hopper, pastor of the church in the 1870s, wrote the words of this hymn with the sailors in his congregation in mind. The poem was printed without the author's name in *The Sailor's Magazine*, March 1871. John E. Gould, a well-known New York musician, saw the poem almost immediately and composed the music for it. He compiled popular collections of Sunday school songs, and his business ventures in piano and music stores in New York City and Philadelphia were very successful. Hopper's words and Gould's tune appeared together for the first time late in 1871 in a hymnal published for Baptists. Very soon other publications included it, still without any acknowledgment of the author's name.

In 1880 Hopper was asked to write a special hymn for the anniversary of the Seaman's Friend Society in New York City. He remembered the hymn he had written nine years earlier and brought it to the meeting. To his surprise, he learned that many already knew the hymn and could sing it heartily, but did not know that Hopper was the author.

A native of New York City, Hopper spent most of his life there. He graduated from New York University in Manhattan and prepared himself for the Presbyterian ministry at Union Theological Seminary. He served two Presbyterian churches in New York, and then in 1870 became pastor of the Church of the Sea and Land. The hymn is based on Matthew 8:23–27, which tells how Jesus stilled the storm on the Sea of Galilee and calmed the anxiety and fear of his disciples.

A NEW TESTAMENT VERSION OF A PSALM

Jesus shall reign where'er the sun
Does his successive journeys run;
His kingdom spread from shore to shore,
Till moons shall wax and wane no more.

In 1701 a new pastor assumed his duties at the Congregational Church that met on Mark Lane Street in London. He was an interesting person, to say the least. Only five feet tall, with a head that seemed much too large for his body and a prominent hooked nose, Isaac Watts was not an impressive-looking person. But his keen mind, literary skills, and radiant personality more than made up for his physical appearance. Always suffering poor health, he kept an assistant standing by in case he could not preach in his pulpit at Mark Lane church. During a serious illness in 1712, he was invited to spend a week at the country mansion of one of his church members, Sir Thomas Abney, one time Lord Mayor of London. The week's stay extended to thirty-six years, for Watts spent the rest of his life with the Abney family.

Isaac was a precocious child. He began the study of Latin at age four, Greek by nine, French at eleven, and Hebrew at thirteen. When he was a teenager, Isaac had complained to his father about the dullness of the church service, particularly the droning of the psalm singing. His father said, "Give us something better, young man." And Isaac did.

He began writing hymns in a simple poetic style, and his hymns were sung to whatever familiar tune was selected by the deacon who led the singing. He not only wrote hymns on many subjects, but he made new poetic versions of Old Testament psalms. Watts was convinced that a New Testament church should sing in the spirit and language of the New Testament. In 1719 he published the *Psalms of David Imitated in the Language of the New Testament,* which included his version of Psalm 72, "Jesus Shall Reign Where'er the Sun."

Watts's vivid imagination envisioned the gospel being preached around the world. Thus, sixty years before William Carey became the champion of world missions, Watts reminded the Christians of his day of the urgent need to take the gospel to every corner of the world, "where'er the sun does his successive journeys run."

MORAVIAN ZEAL FOR FAITHFULNESS

> *Jesus, still lead on*
> *Till our rest be won;*
> *And, although the way be cheerless,*
> *We will follow, calm and fearless:*
> *Guide us by thy hand*
> *To our fatherland.*

Nikolaus Ludwig von Zinzendorf was born of a noble family and was independently wealthy. He left the University at Wittenberg at the age of nineteen after studying law and traveled extensively in Europe. In 1722 he inherited the large estate of Bertelsdorf in Saxony. A group of religious refugees known as the Moravian Brethren came to his attention, and he allowed them to settle on his estate. There they built a village that they called Herrnhut (the Lord's shelter). More than six hundred Moravian Brethren were living at Herrnhut by 1732.

From this settlement, about forty-five miles east of Dresden, came the Moravian Church, with von Zinzendorf as its leader.

Zinzendorf became a prolific hymn writer, and before he died in 1760 he had written more than two thousand hymns. These were published for the use of the Moravian Brethren, who translated them into the languages of the lands to which they went as missionaries. Strong missionary zeal was a trademark of the Moravians, and Zinzendorf encouraged this activity. Their first missionaries—two men—went to the West Indies in 1732, and three years later a missionary group left for the colony of Georgia in America. After a brief stay in Georgia, the group moved to Pennsylvania and joined another group from Herrnhut that had arrived on Christmas Day in 1741. The date of their arrival inspired the name they gave the settlement, Bethlehem.

The Moravians had a significant influence on John and Charles Wesley, who traveled with them on their way to Georgia. During the sea voyage the Moravians sang the hymns Zinzendorf had prepared. The singing through storm and peril greatly impressed on the Wesleys the value of hymn singing. Later a group of Moravians in London in 1738 were responsible for the meeting at Aldersgate Street in which John Wesley's heart was "strangely warmed."

Zinzendorf wrote "Jesus, Still Lead On," in 1721. It reflects his zeal for faithfulness in the Christian pilgrimage and the missionary spirit of the Moravians. The English translation was made in 1846 by Jane L. Borthwick, an English woman who translated many German hymns into English.

A DISPUTED SOURCE

Jesus, the very thought of thee
With sweetness fills my breast;
But sweeter far thy face to see,
And in thy presence rest.

No one knows who wrote the seven-hundred-year-old Latin hymn on which this translation is based. Bernard of Clairvaux, a devout mystic who lived in the twelfth century, is usually credited with being the author of the Latin text. His authorship is questioned by some who point out that the best manuscripts were found in England and seem to be the work of an Englishman writing in Latin. We know the hymn is from the twelfth century, however, and is one of our oldest.

Edward Caswall made his English translation in 1849, two years after he left the clergy of the Anglican Church and followed John Henry Newman, Frederick Faber, and others into the Catholic Church. A skillful translator of Latin hymns, Caswall produced almost two hundred English hymn translations for use by the church.

"Jesus, the Very Thought of Thee" is quiet, devotional, and abounding in adoration and love for Jesus Christ. One can imagine a monk in his private predawn devotions, quietly expressing his love for the Lord in these lines. Hope and joy are to be found in Jesus, for those who know him:

> *O Hope of every contrite heart!*
> *O Joy of all the meek!*
> *To those who fall, how kind thou art!*
> *How good to those who seek!*
> *But what to those who find? ah! this,*
> *Nor tongue nor pen can show*
> *The love of Jesus, what it is*
> *None but his loved ones know.*

The tune found in most of our hymnals for this text is called "St. Agnes." It was composed for the text in 1866 by John B. Dykes, who is probably better known for his tune for "Holy, Holy, Holy." Dykes named the tune for a thirteen-year-old Christian girl in Rome who was martyred on January 21, A.D. 304. A beautiful girl, Agnes refused marriage, saying that she could have no spouse but Jesus Christ. Her suitors exposed her as a Christian and she was eventually murdered during the persecution of the Christians by the Roman emperor Diocletian. She is venerated as the patron saint of young girls in the Roman Catholic Church.

A TWELFTH-CENTURY HYMN

> *Jesus, thou joy of loving hearts,*
> *Thou fount of life, thou light of men,*

> *From the best bliss that earth imparts,*
> *We turn unfilled to thee again.*

Some have attributed the hymn to Bernard of Clairvaux, a twelfth-century French monk, whom they believe to be the author of the Latin hymn "Jesu dulcis memoria," from which this group of stanzas was taken. Others believe that the Latin hymn was written by an unknown English churchman in the late twelfth century. The earliest and best texts were copied in England and passed to France, Italy, and Germany.

In his diary, David Livingstone, the English missionary to Africa, referred to "Jesu dulcis memoria" as "that hymn on the name of Christ, although in which might be termed dog-Latin, pleased me so: it rings in my ears as I wander across the wide, wide wilderness."

Ray Palmer, a Congregational minister in Albany, New York, translated "Jesus, Thou Joy of Loving Hearts" in 1858. Twenty-six years earlier he had written the hymn "My Faith Looks Up to Thee." Educated at Phillips Academy and Yale University, Palmer was ordained to the Congregational ministry in 1835. After several pastorates he served with distinction as the corresponding secretary of the American Congregational Union in New York City.

For translation Palmer chose five stanzas from the original forty-eight Latin stanzas, but not in sequence. Apparently he selected those that appealed to him most and paraphrased them rather than making a faithful word-for-word translation. Palmer's hymn captures the spirit of the unknown twelfth-century writer and communicates clearly to us in nineteenth-century expression. Expressing praise and adoration to Jesus Christ, the hymn concludes with this final stanza:

> *O Jesus, ever with us stay,*
>   *Make all our moments calm and bright;*
> *Chase the dark night of sin away,*
>   *Shed o'er the world thy holy light.*

A GEORGIA COLONY TRANSLATION

> *Jesus, thy boundless love to me*
>   *No thought can reach, no tongue declare;*

O knit my thankful heart to thee,
And reign without a rival there:
Thine wholly, thine alone, I am;
Be thou alone my constant flame.

Paul Gerhardt wrote the German hymn in 1653, about two years after he was ordained to the Lutheran ministry and while he was serving a small church near Berlin. Gerhardt's 123 hymns mark the transition in Lutheran hymnody from the earlier confessional hymns to those of subjective, devotional piety. The personal and optimistic note in this hymn was welcomed after the dreaded period of the Thirty Years' War.

John Wesley translated Gerhardt's hymn into English. In 1736 Wesley left England to go to the English colony of Georgia in America. He was sent as a clergyman by the Church of England to minister to people who had settled in this primitive outpost. On board the ship bound for Georgia were a group of Moravian missionaries. Wesley was fascinated by the enthusiastic singing of this group in their native German language. He began immediately to study German, thinking that by translating these German hymns into English he could retain the enthusiastic spirit of the singing. Wesley's translation of Gerhardt's hymn was made in Georgia but was not published until 1739, after he had returned to England.

The music generally found in our hymnals for this text was written by Henri Frederick Hemy in 1864. The son of German parents, he was born at Newcastle-upon-the-Tyne in England in 1818. A talented church organist, he served in several Roman Catholic churches in England. His collection of hymn tunes, *Crown of Jesus Music,* published in London in 1864, included the tune "St. Catherine." Named for Catherine of Alexandria, a revered fourth-century Christian martyr, it has been used for several hymns that fit this metrical form—a six-line stanza with eight syllables in each line.

A HYMN WRITTEN FOR A LONDON CONGREGATIONAL CHAPEL

Joy to the world! the Lord is come;
Let earth receive her king;

> *Let every heart prepare him room,*
> *And heaven and nature sing.*

This familiar hymn we sing during the holidays first appeared not in a collection of Christmas carols but in a collection of Old Testament psalms rewritten in poetic verse by Isaac Watts.

Watts was displeased with the poetic versions of the psalms being sung in the churches at the turn of the eighteenth century. He strongly felt that the New Testament church should sing in the spirit and fervor of the New rather than the Old Testament. So he set about making new poetic versions of the 150 psalms of the Old Testament, which he published in 1719 under the title *The Psalms of David Imitated in the Language of the New Testament.*

"Joy to the World" is based on Psalm 98, which opens with "O sing unto the Lord a new song." The psalm is a song of rejoicing for the greatness of God and the marvelous ways he has protected and restored his children. The psalmist calls on the whole creation, man and nature alike, to celebrate in the singing of a new song.

Watts turned this Old Testament psalm into a song of praise for the salvation of God's people, which began when God became flesh at Bethlehem. In four brief stanzas—sixteen poetic lines—Watts brings a fresh interpretation to Psalm 98.

For more than 120 years this hymn was sung to numerous tunes that fit its poetic structure ("common meter"). Lowell Mason, a New England music educator, published in Boston in 1839 a tune that has become indelibly associated with these words. He indicated that it is "from Handel," for he borrowed two musical phrases from Handel's "Messiah" ("Lift Up Your Heads," and "Comfort Ye"). Mason named the tune "Antioch" for the ancient Syrian city that was the point of departure for Paul's first two missionary journeys and the place where the disciples were first called Christians.

A HYMN PRESENTED AT BREAKFAST

> *Joyful, joyful, we adore thee,*
> *God of glory, Lord of love,*

Hearts unfold like flowers before thee,
Op'ning to the sun above.
Melt the clouds of sin and sadness;
Drive the dark of doubt away;
Giver of immortal gladness,
Fill us with the light of day!

Henry van Dyke was to speak at Williams College in Massachusetts in 1907 and was a guest in the home of Harry A. Garfield, one of the faculty. At breakfast one morning van Dyke surprised the Garfield family with a hymn he had written, inspired by the beauty and majesty of the Berkshire Mountains. He announced to Garfield, "Here is a hymn for you. Your mountains were my inspiration. It must be sung to the music of Beethoven's 'Hymn to Joy.'"

At this time van Dyke was professor of English literature at Princeton University, where Woodrow Wilson was university president. Earlier van Dyke had served with distinction as pastor of New York City's Brick Presbyterian Church. Wilson and van Dyke became friends at Princeton, and after Wilson was elected president of the United States, he appointed van Dyke to be United States minister to the Netherlands and Luxembourg, where he served three years.

Beethoven's "Hymn to Joy" was a hymn tune that was already well known and had been sung in churches in the last half of the nineteenth century. As he shaped the lines of the hymn, van Dyke carefully fitted them to the tune. The suitability of words for tune and tune for words is exceptional.

The words and music were first published together in the *Presbyterian Hymnal* in 1911, and they have been firmly joined ever since. No doubt Ludwig van Beethoven, who died in 1827, would be quite surprised to find his name and the melody from the final movement of his *Ninth Symphony* in church hymnals today. Concert halls throughout the world resound with performances of his music. But more frequent than these performances is the hearty singing of his "Hymn to Joy" tune by congregations around the world.

LIFE COMMITMENT TO CHRIST

Just as I am, without one plea,
But that thy blood was shed for me,
And that thou bidd'st me come to thee,
O Lamb of God, I come.

Because of its use in evangelical churches as a hymn of commitment, this is probably the most frequently sung hymn in American churches. In the Billy Graham crusades, this hymn is always sung at the time of decision.

Charlotte Elliott, an invalid for most of her life, wrote this hymn in 1834 at Brighton, England. Her family was holding a bazaar to raise money to build a school at St. Mary's Hall in Brighton. Charlotte was not well enough to participate in this worthy project. In the middle of a sleepless night, oppressed with a sense of helplessness, she wrote the formula of her faith in six terse stanzas. Two years later it was published in her *Invalid Hymn Book* with the Scripture reference "Him that cometh to me I will in no wise cast out" (John 6:37).

In her earlier years she had written much humorous poetry, but following her conversion through the influence of Cesar Malan, an evangelist from Geneva, Elliott began writing hymns. Over the years she produced more than 150. Her friendship with Malan was of lasting influence, as they corresponded with each other for forty years. Through pain and suffering she continued her literary pursuits.

Several composers have written tunes for this hymn, but the most widely used is "Woodworth," written in 1849 by William B. Bradbury for another hymn text. Bradbury made his home in New York City and published many collections of Sunday school songs.

THE COMFORTING PRESENCE OF JESUS

Just when I need him, Jesus is near,
Just when I falter, just when I fear;

Ready to help me, ready to cheer,
Just when I need him most.

As a young Methodist minister in his early thirties, William C. Poole had a keen interest in writing poetic verse. He enjoyed fitting words together, finding rhyming sounds, and aligning word accents. Out of his concern for an awareness of the presence of Christ in his life, Poole began shaping poetic lines around this idea. His careful choice of words, the lyric flow of the lines, and the rhymes tying the stanzas together crystallized his thinking as the stanzas began to take shape. When he had completed "Just When I Need Him, Jesus Is Near," he sent it along with several other poems to Charles H. Gabriel, a composer then living in Chicago.

Of the poems he received from Poole, Gabriel was most impressed with "Just When I Need Him, Jesus Is Near" and soon composed a tune for it. The song was published in 1909 by a Chicago publisher, and its use in many evangelical services helped to make it very popular.

In 1912 Gabriel became associated with the publishing firm of Homer Rodeheaver, well-known evangelical song-leader, and maintained this relationship until his death in 1932. He edited thirty-five gospel songbooks, eight Sunday school songbooks, seven books for men's choruses, six for ladies' voices, ten children's songbooks, nineteen collections of anthems, and twenty-three cantatas—an extraordinary output of musical writing.

Following his ordination into the Methodist ministry in 1900, William C. Poole served various pastorates in the Wilmington Conference over a period of thirty-five years. He died in 1949 in Lewes, Delaware. Throughout years of pastoral ministry Poole wrote lyrics for gospel songs. Among his songs are "Sunrise," written in 1924, and "The Church by the Side of the Road," written the following year.

A HYMN WRITTEN ON
THE MEDITERRANEAN SEA

Lead, kindly Light! amid th'encircling gloom,
Lead thou me on;

The night is dark, and I am far from home,
Lead thou me on:
Keep thou my feet; I do not ask to see
The distant scene; one step enough for me.

In the summer of 1833, a young minister of the Church of England was a passenger on a ship in the Mediterranean Sea. There was no wind and the ship was becalmed in a fog bank for a week in the Straights of Bonifacio between Corsica and Sardinia. The usual brilliant landscape of that area was obscured by the motionless fog. Lost were the rocky shores of Sardinia on one side and the stark perpendicular cliffs of Corsica on the other.

John Henry Newman, eldest son of a prosperous London banker, began his ministry at Oxford. While traveling through Sicily in 1833, he became seriously ill. Grave concern about his work in England and the uncertainty of his future weighed heavily on his mind. His faith in the divine purpose of God, even in such circumstances, is evident in this hymn.

Newman returned to his church at Oxford and became a part of the group of Anglican ministers who sought diligently to bring renewal to the church. Twelve years later his intense concern caused him to leave the Church of England and become a Roman Catholic.

Newman was ordained a priest at Rome in 1846. Except for four years at the Dublin Catholic University, he spent the rest of his life at the Oratory of St. Philip Neri near Birmingham, England. Pope Leo XIII made Newman a cardinal in 1879, and he was one of the most revered Catholic leaders in England until his death in 1890.

The tune permanently joined to these words was written by the noted English composer, John B. Dykes. He wrote the tune in the summer of 1865 while walking through the Strand, the famous theater and shopping district of London.

The popularity of the hymn was quite surprising to Newman, who quickly attributed its success to the tune written by Dykes. The composer named the tune "Lux Benigna," meaning "kindly light."

A COMMENCEMENT HYMN
FOR SEMINARIANS

Lead on, O King Eternal,
The day of march has come;
Henceforth in fields of conquest
Thy tents shall be our home:
Through days of preparation
Thy grace has made us strong,
And now, O King Eternal,
We lift our battle song.

Can you imagine this hymn being sung at a commencement for young seminarians? Ernest Shurtleff wrote it for his own graduating class in 1887 at Andover Theological Seminary. He was twenty-six years old, had graduated from Harvard and, after beginning a literary career, had felt called to the ministry.

Shurtleff served Congregational churches in California, Massachusetts, and Minnesota. Then he went to Frankfurt, Germany, where he organized the American Church in 1905. The following year he went to Paris as director of student activities at the Academy Vitt. His work among the American students there was most remarkable.

This stirring hymn deserved a lively tune. It was first set to Henry Smart's "Lancashire" in the 1905 *Methodist Hymnal.*

At the age of twenty-two, Smart was organist at the parish church in the town of Blackburn in Lancashire County, England. In the fall of the year, a music festival was planned in Blackburn commemorating the three-hundredth anniversary of the Reformation in England. Smart wrote the tune "Lancashire," named it for the county, and it was sung in the festival to the words of "From Greenland's Icy Mountain."

The popularity of the tune has grown across the almost 150 years of its life, and it has been used with a variety of hymn texts. The one most frequently associated with the tune is Shurtleff's "Lead On, O King Eternal."

Henry Smart became one of the finest organists of his day in England, though largely self-taught. His overwork as a young man strained his eyes, and by the time he was fifty-two he was totally blind. He continued playing the organ and conducting until his death at the age of sixty-six. His daughter wrote down his compositions as he played them for her.

He composed many works, edited several hymnals, and gave unreservedly of his musical gifts to the church. Today, over one hundred years after his death, his name is found in hymnals around the world with the hymn tune he wrote when he was twenty-three.

"HOLY MR. HERBERT'S" HYMN

Let all the world in every corner sing:
My God and King!
The heavens are not too high,
His praise may thither fly;
The earth is not too low,
His praises there may grow.
Let all the world in every corner sing:
My God and King!

George Herbert was a country preacher, appointed in 1930 to the Anglican Church in the small village of Bremerton near Salisbury, England. An excellent student at Westminster School and Trinity College in Cambridge, he was "perfect in the learned languages, and especially in the Greek tongue." He took holy orders in the Church of England, and, when he was thirty-seven, he and his wife moved to Bremerton. Dearly loved by all, his ministry there was notable; he was called "holy Mr. Herbert." Even those who did not attend his church greatly respected him. When the church bells rang for prayers, those plowing in the fields stopped working and offered their devotion to God. Then they resumed their plowing.

"Let All the World in Every Corner Sing" was in Herbert's poetic collection *The Temple.* Three weeks before his death in 1633, Herbert gave the manuscript to a friend, authorizing him to publish it if he thought it worthy. Herbert's great joy in praise is reflected in the hymn. The first stanza calls for resounding adoration of God in heaven and earth. The second speaks of two kinds of praise: the praise of corporate worship in church ("the church with psalm must shout") and the private devotion of the Christian heart ("the heart must bear the strongest part"). God's praise in church is associated with weekly services, but the individual can praise God in his heart many times throughout the day.

Two or three hymn tunes are found in American hymnals for this text, but one quite widely used is the work of Robert G. McCutchan. While serving as editor of *The Methodist Hymnal* (1935), McCutchan submitted this tune, unsigned. To his surprise, the hymnal committee agreed to use it. When asked about the composer, McCutchan, not wanting to reveal his own writing, replied, "John Porter." Later he said that that was the first name that came to his mind; he really knew no one named that. "John Porter" appeared in the 1935 *Methodist Hymnal,* but subsequent hymnals have corrected this and the tune bears McCutchan's name.

A GATHERING SONG THAT BECAME A COMMUNION HYMN

Let us break bread together on our knees,
Let us break bread together on our knees.
When I fall on my knees,
With my face to the rising sun,
O Lord, have mercy on me.

A spiritual of unknown origin, "Let us break bread together on our knees" is always found in the "Communion" or "Lord's Supper" category in today's hymnals. Originally the song evidently was a "gathering song," beginning "Let us praise God together on our knees." Secret gatherings by slaves hoping to escape to freedom were common. This song, and others such as "Steal Away to Jesus," may have carried hidden meanings about such meetings known only to the slaves.

When the stanza about Communion observance was added is not known. Even with these stanzas there is an obvious awkwardness in the song. Observing communion by the breaking of bread and drinking of the cup does not require that a person kneel, face the east (the rising sun), or do this early in the morning.

Only in recent decades have many spirituals appeared in

the hymnals of major denominations in America. They have been welcomed as hymns for worshipers and have greatly enriched congregational singing. Among those frequently found are "We Are Climbing Jacob's Ladder," "Every Time I Feel the Spirit," "Go Down, Moses," and "Were You There?"

The spirituals, born in the hearts of slaves in America, were sung in fields, homes, and black churches throughout the South. Beyond these circles they were unknown. Eleven students from Nashville's Fisk University left their campus in October of 1871 and shared their songs with the world. From 1871 to 1878, the Jubilee Singers enjoyed a rousing reception in New England, then in Great Britain by both royalty and working people. In Germany they sang before the leading music critics and were received by royalty, nobility, and peasants. Enthusiasm for the spirituals spread around the world. After seven years the Jubilee Singers returned to Nashville with a total of $150,000 for Fisk University. Jubilee Hall, a monument to the dedication and devotion of these singers, stands today on the Fisk University campus on a spot that was once a slave pen.

A FIFTEEN-YEAR-OLD LAD'S METRICAL PSALM

Let us with a gladsome mind
Praise the Lord, for he is kind:
For his mercies shall endure,
Ever faithful, ever sure.

While he was a fifteen-year-old student at St. Paul's School in London in 1623, John Milton wrote the hymn. It is based on Psalm 136 and was first published in a collection of his poems in 1645. At Christ College in Cambridge, he completed his master's degree when he was twenty-four, and for six years after engaged in full-time study while living in his father's home. In 1649, because of his linguistic skills, Milton attained a high position in Oliver Cromwell's government, translating letters from the British government to foreign states and rulers. He became blind in 1653, yet continued to work until

Cromwell's abdication in 1659. That he escaped the scaffold was a tribute to his fame and reputation.

Recognized as a great English poet, second only to Shakespeare, his best-known works are *Paradise Lost* (1667) and *Paradise Regained* (1671). In a strict sense he should not be considered a hymn writer, for his nineteen metrical psalms were not intended to be sung. Perhaps the greatest significance to the development of Christian song was his influence on Isaac Watts and Charles Wesley in poetic style.

The hymn tune most commonly found with "Let Us with a Gladsome Mind" is the work of John Antes, a Moravian composer. It was discovered in an unpublished manuscript about 1790. Without knowledge of this discovery, John B. Wilkes found the tune sometime later, harmonized it, and named it "Monkland" for the village in Hertfordshire, England, where he served as church organist. Born in Fredericks township, in 1740, John Antes was a member of one of the influential families in Pennsylvania. When he was twenty-four years old, he was ordained to the Moravian ministry and spent twelve years as a missionary in Egypt. During his last years there he suffered severe beatings ordered by Osman Bey, a Turk who attempted to extort money from him.

He left Egypt in 1781, spent a couple of years in Germany, then settled in Fulneck, England, for his remaining years. Antes was a devout Moravian and a watchmaker by profession. His avocational interest in music and his music compositions have established him as one of the finest of the early American composers of sacred music.

AN OLD RHINELAND CAROL

Lo, *how a Rose e'er blooming*
 From tender stem hath sprung!
Of Jesse's lineage coming
 As men of old have sung.
It came a floweret bright,
 Amid the cold of winter,
When halfspent was the night.

At the beginning of the Reformation in the sixteenth century, those who followed Martin Luther's followers were confronted with the problem of the popular songs about Mary or addressed to her. Popularized by the Meistersingers in Germany, these songs dealt more with Mary than with her Son. As the central theme, she is referred to as "the queen," "the blooming branch," "the rose without thorns" and "the one who gave birth to God." To make these texts usable, Lutherans attempted to make satisfactory alterations. Sometimes this was accomplished by merely substituting the name of Jesus for Mary.

A carol that has become well known in the English-speaking world is an old Rhineland carol which began

> *Es ist ein' Ros; entsprungen*
> *Aus einer Wurzel zart.*

Dating possibly from the fifteenth century, the German text is based on Isaiah 11:1, "There shall come forth a rod out of the stem of Jesse, and a Branch shall grow out of his roots."

Of all the English translations that have appeared, the one most often used is "Lo, How a Rose e'er Blooming," made about 1900 by Theodore Baker, distinguished American scholar and music editor. The second stanza of his translation is:

> *Isaiah 'twas foretold it,*
> *   The Rose I have in mind;*
> *With Mary we behold it,*
> *   The Virgin mother kind.*
> *To show God's love aright*
> *   She bore to men a Savior,*
> *When halfspent was the night.*

Here the scene at Bethlehem is viewed from the context of Isaiah's prophecy. Upon the soundness of this prophetic backdrop is projected the imagery of the rose tree. To the German people who tended their numerous rose trees with great and tender care, this was a beautiful and meaningful symbol of the Incarnate Son of God.

THE CRUCIFIED AND
EXALTED CHRIST

Look, ye saints! the sight is glorious:
See the Man of Sorrows now;
From the fight returned victorious,
Every knee to him shall bow:
Crown him! crown him!
Crowns become the Victor's brow.

Thomas Kelly was an Irishman ordained in the Church of England. His evangelical preaching in Ireland resulted in opposition from ecclesiastical authorities, and the Archbishop of Dublin closed all pulpits of his diocese to him. Kelly continued preaching, however, and proclaimed a fervent gospel message anywhere he had the opportunity to preach. A man of independent means, Kelly built his own churches and preached there. He was a thorough Bible scholar and was well versed in classical and Oriental languages. Of his 765 hymns, only three are found in hymnals today.

"Look, Ye Saints! The Sight Is Glorious," written in 1809, was published that year under the heading "The Second Advent." The hymn is based on Revelation 11:15: "And there were great voices in heaven, saying, The kingdoms of this world are become the kingdoms of our Lord, and of his Christ; and he shall reign for ever and ever." This same text is used in Handel's "Hallelujah" chorus in his oratorio *Messiah*.

One of the tunes that has come to be associated with Kelly's hymn is "Bryn Calfaria" (meaning Mount Calvary) by the Welsh composer William Owen. Owen wrote the tune for a Welsh text that dealt with Jesus and the cross. The sturdiness of the tune is reflected in the comment of Erik Routley that it is a "piece of real Celtic rock." Owen spent his life in Wales. His father worked in the slate quarries, and as a young man William also worked there. He was a singer and wrote his first hymn tune when he was eighteen. The tune "Bryn Calfaria" had a prominent part in the musical score of the 1941 award-winning motion picture *How Green Was My Valley,* an intense story of Welsh coal miners that features Maureen O'Hara, Walter Pidgeon, and Donald Crisp.

ANTICIPATING THE CHURCH'S GREAT AWAKENING

Lord of our life, and God of our salvation,
Star of our night, and hope of ev'ry nation,
Hear and receive thy church's supplication,
Lord God almighty.

Philip Pusey, a distinguished country gentleman who sat in the House of Commons in Great Britain, wrote the hymn in 1834. Pusey based the hymn on a German hymn written in 1644 in the midst of the Thirty Years' War by Matthaus von Löwenstern in Breslau (now Wroclaw), Poland. A native of Silesia, Löwenstern was born in 1594, son of a saddle and harness maker. Gifted in music and poetry, Löwenstern developed excellent administrative skills. At Bernstadt, a city near Breslau, he served in several administrative and musical posts and was made a noble by Emperor Ferdinand III.

Pusey found the German hymn almost two hundred years after it was written, and made a free English paraphrase of it, for he saw in it an appropriate message to the church of his day. Later Pusey commented that the hymn "refers to the state of the Church, that is to say of the Church of England in 1934, assailed from without, enfeebled and distracted within, but on the eve of a great awakening." The great awakening that he envisioned was the Oxford Movement, which was then in its early stages in the Church of England.

After his student days at Eton and Christ Church, Oxford, Pusey settled on the family estate and devoted himself to agriculture and public service. One of the founders of the Royal Agriculture Society, Pusey represented in turn four different constituencies in Parliament. A connoisseur of art, he owned many valuable prints and etchings.

The tune usually found with this hymn is one of the strong French church melodies that appeared in the seventeenth and eighteenth centuries. These tunes came into use in the churches and cathedrals of the French Roman Catholic dioceses, where they were sung to new Latin hymns. The leaders of the French church were eager for liturgical reform, and by 1791 eighty dioceses had abandoned the Roman rite in favor of the new breviaries and missals. The French church melodies from this year were sung in unison and may have had their roots in plainsong or secular melodies. Their composers or arrangers chose to remain anonymous.

A PRAYER FOR WISDOM AND STRENGTH TO WITNESS

Lord, speak to me, that I may speak
In living echoes of thy tone;
As thou hast sought, so let me seek
Thy erring children lost and lone.

Frances Havergal wrote the hymn in the spring of 1872, while she was living at Bewdley, near Birmingham, England. She titled it "A Worker's Prayer," the prayer of a Christian for wisdom and the will to share with others the blessings and understandings that the Lord provides. The final stanza concludes with an expression of full surrender:

O use me, Lord, use even me,
Just as thou wilt, and when, and where;
Until thy blessed face I see,
Thy rest, thy joy, thy glory share.

A talented musician, Frances Havergal sang beautifully and was much sought after as a concert soloist. She was also a gifted pianist, well schooled in classical piano literature. Many of her hymns first appeared in single leaflets and on ornamental cards. She wrote more than sixty-five hymns, but is best remembered for "I Gave My Life For Thee," "Take My Life and Let It Be," and "Lord, Speak to Me, That I May Speak."

The tune most often used for these words is an adaptation of Robert Schumann's *Nachtstucke in F,* composed for the piano in 1839. Some years later the melody was arranged as a hymn tune and as such has been widely used. The tune, called "Canonbury," was probably named for a street or square in the Islington section of London. Born in Saxony in 1810, Schumann showed remarkable musical talent at an early age.

His career as a concert pianist was halted by an injury to a finger, and he turned his energies to composing, leaving a legacy of great music. He wrote symphonies and secular music but is best known for his works for piano and solo song.

GOD'S LOVE EXTOLLED

Love divine, all loves excelling,
  Joy of heaven to earth come down;
Fix in us thy humble dwelling;
  All thy faithful mercies crown.
Jesus, thou art all compassion,
  Pure, unbounded love thou art;
Visit us with thy salvation;
  Enter every trembling heart.

Few hymns dealt with the idea that God is love when this hymn was first published in 1747. Charles Wesley's opening line declares that God's love exceeds all other loves. The hymn was a welcome addition to Wesleyan hymn singing, for it mirrored the preaching of both John and Charles Wesley.

Wesley imitated both hymnic meter and poetic expression in the opening lines of John Dryden's play "King Arthur":

Fairest Isle, all Isles excelling
  Seats of Pleasure and of Love;
Venus here will choose her Dwelling
  And forsake her Cyprian Groves.

Favorite words of Wesley were "all" and "every," for these occur like a resounding gong or drumbeat all through his hymns. The Wesleys preached that Jesus provides salvation for all persons, not just for a select few. Many scriptural allusions may be found in the four stanzas, for Wesley was highly skilled in putting a maximum of content in a minimum of poetic lines.

The tune most frequently sung to this text was composed in 1870 by John Zundel. Born in Germany, and educated in Russia, Zundel came to America in 1847. Beginning in 1850, he served for thirty years as organist at Henry Ward Beecher's Plymouth Congregational Church in Brooklyn. Zundel's organ playing at Plymouth Church became as popular as Beecher's preaching. Crowds thronged to the services because of the church's reputation for great preaching, skillful organ playing, and thrilling congregational singing.

Zundel assisted Beecher in the compilation of a hymnal, *The Plymouth Collection* (1855), one of the earliest collections designed for church use that contained both words and music on the same page. Though Zundel wrote a number of hymn tunes, only this one survives in our hymnals. It is variously named "Love Divine," or "Beecher," or "Zundel."

THE EXCELLENCIES OF CHRIST

Majestic sweetness sits enthroned
Upon the Savior's brow;
His head with radiant glories crowned,
His lips with grace o'erflow.

Samuel Stennett, author of the hymn, was the fourth of five consecutive generations of Baptist preachers. All five Stennetts served Seventh Day Baptist churches in England, churches that observed Saturday as the Sabbath. He succeeded his father as pastor of the Baptist church at Little Wild Street in London in 1758, serving there until his death in 1795. Many Londoners who belonged to other churches often came to hear him preach. John Howard, the philanthropist, and King George III were among his personal friends. So well was Stennett liked that Church of England leaders offered him a high position in the Anglican Church. But true to his own convictions, he replied, "I dwell among mine own people."

With the heading "Chief Among Ten Thousand" or "The Excellencies of Christ," the hymn was first published in London in 1787. Based on Song of Solomon 5:10–16, the initial stanza borrows the language of these verses and applies them to the brow, head, and lips of Christ.

The hymn tune associated with Stennett's hymn was composed for it by Thomas Hastings in 1837. The composer named the tune "Ortonville" for a small village that no longer exists. Born in Connecticut, Hastings, as a lad, moved with his family to the small village of Clinton, near Utica, New York.

Hastings was an albino and was extremely nearsighted. Amid the hardships of living on the frontier, his only formal education was in a country school. He taught himself the fundamentals of music. By the time he was eighteen, he led the choir in the rural church attended by his family. Later he became active in the Oneida County Musical Society. For several years he edited a religious periodical in Utica, using its columns to promote his ideas regarding the improvement of church music. He became one of America's outstanding music teachers and church musicians, as well as composing more than one thousand hymn tunes and publishing more than fifty collections of music.

A SUNDAY SCHOOL WORKER CONTEMPLATES GOD'S GRACE

Marvelous grace of our loving Lord,
Grace that exceeds our sin and our guilt,
Yonder on Calvary's mount outpoured,
There where the blood of the Lamb was spilt.
Grace, grace, God's grace,
Grace that will pardon and cleanse within;
Grace, grace, God's grace,
Grace that is greater than all our sin.

Julia Harriette Johnston was a gentle lady. When she was six years old her family moved to Peoria, Illinois, where her father was pastor of the First Presbyterian Church. An outstanding student, Julia began teaching in her high school after graduation. She also began working with children in Sunday school, an activity that became a major interest in her life. Her success as a Sunday school worker was widely known, and she was invited to speak and share her expertise at state and district Sunday school meetings.

She was the author of a number of books—devotional, biographical, and missionary. She also wrote many poems and articles for religious periodicals. For several years she wrote Sunday school lesson material for children for the David C. Cook Company, one of the oldest and largest publishers of

Sunday school literature. Her interest in poetic writing led her to write texts for hymns, and she eventually wrote more than five hundred. Except for this present hymn, none of these appear in hymn collections today. "Marvelous Grace of Our Loving Lord," also known by the title "Grace Greater than Our Sin," was written in 1910 and is based on Romans 5:20.

Appropriate music for Johnston's text was composed by Daniel B. Towner, who was then head of the music department of Moody Bible Institute in Chicago. A native of Rome, Pennsylvania, Towner served as music director for Methodist churches for fifteen years in Binghamton, New York, Cincinnati, Ohio, and Covington, Kentucky. In 1885 he became associated with D. L. Moody in his evangelistic work, and in 1893 became head of the music department at Moody Bible Institute. Here he exerted an unusual influence in church music throughout the Midwest as he trained evangelical music leaders and evangelistic singers. He was awarded the Mus.D. degree by the American Temperance University in Harriman, Tennessee, in 1900. He composed many gospel song tunes, but is best remembered for "At Calvary," "Trust and Obey," and this one named "Moody."

CIVIL WAR HYMN POPULAR WITH WORLD LEADERS

Mine eyes have seen the glory of the coming of the Lord;
He is trampling out the vintage where the grapes of
  wrath are stored;
He hath loosed the fateful lightning of his terrible swift
  sword;
  His truth is marching on.
  Glory! glory, hallelujah!
  Our God is marching on!

In the fall of 1861, Julia Ward Howe, Dr. Samuel G. Howe (her husband), Dr. James Freeman Clarke (their pastor), and Governor Andrews (of Massachusetts), were visiting in Washington, D.C. Having been invited to do so, they traveled some distance from the city to watch a military review of federal troops. As they returned to Washington on a road congested with troops, they heard some soldiers singing "John Brown's body lies a-moldering in the grave." Dr. Clarke commented on the stirring character of the music and suggested that Mrs. Howe write a better text for it.

During that night the words began to come to her, and the stanzas were completed before daybreak. After she returned to Boston, she showed the poem to James T. Fields, editor of the *Atlantic Monthly,* who suggested the title "The Battle Hymn of the Republic." Fields published the poem in the February 1862 issue of his magazine.

The song attracted little notice until it caught the attention of Chaplain C. C. McCabe, later a distinguished Methodist bishop. McCabe taught it to his 122nd Ohio Volunteer Infantry regiment and to other troops. In the months that followed, the song spread throughout the North propelled by the rising tide of patriotic emotion.

The music is of obscure origin but was apparently first used as a camp-meeting song from South Carolina, beginning, "Say, brother will you meet me."

The John Brown text seems to involve two people of the same name. The text was written for John Brown, an obscure private in the Northern army. After the abolitionist John Brown's raid on Harper's Ferry on October 16, 1859, and his execution on December 2, 1859, it memorialized him. It was in this form that it came to the attention of Mrs. Howe.

General George S. Patton, Jr., was fond of the hymn and had it played for his men before sending them into action in Europe during World War II. The Mormon Tabernacle Choir sang it at the inauguration of President Lyndon B. Johnson in Washington, D.C., on January 20, 1965. At his own request, it was sung at the funeral service of Winston Churchill at Westminster Abbey on January 30, 1965. At the memorial service for Robert F. Kennedy at St. Patrick's Cathedral in New York City in June 1968, it was sung by Andy Williams, accompanied by the New York Philharmonic Orchestra which was directed by Leonard Bernstein.

EXPRESSING LOVE FOR CHRIST IN SPITE OF POOR HEALTH

More love to thee, O Christ,
More love to thee!
Hear thou the prayer I make
On bended knee;
This is my earnest plea:
More love, O Christ, to thee;
More love to thee.

Elizabeth Prentiss wrote the hymn in 1856 when she was experiencing poor health. The inspiration came in a moment, and she quickly wrote the lines of the four stanzas, though she did not complete the final stanza. Thirteen years later she showed the poem to her husband, George L. Prentiss, professor of preaching at Union Theological Seminary in New York City. He encouraged her to publish the poem in a leaflet in 1869, to be distributed among friends. Before she sent the copy to the printer she completed the final stanza.

The third stanza, often omitted, contains references to her own personal difficulties.

Let sorrow do its work,
Come grief or pain;
Sweet are thy messengers,
Sweet their refrain
When they can sing with me,
More love, O Christ to thee,
More love to thee.

The leaflet came to the attention of William H. Doane, a Cincinnati businessman whose successful hobby was writing gospel-song tunes. His more than 2,200 tunes and more than 40 collections were widely known and popular. His most successful collaboration was with Fanny J. Crosby. Together they wrote "I Am Thine, O Lord," "Jesus, Keep Me Near the Cross," "Pass Me Not, O Gentle Savior," "Rescue the Perishing," and "To God Be the Glory," to name only a few. Prentiss's poem set to Doane's music was included in a collection published by Doane in 1870. During the spiritual awakening of the early 1870s, the hymn was widely used and has remained in our hymnals for more than a century.

SEMINARY STUDENT'S PATRIOTIC HYMN

My country, 'tis of thee,
Sweet land of liberty,
Of thee I sing:
Land where my fathers died,
Land of the pilgrims' pride,
From every mountainside
Let freedom ring.

Samuel Francis Smith, a first-year seminary student, wrote the hymn in 1831. He was studying for the Baptist ministry at Andover Theological Seminary. Because of his knowledge of the German language, he was given some German hymnals and tunebooks by a friend. Smith was intrigued by some of the songs, especially "Gott segne Sachsenland" (God bless our Saxon land). Later he said, "I instantly felt the impulse to write a patriotic hymn of my own, adapted to the tune. Picking up a scrap of paper, I wrote at once, probably within half an hour, the hymn 'America' as it is now known."

Apparently the third stanza of the original five did not survive much beyond the premiere performance at the Boston Sabbath School Union on July 4, 1831. It speaks forcefully against England's treatment of the American colonies and the resulting War of Independence.

No more shall tyrants here
With haughty steps appear,
And soldier bands;
No more shall tyrants tread
Above the patriot dead—
No more our blood be shed
By alien hands.

In addition to his pastoral ministry and teaching, Smith wrote nearly one hundred hymns. A great admirer of Adoniram Judson, missionary to Burma, he toured the mission fields of Asia and Europe in 1880. Because of his continuing interest in missions, he served as editorial secretary for the American Baptist Missionary Union from 1854 to 1869.

At a class reunion at Harvard University, his close friend and classmate, Oliver Wendell Holmes, read a poem he had written for the occasion to honor his friend Smith.

And there's a nice youngster of excellent pith—
Fate tried to conceal him by naming him Smith;
But he shouted a song for the brave and the free—
Just read on his medal, "My country, 'tis of thee!"

FROM A CHANCE MEETING ON A BOSTON STREET

My faith looks up to thee,
Thou Lamb of Calvary,
*   Savior divine!*
Now hear me while I pray,
Take all my guilt away,
O let me from this day
*   Be wholly thine!*

On a street in Boston in 1831, Lowell Mason, a distinguished musician, met Ray Palmer, who had graduated from Yale College the previous year. In the ensuing conversation, Mason mentioned that he was compiling a hymnal. He asked the young man if he had any hymns that might be included. "I just may have," Palmer said, and pulled from his pocket a small morocco-bound notebook in which he had written down poetic verse that came to him in unexpected moments.

Palmer showed Mason a poem he had written a year earlier that began, "My faith looks up to thee." Whether simply to be kind or to indicate genuine interest is not clear, but Mason asked for a copy. The two men stepped into a store and Palmer, standing at the counter, copied the six stanzas.

At his home Mason read the poem again and his interest increased. Soon he had completed a tune for them that he named "Olivet." A few days later, the two men again met by chance on the street. Mason enthusiastically greeted his young friend and exclaimed, "Mr. Palmer, you may live many years and do many things, but I think you will be best known to posterity as the author of 'My Faith Looks Up to Thee.'" How prophetic these words were. Palmer's text and Mason's music were first published in 1832 in Boston in *Spiritual Songs for Social Worship,* edited by Mason and Thomas Hastings.

Mason, a native of Massachusetts, gave evidence of extraordinary musical gifts at an early age. By the time he was sixteen he was leading the village choir and teaching singing schools. From 1812 to 1827 he lived in Savannah, Georgia, where he worked as a bank clerk and studied music with excellent teachers. He returned to Boston, where he began classes for the children of his church to improve the music of both choir and congregation. By 1838 he had gained approval for the teaching of vocal music in the public schools of Boston in "preparation for making the praise of God glorious in families and churches." Because of his commitment to music education he is recognized as the "father of public school music in America."

A FOUR-HUNDRED-YEAR-OLD SPANISH SONNET

My God, I love thee, not because
I hope for heav'n thereby,
Nor yet for fear that loving not
I might forever die;
But for that thou didst all mankind
Upon the cross embrace;
For us didst bear the nails and spear,
And manifold disgrace.

The story of the hymn begins with a sixteenth-century Spanish sonnet that was translated into a Latin hymn a hundred years later. Two hundred years after that, the Latin hymn was translated into English. The Spanish sonnet has been attributed to Francis Xavier, an original member of the Society of Jesus who took Jesuit vows with Loyola in 1534. He became one of the great missionaries of the Roman Catholic Church, serving in India, Japan, and China.

The person who made the Latin hymn from the sonnet is unknown, but Edward Caswall made the English translation in 1849.

As we sing the hymn, we examine our motives for loving Christ. The selfish motives of reaching heaven and escaping hell are set aside as we affirm that our love is motivated by Christ's sacrifice at Calvary—his suffering, anguish, disgrace, and death. Here is God's spectacle of salvation for us.

Jane M. Marshall's beautiful choral setting of this text, which she composed in 1954 and titled "My Eternal King," has become a standard classic for many church choirs. Through its use the text has been introduced to many congregations to whom it was unfamiliar.

THE WRITING OF A MASTER CABINETMAKER

My hope is built on nothing less
Than Jesus' blood and righteousness;
I dare not trust the sweetest frame,
But wholly lean on Jesus' name.
On Christ the solid Rock, I stand;
All other ground is sinking sand.

Edward Mote's mother and father owned a pub in London. In his youth, his parents apprenticed him to a cabinetmaker. He heard the preaching of John Hyatt at Tottenham Court Road Chapel when he was fifteen, and it changed his life. He moved to Southwark, a suburb of London, and became a successful cabinetmaker. His business grew significantly as did the demands on his time, but Mote maintained his church activity and was known for his Christian zeal.

Hymn singing seemed to have great interest for him, and he began to try his hand at hymn writing. One morning in

1834, on his way to work, these lines came to his mind: "On Christ the solid Rock, I stand, all other ground is sinking sand." Before the day was over, he had written the stanzas to go with the lines of the refrain. The next Sunday he visited the home of some fellow church members where the wife was very ill. The husband informed Mote that it was their custom on the Lord's Day to sing a hymn, read the Bible, and pray together. Mote produced the new hymn from his pocket, and they sang it together for the first time.

During his lifetime this master cabinetmaker wrote more than one hundred hymns. Mote published them, together with hymns by other writers, in *Hymns of Praise, A New Selection of Gospel Hymns* in 1836. This was the first usage of the now well-known term "gospel hymn."

When he was fifty-five years old, Mote became pastor of the Strict Baptist Church in Horsham, Sussex. He ministered there for twenty-one years and enjoyed the love and affirmation of his congregation. Because the church building was secured largely through Mote's efforts, the congregation, out of love and gratitude for their pastor, offered to give him the deed to the property. He refused the gift, saying, "I do not want the chapel. I only want the pulpit; and when I cease to praise Christ, then turn me out of that."

A BAPTIST PREACHER'S DISCOVERY

My Jesus, I love thee, I know thou art mine,
For thee all the follies of sin I resign;
My gracious Redeemer, my Savior art thou;
If ever I loved thee, my Jesus, tis now.

Adoniram Judson Gordon, the young pastor of the Baptist church in Jamaica Plain, Massachusetts, was browsing through a new hymnal he had received from England. The opening line of an unfamiliar hymn caught his eye—"My Jesus, I love thee." No author's name appeared with it, but its beauty and intimate expression captured Gordon's attention. He began humming a tune and eventually completed a musical setting for the anonymous text. In a collection he prepared for Baptist churches in 1876, Gordon included the hymn with his tune.

Gordon was born in New Hampshire in 1836, at a time when Baptists had a great interest in foreign mission enterprise. His parents, devout Baptists, named him for Adoniram Judson, then serving in Burma. This pioneer missionary's work caught the interest of not only the Gordons, but many Christians in America as they followed his missionary activities through his frequent letters from the mission field.

For many years after the text's appearance, its author remained unknown. As late as the mid-1940s, many hymnals labeled the text as "anonymous" or attributed it to the "London Hymn Book, 1864." Some years ago someone discovered that the hymn was written by William Ralph Featherston, who lived in Montreal, Canada. He and his parents were members of the Wesleyan Methodist Church of Montreal. Little else is known about him, except that he died in 1873 at the age of twenty-seven. Apparently Featherston wrote the hymn about 1862. For it he borrowed and altered the first two lines of an old camp meeting hymn:

> *O Jesus, my Savior! I know thou art mine*
> *For thee all the pleasures of earth I resign.*

SHAPED BY MANY HANDS

> *Must Jesus bear the cross alone,*
> *And all the world go free?*
> *No, there's a cross for ev'ryone,*
> *And there's a cross for me.*

Thomas Shepherd wrote these lines in 1693. Well, not exactly. The lines he wrote were these:

> *Shall Simon bear the cross alone,*
> *And other saints be free?*
> *Each saint of thine shall find his own,*
> *And there is one for me.*

Some anonymous person changed Shepherd's lines, substituting Jesus' name for Simon's, and making other obvious changes. But were it not for the changes, Shepherd's name would be long forgotten.

Although ordained an Anglican minister, Shepherd left the Church of England in 1694 and served an independent congregation in Nottingham. In 1700 he moved to Bocking, near Braintree, Essex, where he preached in a barn for seven years before a small chapel was erected for his congregation. Here he ministered until his death in 1739.

For almost a century and a half this obscure preacher's poem remained unknown. George N. Allen, a music teacher at Oberlin College in Ohio, discovered the four-line stanza in 1844, added two others of unknown origin, and composed the tune we sing with these words. Allen, who had graduated from Oberlin College in 1838, remained there to teach music until 1864. The choral, instrumental, and music education programs he built became the foundation for the Oberlin Conservatory of Music, one of the fine music schools in the nation.

The three-stanza version in most hymnals is the one selected by Allen. Sometimes two or three additional stanzas by Charles Beecher are used; he added them for the hymnal compiled by his brother, Henry Ward Beecher, in 1855.

Reading the stanzas in our hymnals will call to mind numerous Scripture references, but essentially the hymn reflects the words of Christ, "If any man will come after me, let him deny himself, and take up his cross, and follow me" (Matt. 16:24). We are grateful to the contributors to this hymn, both known and unknown. Its continuing appeal is evident in the large number of hymnals in which it is found today with Thomas Shepherd's name.

SINGING ABOARD A SINKING SHIP

Nearer, my God, to thee,
Nearer to thee!
E'en though it be a cross
That raiseth me;
Still all my song shall be,
Nearer, my God, to thee!
Nearer to thee!

This hymn, expressing a yearning for the nearness of God, was written by Sarah Flower Adams in 1840. It was included in a hymnal compiled for her church congregation, the Unitarian South Place Chapel in London. A gifted and brilliant woman, Adams had many friends in the literary circles of London, including Robert Browning. The basis of the hymn is the account of Jacob's dream found in Genesis 28. Jacob dreamed about a ladder reaching from earth to heaven, with angels descending and ascending.

Lowell Mason, a distinguished Boston musician, was asked to write a suitable hymn tune for these words in 1856. He later recalled that "one night, lying awake in the dark, eyes wide open, through the stillness of the house the melody came to me, and the next morning I wrote down the notes of 'Bethany.'" Besides the tune "Bethany," Mason wrote the tunes that we use today for "Joy to the World," "Blest Be the Tie That Binds," "When I Survey the Wondrous Cross," and "My Faith Looks Up to Thee."

The singing of this hymn by the passengers of the English ship *Titanic,* which struck an iceberg and sank in the Atlantic Ocean on April 14, 1912 with the loss of 1,513 lives, has become legendary. Americans have assumed that Mason's tune "Bethany" was sung by the passengers and played by the ship's band as the ship was sinking. This assumption was reinforced by the use of "Bethany" in the 1953 motion picture about the disaster that starred Barbara Stanwyck and Clifton Webb. After the release of the movie strong protests from England arose saying that Mason's tune had never been associated with this hymn in England and that, at the sinking of the *Titanic,* another tune, probably "Horbury" by John B. Dykes, was surely sung and played. But the legend lives on.

A NEW VERSION OF PSALM 98

New songs of celebration render
To him who has great wonders done;
Awed by his love his foes surrender
And fall before the Mighty One.
He has made known his great salvation
Which all his friends with joy confess;

He has revealed to every nation
*His everlasting righteousness.**

Erik Routley wrote the hymn in 1970 to be sung to the French psalm tune "Rendez à Dieu." The hymn is based on Psalm 98, which begins, "O sing unto the Lord a new song; for he hath done marvelous things: his right hand, and his holy arm, hath gotten him the victory."

Born in Brighton, England, Routley was educated at Magdalen College and Mansfield College in Oxford. Ordained to the Congregational ministry in 1943 at the age of twenty-six, he served churches in Wednesday, Darford, and later in Edinburgh and Newcastle-upon-Tyne. From 1948 to 1959 he served as lecturer in church history, librarian, chaplain and director of music at Mansfield College. His reputation as an organist was widely known and many students in other Oxford colleges attended Sunday services to hear him play. One of these students later commented, "If Routley liked the hymn tune he was playing, he played it magnificently. But, if he did not like it, the tune was played in a very pedestrian manner."

Beginning in 1962, Routley visited the United States eight times in twelve years. He lectured at seminaries and universities, spoke at church music workshops, and preached in churches. His writings and speaking engagements added quickly to his reputation year by year as his influence widened, particularly in the areas of church music and hymnology. Without question Erik Routley became the most influential individual in church music in both England and the United States. He died in 1982 in Nashville, Tennessee, while he was involved in a church music workshop. *Duty and Delight: Routley Remembered* (Hope Publishing Company) was published in 1985. It includes essays and tributes by a number of close friends. A significant section of this work is an extensive bibliography of Erik Routley's writings—books, articles, hymns, hymn tunes, and other music.

A HYMNWRITER BORN OF SLAVE PARENTS

Nothing between my soul and the Savior,
Naught of this world's delusive dream;
I have renounced all sinful pleasure,
Jesus is mine! There's nothing between.
Nothing between my soul and the Savior,
So that his blessed face may be seen;
Nothing preventing the least of his favor,
Keep the way clear, let nothing between.

Charles Albert Tindley, of slave parents, was twelve years old when Abraham Lincoln signed the Emancipation Proclamation. His mother died when he was four, and the following year his father abandoned him. By his own determination he learned to read and write. As a teenager he worked as a janitor in a small church in Philadelphia and went to night school. After completing a correspondence course from the Boston School of Theology, he was ordained to the Methodist ministry and joined the Delaware conference. In 1902 he became the pastor of the Bainbridge Street Methodist Church in Philadelphia, the church where he had been the janitor.

When the building became inadequate for the growing congregation, a larger building was built. This, too, was soon outgrown, and in 1924 a new building was erected at Broad and Fitzwater Streets. In spite of his protests, the church was renamed the Tindley Temple Methodist Church. Here Tindley preached to throngs of people. Both blacks and whites, Italians, Jews, Germans, Norwegians, Mexicans, and Danes were represented in the leadership of the church.

When Tindley died in 1933 at the age of eighty-two, all Philadelphia mourned. Government officials and Chinese laundrymen, priests and scrubwomen, corporation presidents and street cleaners, Jews and Catholics and Protestants, black and white, some five thousand strong, crowded into a church seating three thousand to listen to five hours of inspirational tribute to a man who had been called "Lincoln in Ebony."

A gifted songwriter, Tindley wrote both words and music for "Nothing Between My Soul and the Savior" in 1905. He also wrote "When the Morning Comes," "Stand By Me," and "Take Your Burden to the Lord and Leave It There."

PRAISE IN THE MIDST OF THE THIRTY YEARS' WAR

Now thank we all our God
With heart and hands and voices,
Who wondrous things hath done,
In whom this world rejoices;
Who, from our mother's arms,
Hath blest us on our way
With countless gifts of love,
And still is ours today.

Martin Rinkart wrote these lines in 1636 in the midst of the famine, pestilence, and destruction of the Thirty Years' War. For some time he was the only pastor in the walled city of Eilenburg in Saxony. Many people in the city were casualties of the war or victims of hunger and illness. During the great pestilence of 1637, Rinkart ministered to the people of the city and conducted 4,500 burial services—sometimes as many as forty or fifty a day. One of them was for his wife. A man of frail body but heroic character, Rinkart faithfully served the people of his congregation and the community of Eilenburg from 1617 until his death in 1649.

Rinkart's sturdy Lutheran faith is reflected in the lines of the hymn. The first stanza is an expression of thanksgiving for the blessings of God. The second is a petition for God's care and keeping, and the final stanza is a doxology, praising the Father, Son, and Holy Spirit. The German text was translated into English by Catherine Winkworth in 1858. In four decades it had become well known in England and was sung at the Diamond Jubilee celebration of Queen Victoria in 1897.

Johann Cruger composed the music we use to sing Rinkart's hymn. A distinguished and respected musician, Cruger served as music director at the Lutheran Cathedral of St. Nicholas in Berlin for forty years. He composed many chorale melodies, and his collection of chorale tunes that appeared in 1644 was the outstanding such collection in Germany in the seventeenth century.

THE EMPHASIS OF "NOWNESS"

Now the silence,
Now the peace,
Now the empty hands uplifted,
Now the kneeling,
Now the plea,
Now the Father's arms in welcome,
Now the hearing,
Now the pow'r,
Now the vessel brimmed for pouring;
Now the body,
Now the blood,
Now the joyful celebration;
Now the wedding,
Now the songs,
Now the heart forgiven leaping;
Now the Spirit's visitation,
Now the Son's epiphany,
Now the Father's blessing.
Now! Now! Now!*

Words and phrases of the hymn "Now the Silence" began to take shape in the mind of author Jaroslav J. Vajda one morning when he was shaving. Living in St. Louis, Vajda was editor of *This Day,* a monthly family-religious-cultural magazine. He had served for eighteen years as a Lutheran minister in Indiana and Pennsylvania, and because of this experience, had a continuing concern for worship.

Vajda believed that we get so little out of worship because we anticipate so little. As phrases and words flooded his mind he began to form a list of things that one should expect in worship. The absence of rhyme and well-worn clichés, strengthened by the rhythm and repetition, heighten the impact of the hymn.

The word "now" pounds persistently twenty-one times to remind us of the immediate presence of God, the "nowness" of our Lord. The poem was first published in the May 1968 issue of *This Day*. The text, along with Carl F. Schalk's tune "Now," was included in the Worship Supplement in 1969.

A native of Ohio, Jaroslav J. Vajda is the son of a Lutheran pastor. He completed his studies at Concordia Theological Seminary in St. Louis in 1955, and served as pastor of several churches, some of which were bilingual (Slovak and English). In 1959 he became editor of *The Lutheran Beacon*, published by the Synod of Evangelical Lutheran Churches, and in 1963, editor of *This Day*. Since 1971 he has been an editor for Concordia Publishing House. Because of his knowledge and insight in the areas of poetry, hymnody, and church music, he served on the Commission on Worship of the Lutheran Church (Missouri Synod) and also on the Inter-Lutheran Commission on Worship.

The composer of "Now" is Carl F. Schalk. A graduate of Concordia Teachers College, Eastman School of Music, and Concordia Theological Seminary, he served as music director for the International Lutheran Hour from 1958 to 1965. Since 1965 he has served on the music faculty of Concordia College, River Forest, Illinois. He is well known in the area of church music as author, editor, composer, and lecturer.

INSPIRED BY A TRIP TO WESTERN STATES

O beautiful for spacious skies,
*   For amber waves of grain,*
For purple mountain majesties
*   Above the fruited plain!*
America! America!
*   God shed his grace on thee.*
And crown thy good with brotherhood
*   From sea to shining sea.*

An invitation to lecture on English religious drama at Colorado Springs, Colorado, was an irresistible opportunity for Katherine Lee Bates to go West. Bates, who taught English at Wellesley College in Massachusetts, stopped off at the Columbian World Exposition in Chicago on her way to Colorado. The magnificent "White City" of the exposition celebrating the 400th anniversary of the discovery of America inspired the phrase "alabaster cities" in the fourth stanza.

After her lecture she visited Pike's Peak with friends, a trip that provided inspiration for the expressions "spacious skies," "amber waves of grain," "purple mountain majesties," and "fruited plains." By the time she left Colorado, Katherine Bates had penciled in her notebook the four stanzas of the poem. Two summers later she sent a copy to a church paper, in which it was printed for the first time on July 4, 1895.

The music associated with Bates's hymn was written by Samuel A. Ward for another text, with which it was published in the 1894 Episcopal hymnal. In 1912, the president of the Massachusetts Agricultural College requested permission of the composer's widow to set the music to Bates's poem. The union of words and music became immensely popular during World War I. Ward, a highly respected church organist in Newark, New Jersey, had also established a successful music store there. In 1934, because his hymn tune had become so popular, Ward was memorialized by a brass plaque erected to his memory at Grace Episcopal Church in Newark where he had served as organist.

In the summer of 1960 the United States launched Echo I. This communications satellite, orbiting a thousand miles above the earth, received and relayed back to the United States the hymn "O Beautiful for Spacious Skies," the first music used in the new space-age communications system.

A LATIN CHRISTMAS CAROL FROM FRANCE

O come, all ye faithful,
Joyful and triumphant,
O come ye, O come ye to Bethlehem;

Come and behold him,
  Born the king of angels:
O come, let us adore him, Christ the Lord.

These lines were written in Latin in the middle of the eighteenth century by an Englishman who lived in Douay, France. A Roman Catholic center, Douay was a haven for English religious and political refugees who, in 1745, attempted to restore to the English throne the descendants of the deposed Stuart king, James II.

John Francis Wade, a musician and skilled calligrapher, made his living copying and selling music to Roman Catholic chapels and to families in the community. His beautiful manuscript books were the finest examples of his artistic craft.

The original Latin hymn began:

Adeste, fideles,
  Laeti triumphantes;
Venite, venite in Bethlehem;
  Natum videte
  Regem angelorum.
Venite, adoremus Dominum.

The origins of both text and tune have been shrouded in mystery. Only in recent decades has John Francis Wade's authorship of both been firmly established. The proof has been found in seven manuscript copies of the song that were discovered. They all date from the mid-eighteenth century and, most important of all, they bear Wade's signature.

What a joyful song, that sings of the adoration of Bethlehem's Babe. Unlike the Latin text the English version, made by Frederick Oakley in 1841 for his congregation at Margaret Street Chapel, has irregular lines and no rhyme. The music is simple, unsophisticated, and easily sung. For more than two hundred years, in Latin, in English, and in many other languages, the words and music written by a transplanted Englishman have become one of our most frequently sung songs of the Christmas season.

IN PLAINSONG TRADITION

O come, O come, Emmanuel,
And ransom captive Israel,
That mourns in lonely exile here,
Until the Son of God appear.
Rejoice! Rejoice! Emmanuel
Shall come to thee, O Israel!

Although these lines bore the name of John Mason Neale when they were published in England in 1851, the hymn was inspired by a Latin hymn by an anonymous writer. The Latin hymn was based on seven antiphons which dated from the ninth century or earlier. These antiphons—short verses sung at Vespers before and after the "Magnificat"—were part of the Advent season between December 16 and Christmas Eve.

The seven antiphons were called the "Great O's" because each one began with an "O." Each of the seven saluted the Messiah with one of the many titles found in the Bible—"O Sapientia" (Wisdom), "O Adonai" (Lord), "O Radix Jesse" (Root of Jesse), "O Clavis David" (Key of David), "O Oriens" (Orient), "O Rex gentium" (King), and "O Emmanuel" (God with us). Five of these short verses were made into a Latin hymn by an unknown writer about the twelfth century. From the Latin hymn, Neale made the English paraphrase that is found in most American hymnals today.

The tune we sing with these words had its beginning in a fifteenth-century community of French Franciscan nuns. Neale found a collection containing the tune in the National Library in Lisbon, Spain; Thomas Helmore adapted the tune for a hymnal he published in London in 1856.

HIS FIRST CHRISTIAN BIRTHDAY

O for a thousand tongues to sing
My great Redeemer's praise,
The glories of my God and King,
The triumphs of his grace.

John and Charles Wesley were students at Oxford University, preparing for the ministry in the Church of England. They joined a student club dedicated to strengthening personal religious life. John, a meticulous person, made a list of rules and methods for club members. His fellow students jokingly referred to the group as "The Methodists."

Having been greatly influenced by a group of Moravians on a trip to the American colony of Georgia in 1736, John Wesley, after returning to England, visited a Moravian mission on Aldersgate Street in London. Later he wrote in his journal that during the service, "I felt my heart strangely warmed." Three years earlier Charles had had a similar experience and marked it as his Christian conversion.

The Aldersgate experiences changed the religious history of the world. Charles became a magnetic preacher, preaching to throngs of people in farm communities, prisons, mining camps, and many cities in England, Wales, and Scotland. His 6,500 hymns gave his followers ardent songs to sing.

John Wesley became the stalwart leader of the movement. In his diaries and journals he recorded preaching more than forty thousand sermons in city streets, prisons, barns, hamlets, and cow pastures.

Though John and Charles never left the Church of England, the church leaders disassociated themselves from the Wesleys with great contempt. A contemporary referred to them and their followers as "those dirty, lousy Methodists."

On the first anniversary of his Aldersgate experience, Charles Wesley reflected on the twelve months since his conversion. Inspired by a comment by the Moravian Peter Bohler, he wrote the hymn "O for a thousand tongues to sing my great Redeemer's praise."

His abundant joy is reflected in the lines of his hymn.

SINGING WITH CONFIDENCE IN THE FUTURE

O God, our help in ages past,
Our hope for years to come,

Our shelter from the stormy blast,
And our eternal home.

Isaac Watts wrote the hymn as a paraphrase of the first five verses of Psalm 90. The lines of the hymn embrace strong faith in God on the basis of past experiences and reveal great confidence in the future. In times of stress and crisis, both national and personal, there is renewed hope in the singing of the hymn.

When he was a youth, Watts became disenchanted with the singing at the Congregational church in Southampton, England, where his deacon father and saintly mother took him on Sundays. The singing droned on and on, with some trying to maintain the tune and pace, but with many others either mumbling listlessly or showing no interest at all. Young Isaac thought there might be greater interest in psalm singing if new versions of the psalms were written in simple and singable language, with well-constructed poetic form. In 1719 Watts published his poetic versions of all 150 psalms in the Old Testament. Some of these may still be found in our hymnals.

William Croft, an eighteenth-century English organist, composed the tune we use for singing "O God, Our Help in Ages Past." He named the tune "St. Anne" for St. Anne's Church in Soho, London, where he became organist in 1700. One of the finest musicians of his day, Croft became organist at Westminster Abbey and composer to the Chapel Royal in 1708. He wrote a large amount of secular music in his younger days, but he is remembered for his church music—hymn tunes, anthems, and Anglican service music. The translation of his Latin epitaph in Westminster Abbey reads, "Having resided among mortals for fifty years, behaving with utmost candor, he departed to the heavenly choir on the 14th day of August, 1727, that, being near, he might add his own Hallelujah to the Concert of Angels."

THE JOY OF A BELIEVER

O happy day that fixed my choice
On thee, my Savior and my God
Well may this glowing heart rejoice,

And tell its raptures all abroad.
Happy day, happy day,
When Jesus washed my sins away!

The Walter Hawkins Singers introduced this song in the early 1970s to many people as their ecstatic recording hit the music charts. This gospel choir from Oakland, California, brought the sound of gospel singing to many who were totally unfamiliar with it. The Hawkins Singers had made a new song out of a text that was more than two hundred years old and a tune that dates from the middle of the nineteenth century.

Philip Doddridge, author of "O Happy Day That Fixed My Choice," was a Dissenting minister in England. A brilliant young man, he declined an offer of a university education for the ministry in the Church of England. Instead he enrolled in a Dissenting academy at Kibworth. He was ordained in the Congregational church and ministered for twenty-two years to a congregation in Northampton, England.

Doddridge wrote about 370 hymns, not one of which was published during his lifetime. Copies of some of them were circulated among his friends and sung in the churches they attended. In 1755, four years after his death, his hymns were published by a friend in a collection that included "O Happy Day," which he had titled "Rejoicing in Our Covenant Engagements to God," based on 2 Chronicles 15:15.

The tune "Happy Day" that is associated today with Doddridge's text in the United States, dates from William McDonald's *Wesleyan Sacred Harp,* published in Boston in 1854. The title page indicated that McDonald was a Methodist minister, a member of the Maine Conference. McDonald used this tune with another hymn and included as a refrain the words "Happy day, happy day, When Jesus washed my sins away." Doddridge's hymn was suggested as an alternate text for the stanzas. The tune—at least the refrain—apparently was adapted from an earlier song by Edward Rimbault, noted English composer. It is not known who shaped the tune in the form that McDonald printed it, but that form has remained and is irrevocably associated with Doddridge's hymn, which rejoices in the experience of Christian conversion as a happy, joyful day.

AN ALMOST-FORGOTTEN PHRASE

O how he loves you and me,
O how he loves you and me;
He gave his life, what more could he give?
O, how he loves you:
O, how he loves me:
*O, how he loves you and me.**

Whenever a new idea for a tune or a lyric comes to Kurt Kaiser, he jots it down and files it away for later reference. He frequently refers to this file of bits and pieces for a spark to ignite further creative writing. One day in 1975 he ran across the phrase "O, how he loves you and me" and decided to write a melody for it. In ten minutes he had completed the work— words and music.

Since 1959 Kaiser has been associated with Word, Inc., of Waco, Texas (now located in Las Colinas, Irving, Texas). He has had a significant role in the development of the international image of this firm that is so prominent in the fields of sacred recordings, music, and books. Degrees from the American Conservatory of Music in Chicago and Northwestern University hang on his wall. In 1973 Trinity College awarded him the honorary doctorate in music.

Kurt Kaiser is a deacon in the Seventh and James Baptist Church in Waco, Texas. He and his wife, Patricia, parents of four children and grandparents of two, are active in the fellowship of this church family. His compositions and choral arrangements are familiar in evangelical churches. Records and cassettes of his own piano artistry and his orchestral scorings have been exceedingly popular in the Christian music market.

A CONFIRMATION HYMN FOR THREE CHILDREN

O Jesus, I have promised
To serve thee to the end;

Be thou forever near me,
  My Master and my Friend;
I shall not fear the battle
  If thou art by my side,
Nor wander from the pathway
  If thou wilt be my guide.

A young girl and her two brothers stood for their confirmation on a Sunday morning in 1868 in the country parish of Castle Camps, near Cambridge, England. Their father was the minister of the Anglican church in this quiet community. John Ernest Bode, educated at Eton and Oxford, had taken Holy Orders in the Church of England in 1847. After serving three different parishes he was assigned to Castle Camps, where for fifteen years he ministered to the community.

For the confirmation service for his children, Bode wrote six stanzas, which began "O Jesus, we have promised." More than a century later, four stanzas of the hymn remain in our hymnals, with the pronoun in the opening line changed from plural to first-person singular. Bode's lines express a yearning for the presence of Christ in all the changing circumstances of life, with the promise of a commitment "to serve thee to the end." Bode may be ranked among those who are famous for one piece of writing; his inclusion in today's hymnals is well assured on the basis of this hymn of commitment.

The music we associate with the hymn was written in 1881 for another text, long since forgotten. The composer, Arthur H. Mann, was an outstanding English church organist of his day. His death in 1929 ended his fifty-three years as organist at King's College Chapel in Cambridge, where he contributed much to the great musical tradition of that chapel. His tune is named "Angel's Story" for the text for which it was written. The singable, simple tune is most appropriate for "O Jesus, I Have Promised."

A NIGHT IN BETHLEHEM

O little town of Bethlehem,
  How still we see thee lie!
Above thy deep and dreamless sleep

The silent stars go by;
Yet in thy dark streets shineth
The everlasting Light;
The hopes and fears of all the years
Are met in thee tonight.

In 1865 a young minister from Philadelphia visited Palestine. On the day before Christmas he rode a horse the several miles from Jerusalem to Bethlehem. After riding through the streets of Bethlehem, he went out to the nearby fields, the traditional site where the birth of Jesus was announced to the shepherds. From Shepherds' Field he returned to Bethlehem and attended the Christmas Eve service in the ancient basilica that was built over the traditional site of Jesus' birth.

Phillips Brooks was this young minister who was enjoying a year's travel away from his pulpit of Philadelphia's Holy Trinity Church. After he returned from his trip abroad, and long before he became nationally famous, he wrote the stanzas of this hymn for the children of his Sunday school to sing in a Christmas program. Brooks's vivid memory of his visit to Bethlehem is reflected in its lines.

Brooks was later moved to Trinity Church in Boston and was recognized as one of America's outstanding preachers. His published sermons are found in theological libraries, but his simple Christmas hymn appears in hymnals everywhere, in English and many other languages. For this he is best known.

Lewis Redner, the organist at Brooks' church, composed the music for "O little town of Bethlehem." Besides being the church organist, for nineteen years he served as superintendent of the Sunday school. Largely through his leadership, the enrollment of the Sunday school at Holy Trinity Church increased from thirty-six children to more than one thousand.

First published in 1874, this hymn became increasingly popular. Now, more than a century later, the collaboration of an Episcopal minister and his church's organist is standard fare in our Christmas singing.

PROGRESSION THROUGH
FOUR LANGUAGES

O Lord my God, when I in awesome wonder
Consider all the worlds thy hands have made,
I see the stars, I hear the rolling thunder,
Thy pow'r throughout the universe displayed,
Then sings my soul, my Savior God to thee;
How great thou art, how great thou art.*

The hymn had its beginning in 1886 in the mind of a Swedish lay preacher. Carl Boberg, the son of a shipyard carpenter, preached in his hometown, edited a weekly Christian newspaper, and served for more than twelve years in the Upper House of the Swedish Parliament. Boberg wrote "O Store Gud" and set the words to a Swedish folk melody of unknown origin. "O Store Gud" first appeared in several periodicals, then was published in Boberg's weekly paper in 1891. A German translation appeared in 1907, and the singing of the German text spread throughout Germany.

From the German text, a Russian translation was made and published in Moscow in 1927 in a Russian hymnal. That same year Stuart K. Hine, an English Methodist missionary to the western Ukraine, heard the song. Some years later, while working in a Carpathian mountain village in Czechoslovakia, he translated the first stanza into English during a thunderstorm. The "rolling thunder" of the storm is in the first stanza. Later Hine added the second and third stanzas that were not so much a translation as his own creation.

At the outbreak of World War II in 1939, Hine returned to England. He added stanza four in 1948. Hine printed the hymn in a Russian gospel magazine the following year, and subsequently printed it in leaflet form. One of the leaflets was given to George Beverly Shea during the Billy Graham Crusade in 1954. Shea and Cliff Barrows introduced the song in the meetings of the Toronto Crusade in 1955.

From Boberg's first writing on the southeast coast of Sweden to the Toronto Crusade covered sixty-nine years. Boberg's words passed through Swedish, German, Russian, and then into English. Many other translations have been made from each of these versions, and the song has spread around the world. Through it all, the spirit of Boberg's "O Store Gud" lives on.

INSPIRED BY
A VERSE OF SCRIPTURE

O Lord, our Lord,
How majestic is your name in all the earth;
O Lord, our Lord,
How majestic is your name in all the earth.
O Lord, we praise your name;
O Lord, we magnify your name:
Prince of Peace, Mighty God.
*O Lord God Almighty.**

A recommitment of his life turned things around for Michael W. Smith. After his experience with the Lord, Michael discovered new relationships, new words, new sounds, new melodies to express his love for Jesus Christ. As he read the Old Testament, the words of Psalm 8 seemed to stick in his mind. "O Lord, our Lord, how excellent is thy name in all the earth! who has set thy glory above the heavens."

As he studied the words, music filled his mind that would frame a verse of Scripture—his first attempt of this kind. His church family, Belmont Church, a nondenominational congregation in Nashville, Tennessee, was the first to hear and share in the singing of this new song.

In 1981 Michael met Amy Grant and began touring as the keyboard musician in her band. Two years later he signed with Reunion Records. His first release, *Michael W. Smith Project*, was nominated for several Dove Awards by the Gospel Music

Association. In 1984 he received a Grammy Award from the National Academy of Recording Arts and Sciences for his album *Michael W. Smith 2*.

His 1988 album, *i 2 (EYE)*, shows a more mature and intimate side of the personality and artistry of this multi-talented performer. The songs reflect facets of Michael's own life in their infectious melodies set in open, acoustical-pop production. New songs pour from his creative mind, but this song, based on a portion of God's Word, will continue to be sung by the people of God.

A HYMN BY A BLIND MINISTER

O Love that wilt not let me go,
I rest my weary soul in thee;
I give thee back the life I owe,
That in thine ocean depths its flow
May richer, fuller be.

George Matheson was afflicted with poor eyesight when he was a child. By the time he was eighteen, he was almost totally blind. Nevertheless, he was a brilliant student in the academy and university at Glasgow, Scotland. He became a Presbyterian minister, served churches in Glasgow, Innellan, and Edinburgh, and was loved and admired by his people for his effective ministry.

Perhaps as a compensation for his blindness, Matheson developed an extraordinary memory. Each week he would dictate his sermon to his sister. She would read it back to him twice, and on Sunday he would preach it word for word.

"O Love That Wilt Not Let Me Go" was written in Innellan on the day of his sister's marriage in 1882. The wedding, many thought, brought back to Matheson vivid memories of his teenage romance, which ended when the girl refused to go through with the wedding because of his blindness. He remained single throughout his life. The four stanzas were written in five minutes. He later recalled that "it was the quickest bit of work I ever did in my life. I had the impression of having it dictated to me by some inward voice rather than of working it out myself."

The tune we associate with his words was also written rapidly. Two years after Matheson completed the words, the compilers of the *Scottish Hymnal* asked Albert L. Pearce to write a tune for them. Pearce, music editor for the hymnal, read the words and quickly wrote the melody. He later said, "I wrote the music straight off, . . . the ink of the first note was barely dry when I finished the tune."

A DESIRE TO WALK WITH GOD

O Master, let me walk with thee
In lowly paths of service free;
Tell me thy secret, help me bear
The strain of toil, the fret of care.

Washington Gladden wrote these lines in 1879 while he was pastor of the Congregational Church in Springfield, Massachusetts. Written as a meditation, the poem, titled "Walking with God," was first published in a weekly religious paper called *Sunday Afternoon.* The quiet, meditative nature of the words does not reveal the aggressive, outspoken, crusading spirit of the author. While serving as religious editor of the New York *Independent,* Gladden aided in the exposure of the "Tweed Ring," a group of politicians who controlled New York City's treasury and got away with millions of dollars.

During his eight-year pastorate in Springfield, Gladden's role as a crusader for the practical application of the Christian faith became well known. His Sunday-evening sermons reflected this emphasis, and throngs of people came to hear him preach the social implications of the gospel. In 1882 he became pastor of the First Congregational Church of Columbus, Ohio, where he ministered for thirty-two years. His Sunday-evening services were controversial as he continued to apply the gospel of Jesus to the social, political, and economic life of America and the world.

Gladden's published sermons and articles were widely read, and he was severely criticized in both the secular and religious press. He castigated his denomination's Board of Foreign Missions for accepting from John D. Rockefeller, Sr., a gift of $100,000, which Gladden called "tainted money" because of the unfair and monopolistic practices of Standard Oil. He stated his position in two articles, "Tainted Money" and "Standard Oil and Foreign Missions."

Gladden's poem was first published as a hymn the year after it was written, and set to a tune composed by Henry Percy Smith, a minister in the Church of England. The tune was Gladden's choice and proved a most appropriate setting.

JESUS CHRIST, THE MORNING STAR

O Morning Star, how fair and bright
Thou beamest forth in truth and light!
O Sovereign meek and lowly!
Thou Root of Jesse, David's Son,
My Lord and Master, thou hast won
My heart to serve thee solely!
    Thou art holy,
    Fair and glorious,
    All-victorious,
    Rich in blessing,
Rule and might o'er all possessing.

Philip Nicolai wrote the hymn while he was the Lutheran pastor at Unna, a city about forty miles northeast of Dusseldorf, in what is now West Germany. Born in 1556, the son of a Lutheran pastor, he received his theological training at Wittenberg University. After graduation he assisted his father at Mengringhausen for four years, then was appointed pastor at Herdecke. There he encountered difficulties because Roman Catholics controlled the town council. When Spanish troops invaded the city in 1586, Nicolai was forced to leave.

Following two other appointments, he went to Unna in 1596. There he became involved in controversy with the Calvinists. In the midst of this difficulty, the city suffered the tragedy of the bubonic plague (1587–1598). During these days of suffering he kept a daily record of his thoughts "to leave behind me (if God should call me from the world) as the token of my peaceful, joyful Christian departure, or (if God should spare me in health) to comfort other sufferers." He became so engrossed in his writing about the praise and adoration of God that he was oblivious to all about him, even sometimes forgetting his noon meal. The work was published in 1599 and included three hymns—both words and music. Two of these were "O Morning Star, How Fair and Bright" and "Wake, Awake for Night Is Flying."

Many translations of his German text "Wie schön leuchtet der Morgenstern" have been made into English and other languages. The most used English version was made by Catherine Winkworth in 1963, and published in London that year.

Across almost four hundred years, Nicolai's hymn has been a favorite of many people in many lands. Sometimes it is referred to as the "Queen of the Chorales," and is rivaled only by Nicolai's other great hymn, "Wake, awake for night is flying," called the "King of the Chorales."

A PRESBYTERIAN MINISTER'S TRANSLATION

O Sacred Head, now wounded,
*   With grief and shame weighed down,*
Now scornfully surrounded
*   With thorns, thine only crown;*
How pale thou art with anguish,
*   With sore abuse and scorn!*
How does that visage languish
*   Which once was bright as morn!*

This hymn is based on a medieval Latin hymn that reflected an era when the crucifix had become an important Christian symbol for personal devotion. Artists and sculptors had begun to show the realistic aspects of Christ's sufferings and death, vividly portraying the wounds and anguish of our Lord. In medieval churches, monasteries, and homes, crucifixes became an accepted part of religious worship, providing an object of contemplation and a constant reminder of Christ's death on the cross.

The original Latin hymn, sometimes attributed to Bernard of Clairvaux, consisted of seven parts. Each was designed to be sung on a different day of the week, and each was addressed to a part of Christ's body—his feet, knees, hands, sides, breast, heart, and head. Paul Gerhardt, a Lutheran minister, made a German translation of the Latin hymn and it was published in Berlin in 1656.

The several English translations that have been made of Gerhardt's German text show the popularity of the hymn. The English translation most often in American hymnals was made in 1830 by James W. Alexander while he was pastor of the First Presbyterian Church in Trenton, New Jersey.

LINES WRITTEN DURING BRITISH BOMBARDMENT

O say, can you see, by the dawn's early light,
  What so proudly we hailed at the twilight's last
    gleaming,
Whose broad stripes and bright stars, thro' the perilous
    fight
  O'er the ramparts we watched, were so gallantly
    streaming?
And the rockets' red glare, the bombs bursting in air
Gave proof through the night that our flag was still
    there.
O say does that star-spangled banner yet wave
O'er the land of the free and the home of the brave?

Francis Scott Key wrote these lines "by the dawn's early light" on September 14, 1814. British interference in American commerce caused the United States to declare war on England on June 18, 1812. In August of 1814 the British sailed up Chesapeake Bay and sent ashore a small group who set fire to the Capitol, the White House, and other public buildings in Washington. On their way back to their ships, they took as prisoner a Dr. Beanes.

Because of his political influence, Key was asked to negotiate with the British for the release of Beanes. The British, planning to attack Baltimore immediately, feared that Key might alert the American forces, so they kept him prisoner for several days as they moved up Chesapeake Bay toward Baltimore.

Key and his party were released, and from a small boat they witnessed the British bombardment of Fort McHenry on September 13. The firing continued until after midnight, and it was not until Key saw the United States flag still flying over Fort McHenry in the early morning mist that he knew the British attack had been unsuccessful. Still on the small boat, Key began sketching the lines of the poem inspired by the recent incredible experiences. In his hotel room that evening, he wrote out a clean copy, which is now preserved in the Walters Art Gallery in Baltimore.

Key wrote the words to fit an English tune of unknown origin that was familiar to him and was used for singing various patriotic texts. Within a week Key's poem had appeared in two Baltimore newspapers and caught the excitement of all who saw it. Joseph Carr, a Baltimore music dealer, published words and music in sheet music form within a month.

With the passing years the popularity of the song increased, and it was acclaimed our national anthem by public acceptance long before the Act of Congress gave it official recognition on March 3, 1931, 117 years after its birth.

A SONG OF BETHLEHEM

O sing a song of Bethlehem,
Of shepherds watching there,
And of the news that came to them,
From angels in the air.
The light that shone on Bethlehem
Fills all the world today;
Of Jesus' birth and peace on earth
The angels sing alway.

Louis F. Benson, a distinguished Presbyterian minister, wrote the hymn in 1899. In it he compressed the earthly life and ministry of Jesus into four concise stanzas. Four geographical locations related to Christ's life are mentioned—Bethlehem, Nazareth, Galilee, and Calvary (as related to both his death and resurrection). Each stanza refers to the historical significance of the place, with a present-day application.

The initial stanza concludes with the reminder that the angels that sang at Jesus' birth continue to sing today of "peace on earth." The second stanza refers to Jesus' childhood in Nazareth and concludes

> For now the flowers of Nazareth
> In every heart may grow;
> Now spreads the fame of his dear name
> On all the winds that blow.

Christ's ministry is the focus of stanza three, which concludes:

> For though like waves on Galilee,
> Dark seas of trouble roll,
> When faith has heard the Master's word,
> Falls peace upon the soul.

The final stanza, omitted in some hymnals, begins with Christ's death at Calvary and ends with the Resurrection.

> For he who died on Calvary
> Is risen from the grave,
> And Christ, our Lord, by heav'n adored
> Is mighty now to save.

After enjoying a successful law practice for seven years, Benson enrolled in Princeton Theological Seminary. He was ordained to the Presbyterian ministry in 1886. In addition to a series of hymnals for the General Assembly of the Presbyterian Church, U.S.A., he wrote a number of books in the area of Christian hymnody. He was a highly respected hymnologist. His large and valuable hymnological library was bequeathed to Princeton Seminary upon his death.

A HYMN INSPIRED BY A TRACT

> O soul, are you weary and troubled?
> No light in the darkness you see?

There's light for a look at the Savior,
And life more abundant and free!
Turn your eyes upon Jesus,
Look full in his wonderful face,
And the things of earth will grow strangely dim
*In the light of his glory and grace.**

Helen Howorth Lemmel received a Christian tract from a friend in 1918. A sentence in the tract caught her attention: "Turn your eyes upon Him, look full into His face and you will find that the things of earth will acquire a strange new dimness." So strong was the impression of these lines that both words and melody took shape in her mind, first the chorus and later the stanzas. The song was printed in a pamphlet in London that year, and in 1922 was included in a small collection, *Glad Songs,* which featured sixty-seven songs by Lemmel. This publication introduced the song at the Bible conference at Keswick, England, where it experienced almost instant success.

Born in Wardle, England, Lemmel was the daughter of a Wesleyan Methodist minister. While she was still a small child, her family came to America, settling briefly in Mississippi and then moving to Wisconsin. Sometime after the turn of the century she made her home in Seattle, but traveled extensively in many states. She conducted religious services for children and wrote stories and songs for them. Lemmel was a gifted singer with a beautiful soprano voice. She studied voice in Germany for four years. When she was a young woman, she organized a women's vocal quartet that traveled the Chautauqua Circuit. She also briefly taught voice at Moody Bible Institute in Chicago and at the Bible Institute of Los Angeles. During her years in Seattle she was an active member of the Ballard Baptist Church.

Across more than six decades, Helen Lemmel composed more than four hundred hymns, writing even in her later years in spite of becoming blind after she was ninety. "Turn Your Eyes Upon Jesus," her best-known hymn, is found in most evangelical hymn collections. She died in Seattle, on November 1, 1961, a few days before her ninety-eighth birthday.

THE SPIRIT OF PENTECOST

O spirit of the living God,
*   Thou light and fire divine,*
Descend upon thy church once more,
*   And make it truly thine!*
Fill it with love and joy and pow'r,
*   With righteousness and peace,*
Till Christ shall dwell in human hearts,
*   And sin and sorrow cease.*

Pentecost, the Feast of Firstfruits, was one of the agricultural festivals observed by Israel. The Old Testament festival was observed seven weeks after Passover and involved the consecration of the harvest by offering a sheaf of the first ripe barley. On the first Pentecost after our Lord's ascension, his followers were assembled together in a room in Jerusalem. Suddenly there was a great noise that sounded like a mighty wind (Acts 2). All in the room saw what seemed to be tongues of fire touching each person. All were filled with the Holy Spirit, as promised by Jesus, and were enabled to speak in languages they had not previously known. There were people from fifteen different nations in Jerusalem. The Galilean apostles, touched by the tongues of fire, proclaimed the resurrection of Christ to all the people in their own languages.

To interpret the Pentecost experience, Henry Tweedy wrote the hymn "O Spirit of the Living God." The four stanzas illumine the biblical account, capture the spirit of the event, and make it applicable to contemporary Christian life.

Born of Scottish ancestry, Tweedy was educated at Yale University, Union Theological Seminary, and the University of Berlin. He was ordained to the Congregational ministry in 1898 and pastored churches in Utica, New York, and Bridgeport, Connecticut. For Twenty-eight years he taught practical theology at Yale Divinity School and was in great demand as a preacher and speaker. "O Spirit of the Living God" was published in the *Methodist Hymnal* of 1935.

DESCRIBING THE LOVE OF JESUS

O the deep, deep love of Jesus,
Vast, unmeasured, boundless, free!
Rolling as a mighty ocean
In its fullness over me!
Underneath me, all around me,
Is the current of thy love;
Leading onward, leading homeward,
To my glorious rest above.

Samuel Trevor Francis grew up in the Church of England. Later he joined the Plymouth Brethren, a group of devout Christians who lived in Plymouth, England. They met regularly for prayer and fellowship and placed a strong emphasis on biblical prophecy. Francis became a London merchant of considerable means and contributed generously of his time and fortune to religious and charitable activities. During the Moody-Sankey meetings in England (1873–75), Francis ably assisted Ira D. Sankey in the music of the crusades. His experiences in the crusades seem to have provided the inspiration for writing "O the Deep, Deep Love of Jesus," for it appeared about 1875.

The music for Francis's hymn has both a true and fictional background. The true story is that the music was composed in 1890 by Thomas John Williams, a Welsh musician born in the Swansea Valley of Glamorganshire. Within less than a decade after its writing, the tune became a favorite for the singing of several different hymn texts.

As its popularity grew, a London daily newspaper carried an item that provided the basis for the unfounded story. In Wales the tune was popularly known as "Ton-y-Botel," which in English means "the tune in the bottle." The newspaper story told about a young man who had sung the tune in a private gathering. When asked the source of the tune, the young man laughingly told his friends that it had been discovered in a bottle washed up on the Lleyn coast of Wales. Though untrue, this strange and fascinating story has persisted even though the tune long ago was rechristened "Ebenezer." By any name, it is a delightful melody. When sung enthusiastically by a large group, it has the effect of accumulating grandeur.

A MOONLIT NIGHT

O they tell me of a home far beyond the skies,
  O they tell me of a home far away;
O they tell me of a home where no storm clouds rise,
  O they tell me of an unclouded day.

Josiah K. Alwood, a circuit-riding preacher in the Midwest, wrote both words and music of the hymn. Sometime in the 1880s Alwood was riding home from a preaching appointment on a cloudless, moonlit night. As he rode along on horseback, thinking about the sermons he had preached during the day, the melody and words began to form in his mind. Soon he was urging his horse along and singing at the top of his voice. The next morning he wrote down the words and picked out the melody on the little Estey reed organ in his home. A friend finished the tune, and it was published in Chicago about 1890.

A native of Ohio, Alwood was ordained a minister in the church of the United Brethren in Christ. He spent many years as a circuit-riding preacher, preaching in scattered communities. Many churches had preaching services only once or twice a month because of the distances involved and the scarcity of preachers. Alwood was gone from his family for weeks at a time, holding revival meetings and lecturing on Christian doctrine. Later he was appointed a presiding elder in the North Ohio Conference and was a delegate to several general conferences of the United Brethren church. Always a staunch supporter of the original constitution of his denomination, Alwood was a delegate to the general conference at the time the church divided into two groups in 1889.

The popularity of the hymn, better known as "The Unclouded Day," has diminished in recent years. While it is not found in many hymnals today, it appears in the most unexpected places. On September 19, 1987, it was sung by Willie Nelson on the nationally telecast program "Farm Aid II," an indication that the hymn has not been forgotten.

SINGING OF THE HALLOWED PAGE

O Word of God incarnate,
O Wisdom from on high,
O Truth unchanged, unchanging,
O Light of our dark sky:
We praise thee for the radiance
That from the hallowed page,
A lantern to our footsteps,
Shines on from age to age.

William Walsham How wrote these lines in 1867 in the pleasant English farming village of Whittington on the Welsh border. Ordained in the Church of England, How was assigned as rector at Whittington in 1851. He was a distinguished churchman and highly thought of for his unassuming manner, love for his people, and lack of ambition for higher ecclesiastical positions in the Church of England. Appointed a bishop in East London, he became best known for his ministry among the people of its poverty-stricken slums. Other Anglican bishops of his day lived in palatial residences and rode in private coaches, but How lived among his people in modest accommodations and relied on public transportation.

How wrote more than sixty hymns, but only three or four are found in our hymnals today. "O Word of God Incarnate" expresses beautiful praise for the Bible. The lines mirror How's devotion to God's Word. The initial stanza employs four striking synonyms for the Holy Scriptures—"Word," "Wisdom," "Truth," and "Light."

Metaphors and similes abound in How's hymn, reminding us of the significant influence that God's Word brings to our lives: The Bible is a "banner," a unifying symbol providing courage, strength, and inspiration; a "beacon" to warn of danger, harm, and wrong; a "chart and compass" giving direction to life and providing a ready reference to help us stay on course in the Christian pilgrimage. The final stanza is a prayer that the church may be a faithful steward of the treasure of God's Word, and that the Bible may always be a path to guide individuals to God.

A HYMN THAT MENTIONS
SEVEN NAMES FOR JEHOVAH

O worship the King, all glorious above,
And gratefully sing his wonderful love;
Our Shield and Defender, the Ancient of Days,
Pavilioned in splendor, and girded with praise.

Vivid imagery, poetic language, and elegant style make this a most unusual hymn. Here are majesty, beauty, wonder, and glory. Here are reverence, assurance, and joyful praise. Robert Grant wrote the hymn in 1833. It is based on Psalm 104. Rather than using the Hebrew or English version of this psalm, he based his stanzas on an earlier hymn by William Kethe from the *Anglo-Genevan Psalter* of 1561.

Grant's hymn comes into clearer focus if one reads Psalm 104 and compares the psalm with the hymn. The hymn reflects the spirit of the psalmist as he is caught up in the wonder and beauty of God's magnificent creation. Seven names for Jehovah are found in the hymn—King, Shield, Defender, Ancient of Days, Maker, Redeemer, and Friend.

The descriptive imagery of the second stanza shouts of God's might and grace. It reminds us that his robe is light, his canopy is all of space, his chariots of wrath form thunder-clouds, and his path is on the wings of the storm. Stanza three's action words describe God's loving care for human-kind.

Of Scottish ancestry, Grant was born in Bengal, India, where his father was a director in the East India Company. While still a child he returned with his family to Scotland, was educated at Cambridge, and then was admitted to the bar. His election to Parliament began his career of distinction. Sent to India as governor of Bombay in 1834, Grant was knighted by King William IV before he left India.

Grant wrote more than a dozen hymns, most of which have been forgotten. His name, however, will long remain in our hymnals because of the great expression of God's praise that begins "O worship the king, all glorious above."

A SONG IN THE NIGHT

O Zion, haste, thy mission high fulfilling,
To tell to all the world that God is Light;
That he who made all nations is not willing
One soul should perish, lost in shades of night.
Publish glad tidings, tidings of peace,
Tidings of Jesus, redemption and release.

A weary mother watching over her restless child, who was ill with typhoid fever, hummed familiar hymns to quiet the feverish child. One of the hymns Mary Ann Thomson remembered from her childhood was a favorite tune set to the text "Hark, hark, my soul." When her child was resting quietly, she began to fit other words about world missions to the tune she liked so well. Phrase by phrase and line by line the poem took shape. During that night in 1868 she wrote four stanzas, then left them untouched for almost three years. Finally she completed the poem, added the refrain lines, and had it published in a religious paper. The first hymnal to include Thomson's poem was the Episcopal hymnal of 1892.

Mary Ann Thomson was born in England, the daughter of an Anglican minister. As a young woman she came to America, and met and married John Thomson, the first librarian of the Free Library of Philadelphia. She and her husband were active members of the Church of the Annunciation in Philadelphia; she was a faithful participant in the life and work of this Episcopal congregation until her death in 1923. She wrote more than forty poems that were published in the religious journals of her day. Only "O Zion, haste" survives.

The hymn addresses God's people using the biblical term "Zion." Here is an urgent appeal to God's people to reveal to the world that God is Light and Love. A similar usage may be found in Timothy Dwight's "I Love Thy Kingdom, Lord" in the second line of the final stanza: "To Zion shall be giv'n." The usage is based on the biblical reference, "O Zion, that bringest good tidings, get thee up into the high mountain" (Isa. 40:9).

FROM A FOURTH-CENTURY
SPANISH POET

Of the Father's love begotten,
  Ere the worlds began to be,
He is Alpha and Omega,
  He the source, the ending he,
Of the things that are, that have been,
  And that future years shall see,
    Evermore and evermore.

A Christian poet of the fourth century, Aurelius Clemens
Prudentius was born in northern Spain. Well-educated and a
student of law, he was twice appointed a magistrate. When
Theodosius became emperor in 379, he brought Prudentius to
Rome and appointed him to a high office. Prudentius was
fascinated by the imperial city, the new Christian basilicas, and
the tombs of apostles and martyrs. He became disenchanted
with court life, however, and retired to a life of poverty and
seclusion. At the age of fifty-seven he entered a monastery and
spent his days in prayer, meditation, and writing (sacred
poetry, hymns, and devotional literature).

In his writings Prudentius sought to glorify God and to
speak boldly against heresy and heathen rites. He appealed to
Emperor Honoris to stop the slaughter of animals and
gladiators in the Colosseum, and this was accomplished in 404
after the monk Telemachus was slain trying to stop the
gladiators from killing each other. The hymns of Prudentius
were personal and devotional in character and not intended
for public worship. Selections from them have been appropriately used, however, to the enrichment of the church's song.

Numerous translations have been made of his poem
beginning "Da puer plectrum, choreis ut canam fidelibus," but
by far the most familiar is "Of the Father's Love Begotten" by
John Mason Neale and Henry W. Baker in 1859.

Appropriately, the music in our hymnals for this text is a
plainsong melody associated with the Latin text since the
thirteenth century. Plainsong is the liturgical music of the
Roman Church—beautiful, simple, sung in unison without
accompaniment. The accent of the music is determined by the

accent of the words, not the rhythmic beat of the music. The most generally used version of this melody was made by Canon Winfred Douglas for the 1940 Episcopal *Hymnal.*

A MAN FAMOUS FOR WRITING ONE HYMN

On a hill far away stood an old rugged cross.
  The emblem of suffering and shame;
And I love that old cross where the dearest and best
  For a world of lost sinners was slain.
So I'll cherish the old rugged cross,
  Till my trophies at last I lay down;
I will cling to the old rugged cross,
  And exchange it someday for a crown.

The Delta Tau Delta fraternity house is one block from the campus of Albion College, a United Methodist school in Albion, Michigan. In front of this three-story house stands a marker erected by the Michigan Historical Commission that reads: "The Old Rugged Cross, one of the world's best loved hymns, was composed here in 1912 by Rev. George Bennard (1873–1958)."

Bennard began writing the hymn late in the fall of 1912. He was engaged in revivals in Michigan and New York State and carried the words with him in these meetings. He may have made some revisions or additions at Sturgeon Bay, Wisconsin; a Friend's church claims that Bennard completed the song during a revival there from December 29, 1912, through January 12, 1913. They say it was sung there for the first time. Charles H. Gabriel, well-known gospel-song composer, helped Bennard complete the manuscript of the music and "fix up" the harmonies.

Homer Rodeheaver, the popular song leader for evangelist Billy Sunday, used this new song immediately and was greatly responsible for its early popularity.

A coal miner's son, Bennard was born in Youngstown, Ohio. At the age of fifteen he worked in the coal mines to support his widowed mother. During a Salvation Army meeting he was converted, and later he and his wife became ardent Salvation Army workers. He became a brigade leader in the corps before he left the Salvation Army to become an independent evangelist. He later joined the Methodist church. For several years he was an evangelist in Methodist churches in the northern states of the Midwest and in Canada.

Bennard died in 1958 at the age of eighty-five. His last years were spent in Reed City, Michigan, where he was loved and honored. In 1956 the Reed City Chamber of Commerce erected a wooden cross twelve feet high near his home with an inscription honoring him.

THE SCENE IS THE JORDAN RIVER

On Jordan's stormy banks I stand,
And cast a wishful eye
To Canaan's fair and happy land,
Where my possessions lie.

Those who have visited the Middle East and have seen the Jordan River as a narrow, fordable stream may wonder why "stormy banks" is applied to it. From its sources at the foot of Mount Herman, 1800 feet above sea level, the Jordan River is 223 miles long. However, the actual distance between its sources and the Dead Sea, 1,292 feet below sea level, is only 124 miles. Seasonal conditions in that area and the sharp decline of the riverbed downstream make for rapid currents and sometimes "stormy" conditions.

Samuel Stennett wrote the hymn in 1787, borrowing the scene from the Old Testament account of the Children of Israel crossing the Jordan River into Canaan, the Promised Land (Josh. 3). Stennett paints a word picture of the Christian gazing into the future and anticipating the joy of life beyond the grave—the Promised Land. His reference to "possessions" in the fourth line is based on the words of Jesus, "lay up for yourselves treasures in heaven" (Matt. 6:20).

For almost forty years before his death in 1795, Stennett ministered to the Baptist congregation that met on Little Wild Street, Lincoln's Field, London. He held a prominent position among the non-Anglican ministers of London and was a personal friend of King George III. Stennett used his strong influence in both religious and political circles to support the principle of religious freedom. He wrote quite a number of hymns, but only this one and his "Majestic Sweetness Sits Enthroned" survive in some American hymnals.

The survival of "On Jordan's Stormy Banks I Stand" may be attributed in part to the Southern folk tune to which it is sung. The tune, called "Promised Land," seems to have first appeared in William Walker's *Southern Harmony,* a collection of shape-note music published in 1835. Walker, a singing-school teacher living in Spartanburg, South Carolina, was a devout Baptist layman whose musical influence extended far beyond his native state.

A HYMN OF PROTEST

Once to every man and nation
Comes the moment to decide,
In the strife of truth with falsehood,
For the good or evil side;
Some great cause, some great decision,
Offering each the bloom or blight,
And the choice goes by forever
'Twixt the darkness and that light.

A year before these lines appeared in 1845, the poet James Russell Lowell married Maria White. Her fervent interest in human welfare causes greatly impressed this gifted member of a distinguished New England family. Mrs. Lowell was an ardent abolitionist. Soon after her marriage to Lowell, antislavery verses began to appear in his poetic writings.

Lowell contributed a poem titled "The Present Crisis" to the *Boston Courier* on December 11, 1845. The eighteen stanzas voiced his protest against the war with Mexico over the territory of Texas. The injustice of war and the conviction that the acquisition of new territory would only enlarge the area of slavery in the United States were the concerns that inspired this writing. On the same day that the poem appeared in the Boston newspaper a House Committee in Washington reported favorably on the resolution to admit Texas to the Union, and a similar bill was introduced in the Senate.

Although Lowell's writing was inspired by political conditions in our nation 135 years ago, the hymn is valid for today. The "strife of truth with falsehood" continues, and we need to be reminded of what this hymn says. The last lines of the final stanza are often quoted.

> *Yet that scaffold sways the future,*
> *And, behind the dim unknown,*
> *Standeth God within the shadow,*
> *Keeping watch above his own.*

The tune most generally used for singing this hymn was written in 1890 by a Welshman, Thomas J. Williams. For some unknown reason it is called "Ebenezer," the name mentioned in 1 Samuel 7:12. (Samuel set a stone marker between Mizpeh and Shen, saying, "hitherto hath the Lord helped us.") Because of an erroneous legend the tune is also called "Ton-y-Botel" (tune in a bottle).

BORN AT A BIBLE CONFERENCE

> *One day when heaven was filled with his praises,*
> *One day when sin was as black as could be,*
> *Jesus came forth to be born of a virgin,*
> *Dwelt among men, my example is he!*
> *Living, he loved me; dying, he saved me;*
> *Buried, he carried my sins far away;*
> *Rising, he justified freely forever:*
> *One day he's coming—O glorious day!*

J. Wilbur Chapman, well-known evangelist and Bible teacher, conducted a Bible conference at Stony Brook, Long Island, in the summer of 1909. Several months before, in Pittsburgh, Chapman had met Charles H. Marsh, a talented young musician who played the piano with extraordinary skill. He had just graduated from high school and accepted Chapman's invitation to be the pianist for the Stony Brook Bible Conference. Chapman had written the words to a hymn titled

"One Day." At the conference he gave Marsh the words and asked him to compose a tune for them. The music was completed during the weeks of the Bible conference.

A Presbyterian minister, Chapman served churches in Albany, Philadelphia, and New York City for twenty years. He spent more than a decade as an evangelist and teacher of Bible conferences. In 1917 he was elected moderator for the General Assembly of the Presbyterian Church, U.S.A., in recognition of his respected leadership.

Charles H. Marsh was born a few months after his parents arrived in America from England in 1886. His father, a Congregational minister, first served a church in Iowa, then moved his family to Pittsburgh. Later Marsh spent several years in Paris where he studied under Charles-Marie Widor and Henri Libert in organ, Camille Decreus in piano, Marcel Dupre in organ, and Nadia Boulanger in composition. These were some of the world's finest music teachers, and they had great influence on his musical development and his life. After Marsh's return to America he taught music and served as organist in several churches. He was organist-choirmaster for the St. James-by-the-Sea Episcopal Church in La Jolla, California, for twenty years until his death in 1956.

A COLORFUL CHILDREN'S PROCESSION

Onward, Christian soldiers
Marching as to war,
With the cross of Jesus
Going on before!
Christ, the royal Master,
Leads against the foe;
Forward into battle,
See his banners go!

The Yorkshire village of Horbury welcomed a new Anglican minister in 1864. Not long after he arrived, he rescued a young girl who worked in the mill when the nearby Calder River flooded. Out of this experience a romance developed, and later they were married. Sabine Baring-Gould was an extraordinary man. During his lifetime he produced eighty-five books on such varied subjects as religion, travel, folklore, biography, fiction, history, mythology, theology, and his own sermons. He did all his own writing without the aid of a secretary, saying, "The secret is simply that I stick to a task when I begin it." All his writing was done not while he was sitting at a desk, but while standing at a writing table. Because of this persistent discipline, the list of books under his name in the British Museum exceeds that of any other writer of his time.

In England, the Monday following Whitsunday is a holiday, and children's festivals with colorful processions are a major part of the holiday activities. Baring-Gould wrote "Onward, Christian Soldiers" for this festival in 1865. It was sung by the children of his church school as they marched from village to village following the cross and banners. The spiritual warfare of the Christian and the military image of the church are found in numerous references in the Bible, and Baring-Gould's hymn reflects this imagery as he compares the church to a "mighty army."

The language of the hymn is consistent with Paul's exhortation to the church at Ephesus to "put on the whole armor of God." It mentions such armament as the "breastplate of righteousness . . . shield of faith . . . helmet of salvation . . . sword of the Spirit." The martial spirit of the hymn may have less appeal today, and the song may be sung in our churches less frequently than in earlier times. Nonetheless, spiritual warfare is a reality to every Christian. A vigorous singing of the hymn can be inspiring and affirming to the congregation.

OPEN EYES, EARS, MOUTH
FOR TRUTH

Open my eyes that I may see
Glimpses of truth thou hast for me;
Place in my hands the wonderful key
That shall unclasp and set me free:
Silently now I wait for thee,

Ready, my God, thy will to see;
Open my eyes, illumine me,
Spirit divine.

People in Dubuque, Iowa, were shocked to read in the morning paper of June 22, 1897, of an accident involving a runaway horse the previous morning. Three women in a two-seated carriage were returning from the funeral of a former classmate. Their horse, frightened on a sharp incline, became completely unmanageable. Two of the women were instantly killed in the wreck that occurred. One of them was Clara H. Scott of Chicago, who had returned to Iowa for the funeral. Two years earlier Scott had written both words and music of "Open My Eyes That I May See."

Born in a Chicago suburb, Clara Scott was reared in a musical home. She began to study composition in 1856, when she was fifteen, in one of the first musical institutes conducted in Chicago. Three years later she began teaching music at a girls' school in Lyons, Iowa, a small community along the Mississippi River near Clinton. Three years later she married Henry Clay Scott and settled down to an active musical life in Chicago. She met Horatio R. Palmer and contributed to his music publication. She also became interested in sacred compositions. Aided by her wide experience in church choir work, she compiled a collection of anthems. Her *Royal Anthem Book,* published in 1882, was the first of its kind ever published by a woman. It was quite successful.

In the spring of 1897 Clara Scott compiled a collection of songs entitled *Truth in Song,* which was published in the fall of the year after her tragic death. "Open My Eyes That I May See" was included in it. Her untimely death kept her from knowing of the widespread popularity of her hymn.

INSPIRED AT A PRISON SERVICE

Pass me not, O gentle Savior,
Hear my humble cry;
While on others thou art calling,
Do not pass me by.

Here is one of the earliest hymns written by Fanny J. Crosby and the Cincinnati manufacturer William Howard Doane. When he first visited Fanny Crosby in New York City, Doane discovered that they were kindred souls. He inquired if she would write a poem using the phrase "Pass me not, O gentle Savior." She smiled and said she would, but she did not seem to have an inspiration at that time.

As the popularity of Crosby's hymns increased, more invitations came to her to speak at churches, conventions, YWCAs, and even prisons. In the spring of 1868, after the visit with Doane, she spoke at a religious service in a Manhattan prison. After she had spoken and some of her hymns had been sung, she heard one of the prisoners cry out in a pleading voice, "Good Lord, do not pass me by." She immediately recalled Doane's suggested line; here was the needed inspiration. That evening in her room she completed the poem. Doane composed the music and the hymn first appeared in a collection he published in 1870.

Three years later evangelist Dwight L. Moody and his music director, Ira D. Sankey, began their evangelistic campaigns in England. One of the first hymns used by Sankey was "Pass Me Not, O Gentle Savior." Sankey wrote, "No other hymn in our collection was more popular than this at our meetings in London in 1874. It was sung every day at Her Majesty's Theatre in Pall Mall." Several years later, Sankey was on vacation in the Swiss Alps. From his hotel room one day, he heard the people in the street below his window singing heartily in German, "Pass me not, O gentle Savior."

The scriptural basis for the hymn is found in the account of Jesus' encounter with a blind beggar, recorded in Luke 18:35–42. When the beggar heard the noise of the crowd and asked what was going on, he was told that Jesus of Nazareth was passing by. Immediately he turned and cried out, "Jesus, thou Son of David, have mercy on me."

A GREAT DOXOLOGY

Praise God, from whom all blessings flow;
Praise him, all creatures here below;

Praise him above, ye heavenly host;
Praise Father, Son and Holy Ghost.

This doxology, which may be the most frequently sung hymn in Christendom, was written in 1674 by Thomas Ken. At the time Ken was chaplain to the bishop of Winchester Cathedral in England. He wrote three hymns for the boys at Winchester College. To each of them—one for morning, one for evening, and one for midnight services—Ken added these four lines as a final stanza.

Orphaned as a child, Ken lived with his half-sister Anne. She was married to Izaak Walton, the author of *The Compleat Angler*. Walton reveals in this work his enthusiasm for outdoor recreation and the life of a gentle, philosophical fisherman.

As an Anglican clergyman, Ken's days were never dull or monotonous. After more than a decade at Winchester Cathedral, Ken was appointed royal chaplain to Charles II. Shortly afterward the King declared his intent to visit Winchester and to lodge the actress Nell Gwyn, his mistress, in Ken's house. Ken opposed the plan strenuously, and to thwart it he had a builder begin repairs on his house and in the process remove the roof. When the king arrived with his entourage, he had to make other plans since Ken's house was roofless.

In 1688, after James II became king, Ken and six other bishops were imprisoned in the Tower of London for refusing to subscribe to the king's Declaration of Indulgence. They not only refused to publish it in their dioceses, but also published an order against it. After his trial and acquittal, Ken resigned his bishopric and spent the rest of his life in peaceful retirement. He died in 1711 at the age of seventy-four.

Only a few hymnals today include the morning and evening hymns Thomas Ken wrote for the boys at Winchester, but hymnals throughout the English-speaking world include his four-line stanza, a universal doxology of praise to God.

IN THE SPIRIT OF PSALM 103

Praise my soul, the King of heaven,
To his feet thy tribute bring;
Ransomed, healed, restored, forgiven,

Evermore his praises sing:
Alleluia! Alleluia!
Praise the everlasting King.

Henry Francis Lyte, born in Scotland, was still a child when he lost his parents. He became a charity student at a boys' school in Ireland, continuing his education with great diligence at Trinity College in Dublin. At the age of twenty-one he was ordained in the Church of England and assigned to a small parish in Ireland. When he was thirty he was appointed to Lower Brixham in Devonshire, a picturesque village on the coast. Famous for its fishing, Lower Brixham was the port for the fleets of trawlers that fished in the English Channel.

For twenty-four years Lyte ministered faithfully to the people of this village. More than eight-hundred children were involved in his Sunday school, and he was dearly loved in his parish. His hymn "Praise, My Soul, the King of Heaven" was written in 1843 and is cast in the spirit of Psalm 103. Lyte had undergone a deep spiritual experience about two decades earlier, and the change in his life was evident in his pastoral work. The line "ransomed, healed, restored, forgiven" in the first stanza describes the experience of one who has known despair, yet has found the rich, abundant life in Christ.

The four words "ransomed, healed, restored, forgiven" provide a summation that is unequaled regarding the meaning of salvation. This is the message of Psalm 103, which praises God for his loving provision for humankind. Without question this is the most evangelical of David's psalms as it reveals a portrait of God the Savior.

At her wedding at Westminster Abbey on November 20, 1947 (also the one-hundredth anniversary of Lyte's death), Queen Elizabeth II chose the hymn as the processional. What unusual recognition for an obscure country preacher with no claim to fame other than his own gracious spirit and a handful of hymns.

ONE GRAND ALLELUIA!

Praise the Lord who reigns above,
And keeps his court below;

Praise the holy God of love,
  And all his greatness show;
Praise him for his noble deeds,
  Praise him for his matchless pow'r;
Him from whom all good proceeds
  Let earth and heav'n adore.

The Book of Psalms in the Old Testament concludes with six psalms that express continuous praise to God. All of these climax in a burst of sheer intensity in the final psalm, Psalm 150. As though the previous psalms had exhausted all expressions of human language, the psalmist now turns to the moving power of musical metaphors to express the exuberance of his feelings. More than literal language, more than all other phenomena of life, music is destined to glorify God. After the initial alleluia, the psalmist's exhortation is to praise God in his sanctuary, the holy place symbolic of God's heavenly dwelling. God is also to be praised in the "firmament of his power," the vaulted sky.

God is to be praised because of his mighty acts "according to his excellent greatness"—because of what he has done and who he is. Then comes a call for the full resources of musical instruments: the trumpet, the shofar, the ram's horn (which signaled the presence of God); the lute and harp (instruments of harmony—beautiful, rich, sweeping, strummed, plucked, struck gently, struck vigorously); the hand drum (the timbrel with its throbbing, pulsating, exciting rhythm); the organ (the generic word for all the wind instruments); and the loud cymbals and high-sounding cymbals that may be heard over all. Also included is the dance with its physical involvement and personal expression. Finally, the psalmist calls for everything that breathes to join in praise to God.

"Praise the Lord who Reigns Above" is Charles Wesley's poetic version of Psalm 150. It was published in London in 1743. We sing this text to "Amsterdam," one of John Wesley's favorite tunes, which he had found in a collection published almost forty years earlier in Halle, Germany.

A PARAPHRASE OF PSALM 148

Praise the Lord, ye heavens, adore him;
Praise him, angels, in the height;
Sun and moon, rejoice before him;
Praise him, all ye stars of light.
Praise the Lord! For he hath spoken;
Worlds his mighty voice obeyed;
Laws which never shall be broken
For their guidance hath he made.

This anonymous hymn, along with four others, was pasted in the back of a hymnal in the chapel of London's Foundling Hospital about 1801. The Foundling Hospital was not really a hospital. Established in 1739 by Thomas Corum, a wealthy shipbuilder, it was a home for children abandoned on London's streets. By 1760 it had become a home for illegitimate children.

George Frederick Handel, a generous friend of the Foundling Hospital, was a frequent visitor. He donated a pipe organ for the chapel. He also conducted performances of his oratorio *Messiah* for several years to raise funds for the home. Fashionable people from the wealthiest sections of London frequently visited the Foundling Hospital, especially on Sundays to hear the music of the chapel services.

A paraphrase of Psalm 148, the hymn praises God for his wonderful works of creation, his laws that govern creation, and his promises to humankind for victory over sin and death. "Praise the Lord! Ye Heavens, Adore Him" captures the spirit of Psalm 148.

Apparently the tune first associated with this hymn was "Austrian Hymn," composed by Franz Joseph Haydn as a national anthem for Austria. It was first sung on February 12, 1797, on the birthday of Emperor Francis II. The first three measures of the melody are identical with an existing Croatian folk song, which Haydn borrowed for his tune.

Another hymn tune frequently used for the hymn is "Hyfrydol" (meaning "Good Cheer"). Composed by Rowland Prichard about 1831, the tune has been widely used with a variety of hymn texts that fit its metrical form. Prichard lived in the village of Bala in North Wales. Blessed with a good singing voice, he led the hymn singing in his church for many years. He also composed a number of hymn tunes that appeared in Welsh periodicals of that day. His name will long remain in our hymnals because of this excellent hymn tune.

PROLIFIC HYMNWRITER INSPIRED BY THE GERMAN COUNTRYSIDE

Praise to the Lord, the Almighty, the King of creation!
O my soul, praise him, for he is thy health and
salvation!
 All ye who hear,
 Now to his temple draw near;
 Praise him in glad adoration.

The beautiful hills, valleys, and flowing streams in the Düsseldorf area of what is now West Germany provided the inspiration for the hymn. Joachim Neander, a teacher who was the son of a schoolteacher, wrote the hymn a few months before his death at age thirty. A brilliant young man with great promise, Neander became headmaster of the Latin Grammar School in Düsseldorf in 1674 when he was only twenty-four. During his five years as headmaster he wrote more than sixty hymns and more than a dozen melodies. He is best remembered as the author of the German original of "Praise to the Lord, the Almighty," based on Psalms 103 and 150.

 Neander enjoyed the seclusion he found in the valley of the small stream of Düssel, a tributary of the Rhine, seven miles east of Düsseldorf. This valley was named the Neander-thal Valley for him, and almost two hundred years later, in 1856, a skeleton was discovered there that was thought to represent a race of people who lived in western Europe as early as 4,000 B.C. It was named the Neanderthal man.

 Neander left his valley and returned to his hometown of Bremen in 1679 to be the assistant pastor at St. Martin's Church, where he had been converted through the influence of the pastor. His health rapidly declined and he died the following year, a few months after writing this hymn.

While the German hymn was written more than three hundred years ago, the English translation was made and published in 1863. Sixteen years later it appeared in America in a Lutheran hymnal printed in Decorah, Iowa.

The tune we sing for the hymn is one of the classic Lutheran melodies. Of unknown origin, it seems to have first appeared in a collection of tunes published in Stralsund, Germany, in 1665. Its name, "Lobe den Herren," is taken from the first words of Neander's German text.

THE ESSENCE OF PRAYER

> *Prayer is the soul's sincere desire,*
> *Unuttered or expressed,*
> *The motion of a hidden fire*
> *That trembles in the breast.*

No other hymn describes prayer as vividly as these stanzas. The metaphors found in the hymn portray prayer as a hidden fire, the burden of a sigh, the falling of a tear, the simplest form of speech, the contrite sinner's voice, the Christian's vital breath—and it is all of these. The concluding stanza is addressed to God and humbly pleads:

> *O Thou, by whom we come to God,*
> *The Life, the Truth, the Way:*
> *The path of prayer thyself has trod;*
> *Lord, teach us how to pray!*

At the request of Edward Bickersteth, James Montgomery wrote the hymn in 1818, to be included in Bickersteth's work *Treatise on Prayer.* Soon after writing it, Montgomery published it in a pamphlet with three other hymns for use in the Nonconformist Sunday schools in Sheffield, England, where he lived.

Although he wrote more than four hundred hymns, Montgomery stated that he received more inquiries about this hymn than any other he had written. The night before he died he conducted family prayers with greater devotion than usual. The next morning he was discovered lying unconscious on the floor of his room. He died that afternoon experiencing what he had described in the hymn:

> *Prayer is the Christian's vital breath,*
> *The Christian's native air,*
> *His watchword at the gates of death;*
> *He enters heaven with prayer.*

John Julian described Montgomery's hymns as being "richly poetic without exuberance, dogmatic without uncharitableness, tender without sentimentality, elaborate without diffusiveness, richly musical without apparent effort." With his hymns he has "bequeathed to the church wealth which could only have come from a true genius and a sanctified heart."

The hymn tune most frequently found with this text is based on an old camp-meeting chorus of the early nineteenth century and was arranged by Robert G. McCutchan for *The Methodist Hymnal* (1935). He named the tune *"Campmeeting." The early printings of this chorus used these words:*

> *I do believe, I do believe,*
> *That Jesus died for me;*
> *And through His blood, His precious blood,*
> *I am from sin set free.*

STRONG FAITH IN DEEP SORROW

> *Precious Lord, take my hand,*
> *Lead me on, let me stand,*
> *I am tired, I am weak, I am worn;*
> *Through the storm, through the night,*
> *Lead me on to the light,*
> *Take my hand, precious Lord, lead me home.**

In August of 1932, Thomas A. Dorsey and his wife, Nettie, were living in south Chicago; they were expecting their first child. Responding to an invitation from a friend to sing in a revival meeting, Dorsey left his wife and drove to St. Louis. He had been in St. Louis only two days when he received a telegram that his wife had died in childbirth. Some friends drove him home to Chicago, and a few hours after he arrived the baby boy died also.

In the weeks that followed sorrow and anguish possessed him. One day he was with a gospel-singer friend, Theodore Frye. Dorsey sat for a while quietly fingering the keyboard of an old piano. He remembered fragments of an old melody he had known and began to put some words to it. When he was done he sang the song for Frye. Frye was greatly impressed and made only one suggestion, to change the opening words from "blessed Lord" to "precious Lord." The following Sunday morning the song was performed by Frye's choir at the Ebenezer Baptist Church in Chicago, with Dorsey playing the accompaniment. Years later, as he told of this experience, Dorsey quietly recalled, "It tore up the church!"

Thomas A. Dorsey was born in Villa Rica, Georgia, in 1899. His father was an itinerant Baptist preacher and his mother played the pump organ. He got his love for traveling from his father and his love for music from his mother. When he was thirteen, his family moved to Atlanta. He had a knack for the piano and in a few years had his first professional experience playing piano in a local vaudeville house; later he played for dancers in "sporting houses." All this was unknown to his father, for he continued to play for services.

Shortly before he was twenty Dorsey left home to go to Chicago. He had heard that black musicians could find better opportunities there. The 1920s ushered in the era of the blues, a style of music with which Dorsey felt right at home. He wrote more than two hundred blues songs, writing and arranging for blues singers Bessie Smith, Ida Cox, and Ma Rainey. In the depths of the Depression he turned to the Christian faith of his father and mother. Through his writing and influence, black gospel music found a new dimension of expression. For many years Dorsey led the music at the Pilgrim Baptist Church in Chicago; he was the most influential person in black gospel music in America.

THE JOY OF SALVATION

Redeemed, how I love to proclaim it!
Redeemed by the blood of the Lamb;
Redeemed through his infinite mercy,
His child, and forever, I am.

Hymnwriter Fanny J. Crosby wrote these lines in 1882. She and her husband, Alexander Van Alstyne, were living on Frankfort Street in Lower Manhattan in New York City. Fanny Crosby was an extraordinary person. She maintained a vigorous life throughout her ninety-five years. As an infant she was blinded by a quack physician who applied a strong poultice to her eyes. Educated at the New York Institution for the Blind, she later taught there for several years.

Her hymnwriting did not begin until she was almost forty years old. Her phenomenal memory, which was evident at an early age, was a great aid to her in her hymnwriting. By the time she was twelve she knew by memory the first five books of the Old Testament, Proverbs, Ruth, Song of Solomon, and many of the Psalms. During her prolific hymnwriting years she usually put together her poems in the evenings after she had retired to her room. She would finish the text and retain it. The following morning she would dictate to a friend what she had completed the night before. She did not use Braille because years of playing the guitar and harp had made calluses on her fingers that made the use of Braille difficult.

William J. Kirkpatrick composed the music for many of Fanny Crosby's texts, but none achieved the popularity of "Redeemed." Kirkpatrick was an excellent musician, playing flute, violin, fife, cello, and organ. During the Civil War he was fife-major in the 91st Regiment of the Pennsylvania Volunteers. For a number of years he served as music director for the Grace Methodist Episcopal Church of Philadelphia, where he made his home. In addition to writing tunes for gospel hymnwriters, Kirkpatrick was a successful publisher and teacher. Other familiar hymn tunes he wrote are: "We Have Heard the Joyful Sound," "A Wonderful Savior Is Jesus My Lord," and "'Tis So Sweet to Trust in Jesus."

In 1967 A. L. Butler composed a new tune for this text. It

has become quite popular and is included in several hymnals. Butler, a member of the faculty of Midwestern Baptist Theological Seminary in Kansas City, named the tune "Ada" for the city in Oklahoma where he was serving as a minister of music at the time this tune was composed.

REJOICE! REJOICE!

Rejoice, the Lord is King:
  Your Lord and King adore!
Rejoice, give thanks and sing,
  And triumph evermore:
    Lift up your heart, lift up your voice!
    Rejoice, again I say, rejoice!

In 1744, Charles Wesley wrote a hymn based on Philippians 4:4, "Rejoice in the Lord always: and again I say, Rejoice." Rejoicing is central in many songs of praise and celebration. Christians have been exhorted to confront the stress of daily living with unfailing courage and to rejoice.

Charles and John Wesley were frequently the objects of strong and hostile opposition. An example of the hostility they experienced occurred in 1747 in Devizes, a small village about twenty miles southeast of Bristol, England. The local Anglican minister went from house to house telling the people that Charles Wesley had preached blasphemy at the university. A crowd was stirred up by the town leaders and the minister and surrounded the house where the Wesleys were staying. They broke windows, ripped off shutters, and drove the Wesleys' horses into the pond. The following day the crowd used the fire engine to pour water into the house, flooding all the rooms the Wesleys were using and ruining the merchandise of the shopkeeper on the street floor. Charles and John Wesley and their companions rode out of town singing a hymn Charles had written, "Thine Arm Hath Safely Brought Us."

Anglican clergy looked with great disdain upon the Wesleys and their followers. In many villages the Wesleys' converts were threatened, stoned, hounded with dogs, had their homes looted and their businesses ruined. The clergy regarded the Wesleys and their followers as intruders who proclaimed a false doctrine, and they were jealous of their tremendous success. The poor and downtrodden responded to the Wesleys and sang with great enthusiasm Charles Wesley's hymns of praise and celebration. They sang of the assurance that God would take his servants to "their eternal home."

A FESTIVAL AT PETERBOROUGH CATHEDRAL

Rejoice, ye pure in heart,
Rejoice, give thanks and sing,
Your glorious banner wave on high,
The cross of Christ your king:
Rejoice, give thanks and sing.

Annual choral festivals have long been a tradition in many of the magnificent cathedrals in England. Choirs from neighboring communities would join together and make such glorious music that the experience was worth remembering. Distinguished Anglican clergyman Edward H. Plumptre wrote "Rejoice, Ye Pure in Heart" in 1865 for such a festival at the Cathedral at Peterborough, England. Begun in the twelfth century, Peterborough Cathedral is an important example of late Norman architecture. Among its many interesting features are the painted ceiling, dating from about 1200, and the Hedda Stone, a black stone with figures of the apostles carved in relief.

Plumptre's hymn was ten stanzas long to accommodate the long processional in the cathedral. It was not unusual for a cathedral processional to take from ten to thirty minutes, and the hymn that was sung by both the choir and the congregation needed to have enough stanzas for this. A review of a hymnal published more than thirty years ago included a comment that some of the processional hymns were so long that some of the congregation would need to walk about in order to stay awake.

Ordained in the Church of England in 1846, Plumptre soon won fame as a scholar, theologian, and preacher. He was one of the most respected clergymen of his day, and his literary writings include classic literature, history, theology, biblical criticism, biography, and poetry. He was a member of the Old Testament committee for the revision of the Authorized Version of the Holy Scriptures.

In our hymnals today only four or five of Plumptre's original ten stanzas may be found. These we sing with great joy. The lines clearly reflect the apostle Paul's exhortation to the church at Philippi (Phil. 4:4).

The tune we sing with the hymn is called "Marion." It was composed in 1883 by Arthur H. Messiter and named for his mother. A native of England, Messiter came to the United States in 1863. Three years later he became organist at Trinity Church in New York City. During his thirty-one years in this position, he maintained the highest standards of the English cathedral tradition. His choir of men and boys served as a model for many other Episcopal churches in this country.

TELL THEM OF JESUS

Rescue the perishing,
Care for the dying,
Snatch them in pity from sin and the grave;
Weep o'er the erring one,
Lift up the fallen,
Tell them of Jesus the mighty to save.

Fanny Crosby visited her friend William H. Doane in 1869 in Cincinnati. She had known him for barely a year, but already they had collaborated on such hymns as "Pass Me Not, O Gentle Savior," and "Safe in the Arms of Jesus." Doane had the unusual gift for writing singable melodies. He was immediately attracted to the gospel-song lyrics of the blind poetess.

During her visit in Cincinnati, Fanny gave her Christian testimony to a group of working men. At the end of her speech she made a personal appeal for Jesus Christ. She said, "If there is a dear boy here tonight who has perchance wandered away from his mother's home and his mother's teaching, would he please come to me at the close of the service?" A young man in his late teens came to her and said,

"Did you mean me? I promised my mother to meet her in heaven, but the way I have been living, I don't think that will be possible." Fanny Crosby prayed with the young man and he accepted Christ as his Savior. He turned and whispered to Fanny, "Now I can meet my mother in heaven. I have found her God."

When she went to her room that night, Crosby could not erase this experience from her mind. Only recently Doane had suggested that she write a hymn emphasizing evangelism and home missions and had given her the title "Rescue the Perishing." Now the inspiration came, and before she went to sleep that night she had completed the poem. The next day she recited the poem to Doane, and he quickly composed the tune. A few months later he published it in his next collection.

JOY IN THE PRESENCE OF THE ANGELS

Ring the bells of heaven! There is joy today,
For a soul, returning from the wild!
See, the Father meets him out upon the way,
Welcoming his weary, wandering child.
Glory! Glory! How the angels sing;
Glory! Glory! How the loud harps ring!
'Tis the ransomed army, like a mighty sea,
Pealing forth the anthem of the free.

The melody of a new secular song intrigued a young Christian minister. As he hummed it over and over, William O. Cushing wished for sacred words to enhance the strong, singable tune. Before long he had written a new set of words based on two parables recorded in Luke 15. In the parable of the prodigal son, Jesus said that the father, when he saw his son returning, "ran, and fell on his neck, and kissed him," and there was great rejoicing. In the parable of the lost coin, Jesus commented that when the lost had been found there was great rejoicing. "Likewise, I say unto you, there is joy in the presence of the angels of God over one sinner that repenteth" (v.10). Putting together these ideas, Cushing wrote three stanzas and a joyful refrain and made a sacred song out of a secular tune that had been composed by George F. Root.

William O. Cushing, a native of Massachusetts, was ordained to the ministry and pastored Christian churches in five New York cities. Following the death of his wife in 1870, ill health forced his retirement. He became interested in hymn writing and wrote more than three hundred hymns. Well-known among them are "When He Cometh," "Down in the Valley," "There'll Be No Dark Valley When Jesus Comes," and "Ring the Bells of Heaven."

George F. Root, also born in Massachusetts, discovered his love for music at an early age. In 1855, at the age of thirty, he spent a year in Paris in intensive music study. Back in New York City he composed a great deal of music. The famed Christy's minstrel troupe made popular many of his songs. By 1858 Root had settled in Chicago and built a successful business, both teaching and publishing. However, the Chicago fire of 1871 brought great losses and the business was dissolved. He continued to make his home in Chicago, but published his music with an established firm in Cincinnati. Root's popular song, written in 1875, became even more popular with Cushing's new text which sings about finding eternal life through Jesus Christ.

A STIRRING HYMN WRITTEN
FOR MEN

Rise up, O men of God!
Have done with lesser things;
Give heart and mind and soul and strength
To serve the King of kings.

The hymn was written for men at a time when the brotherhood movement was emerging among Presbyterians. William Pierson Merrill, pastor of Chicago's Sixth Presbyterian Church, was sympathetic to the movement. A friend of his, the editor of a Presbyterian weekly newspaper, mentioned to Merrill that an appropriate hymn was needed for the movement. Some weeks later, while crossing Lake Michigan on a lake steamer, Merrill read an article by Gerald Lee entitled "The Church of Strong Men." His mind was stirred by the article and he recalled the suggestion regarding a new hymn. As the ship made its way across the lake, the four stanzas took shape rather quickly. It was published in the Presbyterian newspaper *The Continent* on February 16, 1911. A year later it appeared in the *Pilgrim Hymnal*.

Following pastorates in Philadelphia and Chicago, Merrill became the pastor of the Brick Presbyterian Church in New York City in 1911. He served this congregation with distinction until his retirement in 1938.

In recent years the hymn has been the object of much criticism. Its sexist language makes it something less than appropriate for a congregational hymn. Some critics would remove it from our hymnals, while others suggest altering the text to avoid the problem. The recent hymnals *Lutheran Book of Worship* and *Rejoice in the Lord* replace Merrill's hymn with an entirely new one by Norman O. Forness which begins "Rise up, O saints of God!" Here is the same construction, the same metrical form, sung to the same tune. *The Seventh-day Adventist Hymnal* retains stanzas one and four by Merrill, but adds new second and third stanzas. Stanza two begins "Let women all rise up" and in this way balances the exclusive language of the first stanza. The 1982 Episcopal hymnal retains three stanzas of Merrill's hymn, altering "O men" to "Ye saints." Future hymnals will no doubt follow a similar pattern of altering Merrill's hymn to avoid exclusive language.

A PLACE OF REFUGE

Rock of Ages, cleft for me,
Let me hide myself in thee;
Let the water and the blood,
From thy wounded side which flowed,
Be of sin the double cure,
Save from wrath and make me pure.

The initial stanza of the hymn appeared in the October 1775 issue of a religious magazine published in London. Six months later, in the same magazine, the full hymn appeared with an article by Augustus Toplady. From that time he has been acknowledged as the author of the hymn. The subject of Toplady's article was the absolute impossibility of one's paying his indebtedness to God. He calculated the number of sins a person could commit by the day, the hour, the minute, and the second. According to his calculations, a person who lived eighty years could commit 2,522,880,000 sins.

Having been converted by the preaching of a Wesleyan preacher in a service conducted in a barn, Toplady was ordained in the Church of England in 1762. At first he was John Wesley's close friend, but later he openly criticized Wesley because of his strong Calvinistic beliefs. Bitter feelings existed between them for many years.

The term "Rock of Ages" is not found in the King James Bible. The meaning of the term, however, is found in Isaiah 26:4, "Trust ye in the Lord for ever, for in the Lord Jehovah is everlasting strength." The New American Standard Bible and the New English Bible translate the last portion, "we have an everlasting Rock." The New International Version translates this, "the Lord is the Rock eternal."

Toplady drew from the Old Testament Hebrew the idea of "Rock of Ages." Old Testament writers used the image of the rock as a place of refuge, as a hiding place, as a source of life-giving water. Toplady points to Jesus Christ as the Rock of Ages, in whom one can find not only shelter from the buffeting storms of life but also forgiveness of sin and salvation. Erik Routley said, "All sociology, all psychology, all medicine and science come to this at last, that a man needs friendship with God, and in that will find friendship with the world. He needs a rock for shelter, a rock for refreshment, a rock for forgiveness. That Rock is Christ."

LEAD US LIKE A SHEPHERD

Savior, like a shepherd lead us,
Much we need thy tender care;
In thy pleasant pastures feed us,
For our use thy folds prepare;
Blessed Jesus, Blessed Jesus,
Thou hast bought us, thine we are.

The names of those who wrote many of the hymns we sing are well known. But there are a number of familiar hymns whose writers are not known. Among these are "Come, Thou Almighty King," "Fairest Lord Jesus," "Away in a Manger," "How Firm a Foundation," "Jerusalem, My Happy Home," and "Savior Like a Shepherd Lead Us." Attempts to discover the identities of the persons who wrote the words of these hymns have been unsuccessful. It may have been the intent of the writer to remain anonymous. Or, carelessness on the part of an editor of publisher may have resulted in the writer's name being omitted and never subsequently identified.

"Savior Like a Shepherd Lead Us" first appeared in England in 1836 in a collection of songs and poems compiled by Dorothy A. Thrupp. Some think Thrupp was the author, but there is no evidence to support this. Other hymns she contributed to this collection were signed "D.A.T.," but this hymn had no such identification.

The twenty-third Psalm and the parable of the good shepherd provide the basis for the hymn. The major theological emphasis is found in the last line of the first stanza, "Thou has bought us, thine we are," reminding us of Paul's words in 1 Corinthians 6:20.

While the writer of the hymn text is anonymous, we do know who wrote the music. William B. Bradbury composed the tune and included it in a collection of Sunday school songs that he published in New York City in 1859. In twenty-five years he published fifty-nine collections of songs, sacred and secular. His hymn tunes are still sung today more than a century after they first appeared. (For more information see "Sweet hour of prayer," page 265.)

A SENSE OF STEWARDSHIP

> Savior, thy dying love
>   Thou gavest me,
> Nor should I aught withhold,
>   Dear Lord, from thee:
>   In love my soul would bow,
>   My heart fulfill its vow

Some off'ring bring thee now,
Something for thee.

Sylvanus Dryden Phelps, author of the hymn, was educated at Brown University and Yale Divinity School. Ordained to the Baptist ministry, he served for thirty years as a pastor at two churches, one in Connecticut and one in Rhode Island. Later he became editor of a religious journal, *The Christian Secretary*. His poem appeared in this journal in 1864. Phelps submitted it to Robert Lowry, and Lowry composed the music. The words and music first appeared together in 1871. On Phelps's seventieth birthday he received a letter from Lowry saying, "It is worth living seventy years even if nothing comes of it but one such hymn as 'Savior, Thy Dying Love.'"

The author's son, William Lyon Phelps, was a distinguished scholar. He was a professor of English at Yale University for forty-one years. In his autobiography William Phelps shares the following humorous incident about his father, then seventy-six years old and experiencing failing eyesight.

"In 1892, I was reading aloud the news to my father. My father was an orthodox Baptist minister; he was a good man and is now with God. I had never heard him mention a prize fight and did not suppose he knew anything on the subject of boxing or cared anything about it. So when I came to the headline "Corbett Defeats Sullivan," I read that aloud and turned over the page. My father leaned forward and said earnestly, 'Read it by rounds.'"

Over the years Phelps wrote quite a number of hymns on various subjects. But only this one remains in our hymnals.

WORDS WRITTEN IN NEW ZEALAND

Search me, O God, and know my heart today;
Try me, O Savior, know my thoughts I pray;
See if there be some wicked way in me;
Cleanse me from every sin and set me free.

J. Edwin Orr, an evangelist, was participating in an Easter Conference in Ngaruawahia, New Zealand, in 1936. An extraordinary revival experience was in progress, and evangelistic fervor was very much in evidence as God's Spirit worked in the hearts of many people. Orr had heard some young women sing a native melody of the Maori, the Polynesian people of New Zealand. The melody stuck in Orr's mind, and to this melody he began to fit the words "Search me, O God, and know my heart today." Standing in the post office in Ngaruawahia, he completed the four stanzas in five minutes. Set to the Maori melody, the four stanzas were first published in London later that year.

Born in Belfast, Ireland, in 1912, J. Edwin Orr emigrated to the United States in 1933. He began the evangelistic work that eventually took him around the world many times preaching in 135 countries. He moved to Toronto in 1936, where he became the assistant pastor to Oswald J. Smith at The People's Church. Orr studied at Northwestern University and Northern Baptist Theological Seminary and was ordained to the Baptist ministry in 1940. During World War II he was a chaplain in the United States Air Force, and following the war he completed a doctoral degree at Oxford University.

After extensive evangelistic work, Orr joined the faculty of the School of World Missions of Fuller Theological Seminary in California in 1967. His growing concern for historical and contemporary spiritual awakenings led him to write a number of significant books on the subject. He was instrumental in forming the Oxford Association for Research in Revival in 1974. This organization sponsored conferences, published a journal, and encouraged the publication of scholarly works. He died in Asheville, North Carolina, in 1987.

A FAVORITE HYMN OF
A SUPREME COURT JUSTICE

Shall we gather at the river,
Where bright angel feet have trod;
With its crystal tide forever
Flowing by the throne of God?
Yes, we'll gather at the river,

The beautiful, the beautiful river;
Gather with the saints at the river
That flows by the throne of God.

The sound of this old, familiar song, sung by the United States Army Chorus, reverberated through the National Presbyterian Church in Washington, D. C. The occasion was the funeral service of Justice William O. Douglas. Douglas had requested this song because he remembered his parents singing it when he was a boy in Goose Prairie, Washington, where his Presbyterian-preacher father had eked out a meager existence for his family.

"Shall We Gather at the River," both words and music, was written on a hot sultry day in July of 1864 by Robert Lowry, a Baptist preacher in Brooklyn. The extreme heat had brought on physical exhaustion, and he had flopped down on a couch to rest. He had often wondered why hymn writers had written so much about the "river of death," and so little about the "river of water of life, clear as crystal, proceeding out of the throne of God and of the Lamb" (Rev. 22:1). As he pondered this, some words began to come together in his mind. First there was the question of Christian inquiry, "Shall we gather?" Then the answer of Christian faith, "Yes, we'll gather." Soon words and tune were completed.

The preacher-musician Lowry was a man of many gifts who had a keen sense of humor. Pastor of the Hanson Place Baptist Church, he was an excellent preacher who loved to preach. Yet he found great joy in writing music. His tunes for "We're Marching to Zion," "All the Way My Savior Leads Me," "I Need Thee Every Hour," and "Where Is My Wandering Boy Tonight" were singable and dearly loved. But none of his songs has been more popular than "Shall We Gather at the River."

This song crossed the nation to the state of Washington, and in the early years of the twentieth century, touched a lad who would serve thirty-six years on the United States Supreme Court, longer than any other justice. As his life came to a close, his memory recalled the song of his childhood.

WITNESSING TO ONE'S FAITH

Share his love by telling what the Lord has done for
you,
Share his love by sharing of your faith,
And show the world that Jesus Christ is real to you
*every moment, every day.**

This refrain emphasizes the need for us as Christians to share our own experiences. This is far more appropriate and effective than merely repeating what has happened to someone else. God's love is shared when we tell "what the Lord has done" for us. Our most striking witness occurs when our lives reveal that Jesus is real to us "every moment, every day."

Words and music were written in 1972 by William J. Reynolds as part of a larger work entitled *Reaching People.* The initial stanza speaks of the dimensions of God's love.

The love of God is broader than earth's vast expanse,
'Tis deeper and wider than the sea.
Love reaches out to all to bring abundant life,
For God so loved the world his only Son he gave.

That is the basis for sharing God's love.

After twenty-five years in denominational church music work, Reynolds joined the faculty of the School of Church Music at Southwestern Baptist Theological Seminary. In addition to writing and lecturing about Christian song, he has collaborated with Milburn Price on *A Survey of Christian Hymnody* (1987), a textbook for the study of hymnody. He has served internationally as a consultant for a number of hymnals involving several denominations. His weekly column "History of Hymns" has appeared in several significant newspapers. An active member of the Hymn Society of America, he served as its president from 1978 to 1980.

The hymn tune for "Share His Love" was named "Sullivan," honoring Dr. James L. Sullivan of Nashville,

Tennessee, a distinguished pastor, executive, and church denominational leader.

CHRISTMAS EVE WITHOUT AN ORGAN

Silent night, holy night,
All is calm, all is bright
Round yon virgin mother and child!
Holy Infant so tender and mild,
Sleep in heavenly peace.

An imaginative writer of fiction would find it difficult to write a more vivid story than the true facts about the Christmas favorite, "Silent Night, Holy Night." The story spans two decades and involves a village priest, an organist, an organ repairman, and a family of glovemakers.

It all began on Christmas Eve in 1818 in the village of Oberndorf in Upper Austria. Father Joseph Mohr, at St. Nicholas Church, discovered that the organ would not play. Since the music of the Christmas service depended on this instrument, he faced a major crisis. He fell upon the idea of writing a new song and substituting it for the music previously planned. Father Mohr wrote out some words which began "Stille nacht, heilige nacht," and asked his organist friend, Franz Gruber, to write a suitable tune.

All of this happened rather quickly, and in the Christmas Eve service the carol was heard for the first time by the worshipers at Oberndorf. The two men sang it as a duet as Gruber provided the accompaniment on the guitar.

Later when Karl Mauracher came to Oberndorf to repair the church organ, he heard about the Christmas Eve service. Father Mohr sang the song for him and gave him a copy of words and music. As Mauracher traveled about the country repairing organs, he shared the carol with many people.

The Strasser family of Zillertal were glovemakers who took great pride in exhibiting their gloves at fairs in various cities. They were also singers who sang their folk songs at the fairs. Somewhere in their travels they discovered "Stille nacht, heilige nacht" and sang it at the Leipzig fair in 1831. From Leipzig the song traveled in every direction. It was first published in a Catholic hymnal in Leipzig in 1838, twenty years after that "organless" Christmas Eve service at Oberndorf.

German-speaking immigrants brought the song to America; the first English version appeared in an 1849 collection intended for Methodists. Nine years later it was published in England. By far the most popular translation in America is that made by John Freeman Young, an Episcopal minister, who from 1845 to 1855 served pastorates in Florida, Texas, Mississippi, and Louisiana.

A TRANSLATION OF
A GERMAN HYMN

Sing praise to God who reigns above,
The God of all creation,
The God of power, the God of love,
The God of our salvation;
With healing balm my soul he fills,
And every faithless murmur stills:
To God all praise and glory!

Here is another of the great hymns that began as a German text and have been successfully translated into an English expression of praise. Written by Johann Jacob Schutz in 1675, the German text is based on a single verse from the song of Moses found in Deuteronomy 32:3: "Because I will publish the name of the Lord: ascribe ye greatness unto our God."

Schutz practiced law in Frankfurt, Germany, for many years. An ardent Lutheran, he published a collection of hymns in Frankfurt in 1675 for Lutheran congregations. "Sing Praise to God Who Reigns Above" was one of the hymns in this collection. Schutz became a friend of Philipp Spener, whose devotional gatherings marked the beginning of the Pietistic movement in Germany in the late seventeenth century. Emphasizing a more devout lifestyle, the Pietists encouraged personal spiritual growth, prayer, and Bible study. Schutz's involvement in these activities eventually led him to become a Separatist, and he no longer attended Lutheran services.

The English translation found in most hymnals today was made by Frances Cox, a German scholar who lived in Oxford, England. Her translation was published in 1864, almost two hundred years after the German original.

The tune most frequently used for this text is called "Mit Freuden Zart" (meaning "with great delight"). Its earliest appearance dates from a collection of hymn tunes published for the Bohemian Brethren in 1566. The music fits the hymn and brings joy in the singing of these stanzas, all of which end with, "To God all praise and glory."

A SUNDAY SCHOOL SONG

Sing them over again to me,
Wonderful words of life:
Let me more of their beauty see,
Wonderful words of life;
Words of life and beauty,
Teach me faith and duty;
Beautiful words, wonderful words,
Wonderful words of life.

Philip P. Bliss wrote both words and music for this joyful song about God's Word—the Bible. The lilt of the tune reflects the abounding joy of the "wonderful words of life."

Born in a log cabin in Clearfield County, Pennsylvania, Bliss left home at the age of eleven to work in lumber camps. At the age of twelve he was converted and joined the Baptist church near Elk Run, Pennsylvania. In his early years his musical talents were very evident, and he was an eager student who attended singing schools as often as possible. With a new wife, his horse named Fanny, and a twenty-dollar reed organ, he set out at the age of twenty-two to be a professional music teacher.

In 1874 Bliss wrote "Sing Them Over Again to Me" for the first issue of a Sunday school paper published by Fleming H. Revell in New York City. During the same year, at the urging of Dwight L. Moody and other friends, Bliss gave up his singing schools and became a singing evangelist, traveling with D. W. Whittle. In two years Whittle and Bliss conducted twenty-five revivals in ten states with great success.

In December 1876, after spending the Christmas holidays with his family in Rome, Pennsylvania, Bliss and his wife left for Chicago for an engagement in Moody's Tabernacle on the following Sunday. As the train crossed a ravine approaching Ashtabula, Ohio, the cast-iron bridge gave way. Seven cars plunged into the icy riverbed, and burst into flames. Bliss survived the fall and escaped through a window, but he returned to the wreckage in a desperate attempt to rescue his wife and both perished in the fire. Among the many hymn tunes that Bliss composed are, "I Gave My Life for Thee" and "When Peace Like a River" ("It is Well with My Soul").

AN ALTERNATE TEXT FOR AN EXISTING TUNE

Sing we the King who is coming to reign,
Glory to Jesus, the Lamb that was slain.
Life and salvation his empire shall bring,
Joy to the nations when Jesus is King.
Come let us sing praise to our King,
Jesus our King, Jesus our King,
This is our song who to Jesus belong:
Glory to Jesus, to Jesus our King.

These lines were written in 1910 to replace a text that was entitled "O That Will Be Glory for Me," written ten years earlier. Through the efforts of Charles M. Alexander, the first of the flamboyant evangelistic song leaders, the song became very popular. The spiritual awakening that began in Wales at the turn of the century and swept around much of the world provided an opportunity for Alexander to use the song.

Charles Silvester Horne, an English Congregational minister, greatly enjoyed the jubilant sound of Gabriel's tune but was bothered by the repetition of "that will be glory for me." To Horne this expression was too self-centered and inadequately expressed the Christian faith. He felt that the words should bring "glory to Jesus" rather than "glory for me." So he wrote an alternate text in 1910. A student in the first class of Mansfield College in Oxford, England, Horne was ordained to the Congregational ministry in 1889 and served a congregation in Kensington. Later he served at Whitefield's Central Mission in London, where his reputation became widespread and throngs came to hear him preach. It was for this congregation that he wrote the hymn.

TO PRESERVE THE SIMPLICITY OF THE FAITH

Sinners Jesus will receive:
Sound this word of grace to all
Who the heavenly pathway leave,
All who linger, all who fall.

The original German hymn, by Erdman Neumeister, was published in Hamburg in 1718. One of eighty-six original hymns Neumeister wrote to conclude his sermons, "Jesus nimmt die Sünder an!" (Sinners Jesus will receive) was written to follow a sermon on the parable of the lost sheep (Luke 15:1–7). Educated at the University of Leipzig, Neumeister held several positions as a Lutheran minister before he became pastor of St. James church in Hamburg in 1715. He remained there until his death in 1756, at the age of eighty-five.

An eloquent preacher, Neumeister was an ardent champion of the older, conservative Lutheranism. He sought to preserve the simplicity of the faith from the influence of what he referred to as "subjective novelties." The author of about six hundred hymns, Neumeister is recognized as a significant contributor to the development of the church cantata. His cantata texts, mostly poetic paraphrase of Scripture appropriate for various feasts of the church year, were used by Johann Sebastian Bach and other composers.

Several English translations of the German text have been made, but the one most often used is the work of a London banker's wife, Emma Frances Bevan. Her father was the Reverend Philip Shuttleworth, an official of New College,

Oxford University, and later Bishop of Chichester. Notwithstanding her strong ties to the Church of England, she became identified with the Plymouth Brethren, a group of Christians that began in Ireland and England. Their emphases involved biblical prophecy and the second coming of Christ.

James McGranahan, composer and evangelistic singer, discovered Bevan's translation, adapted the stanzas, added a refrain text, and composed an appropriate tune in 1883. It was introduced in evangelistic crusades at the end of the nineteenth century and is still frequently sung in evangelical churches. What a joyful refrain:

> Sing it o'er and o'er again.
> Christ receiveth sinful men.

A MAJOR REVISION

> So send I you to labor unrewarded,
>   To serve unpaid, unloved, unsought, unknown,
> To bear rebuke, to suffer scorn and scoffing—
>   So send I you to toil for me alone.*

E. Margaret Clarkson wrote these lines in 1937, and the following year they were published in a religious periodical. She completely forgot about the poem until she saw it one day, seventeen years later, as a hymn for which John W. Peterson had composed a tune. She was quite surprised at the reception that this new hymn received.

Some years later she became quite concerned about some of the lines she had written. Throughout her childhood she had grown up in an atmosphere where, as she said, "laying all on the altar" was preached "to the n'th degree." She commented: "The full orbed glory of the great commission was not declared. Consequently, my song was all in one vein, and not really true to the gospel, although I was not aware of this."

In 1963, with this full understanding now in her heart, she wrote four new stanzas with the same poetic structure and rhyme to fit the excellent tune by John W. Peterson. These stanzas capture the spirit of Christ's words, "Peace be unto you: as my Father hath sent me, even so send I you" (John 20:21). The new first stanza reads:

> So send I you—by grace made strong to triumph
> O'er hosts of hell, o'er darkness, death and sin,
> My name to bear and in that name to conquer—
> So send I you, my victory to win.*

Born in Saskatchewan, Canada, E. Margaret Clarkson was educated at Toronto Teachers College. She first taught school in a lumber camp and a gold-mining camp, then in the public schools of Toronto until her retirement in 1973. A member of the Knox Presbyterian Church in Toronto, she was also active in the work of InterVarsity Christian Fellowship. Author of public school textbooks, devotional books, and collections of poetry, she is well known for her writing.

John W. Peterson, a native of Kansas, was educated at Moody Bible Institute and the American Conservatory of Music. In 1954 he became associated with Singspiration, Inc., then located in Montrose, Pennsylvania. The firm moved to Grand Rapids, Michigan, in 1963, when it was acquired by the Zondervan Publishing House. For more than three decades Peterson has written a tremendous amount of music, including gospel songs and seasonal choral cantatas. His cantatas have been extremely popular and are reputed to have sold more than seven million copies. He makes his home in Arizona, where he has his own music publishing company.

AN EAST LIVERPOOL, OHIO, COMPOSER

> Softly and tenderly, Jesus is calling,
> Calling for you and for me;
> See on the portals he's waiting and watching,
> Watching for you and for me.

Will Thompson, writer of both words and music, was born in 1847 in Beaver County, Pennsylvania. His father was a banker, manufacturer, and merchant. When Will was a small boy his family moved to East Liverpool, Ohio. Will majored in commerce and business in college, and upon graduation he combined these skills with his first love—music. With a small stock of pianos, reed organs, and music, he began his business in the back of his father's general store. Later he enrolled in the New England Conservatory of Music in Boston, and in 1876 he went to the conservatory of music in Leipzig. He began writing songs, and one of his earlier secular songs, "Gathering Shells from the Seashore," became a national hit.

Nineteenth-century evangelism blossomed through the efforts of such evangelists as D. L. Moody, Ira D. Sankey, and others. Thompson attended their meetings as well as the summer-camp meetings, where he heard the singing and preaching and caught the spirit of this movement. Thompson wrote gospel songs appropriate for his time, and these were sung in the evangelical services. Nothing is known about the circumstances surrounding the writing of "Softly and Tenderly, Jesus Is Calling." After it was written in 1880, it became a favorite hymn of invitation to unbelievers. It was sung in camp meetings, revival services, and evangelistic crusades in large tabernacles and in small country churches.

In 1899, when D. L. Moody was on his deathbed, Thompson went to his home in Northfield, Massachusetts. No visitors were allowed in his room, but when Moody heard that Thompson was there, he insisted that Thompson be admitted. As Thompson quietly entered the room, Moody greeted him cordially and said, "Will, I would rather have written 'Softly and Tenderly, Jesus Is Calling,' than anything I have been able to do in my whole life." At the memorial services for Martin Luther King, Jr., in Atlanta, Georgia, on April 8, 1968, one of the songs sung by the choir of the Ebenezer Baptist Church was Will Thompson's "Softly and Tenderly, Jesus Is Calling."

A NEW AWARENESS OF HEAVEN

Some day the silver cord will break,
And I no more as now shall sing;

But oh, the joy when I shall wake
Within the palace of the King!
And I shall see him face to face,
And tell the story—saved by grace!

At a Methodist camp meeting in 1891 at Poughkeepsie, New York, Fanny Crosby was impressed by one of the speakers. A few days later, the speaker's sudden death brought a new awareness of heaven to all the participants. After a conversation with some friends, Fanny Crosby stepped into an adjoining room, closed the door, and in an hour had completed the stanzas beginning "Some day the silver cord will break." She sent the poem to her publisher, Biglow and Main of New York City, who apparently filed it and forgot it.

Two years later Crosby attended a Christian Workers' Conference in Northfield, Massachusetts, begun by D. L. Moody twelve years earlier. Ira D. Sankey had asked Fanny Crosby to speak. She closed her remarks by quoting the stanzas of this poem. A reporter from a London newspaper asked permission to take it back to London and publish it. When it appeared in the newspaper, Sankey sent a copy to George S. Stebbins, suggesting that he compose appropriate music for the words. This Stebbins did. He sang it for the first time in a Moody meeting in Newport, Rhode Island.

George C. Stebbins was a gifted musician, a soloist of unusual ability, and a composer of hymn tunes. In the fall of 1877 he began his association with Ira D. Sankey in publishing gospel song collections, which were so popular at that time. As a song leader he assisted evangelist Major D. W. Whittle, and he also substituted for Sankey, since Sankey's failing voice was diminishing his ability to be Moody's music director.

REJOICING IN THE PROVIDENCE OF GOD

Sometimes a light surprises
The Christian while he sings;
It is the Lord who rises
With healing in his wings.

When comforts are declining,
He grants the soul again
A season of clear shining,
To bring it after rain.

What a delightful opening couplet for a hymn! William Cowper, one of England's great poets, wrote these lines in 1779 while living in the village of Olney. Though Cowper often experienced depression, here he writes in a mood abounding in cheerfulness, singing of the providence of God. The lessons Jesus taught about not worrying (Matt. 6:25–34; Luke 12:22–30) are evident here.

Here also are the triumphant words of Habakkuk the prophet: "Although the fig tree shall not blossom, neither shall fruit be in the vines; the labor of the olive shall fail, and the fields shall yield no meat; the flock shall be cut off from the fold, and there shall be no herd in the stalls: yet I will rejoice in the Lord, I will joy in the God of my salvation" (Hab. 3:17–18).

While no one tune has become permanently identified with Cowper's hymn, one of the most frequently used is "Llanfyllin," a version of an anonymous Welsh tune first printed in Wales in 1865. Like most Welsh tunes, "Llanfyllin" is a hardy melody that sings easily and joyfully—most appropriate for the hymn.

Hymnbook 1982 uses a melody from *The Christian Lyre* (1932) that Winfred Douglas arranged for *The Hymnal 1940*, called "Light."

A HYMN FREQUENTLY HEARD
IN WESTERN FILMS

Sowing in the morning, sowing seeds of kindness,
Sowing in the noontide and the dewy eve;
Waiting for the harvest, and the time of reaping,
We shall come rejoicing, bringing in the sheaves.

When the script for a western motion picture calls for a church scene on the western frontier, frequently the scene will open with the singing of a hymn accompanied by an old reed organ. Generally the hymn will be "Bringing in the Sheaves." The hymn has become a trademark of movies set in the romantic West of the nineteenth century.

Knowles Shaw wrote words and music of the hymn in 1874, when he was forty years old. A native of Butler County, Ohio, Shaw learned to play the violin as a teenager and played well. When the young people gathered for community dances, he was much in demand to provide the music.

Before he was fifty, Shaw was converted, was baptized in Mud Creek near Homer, Ohio, and joined the Big Flatrock Christian Church across the road from the farm where he lived. He was ordained to the Christian ministry and became a successful evangelist, serving in a dozen states for more than twenty-five years. Some twenty thousand persons are reported to have been converted under his preaching.

He made much use of his musical talents. His organ playing and singing were attractive features of his work. He composed more than 110 gospel songs and published five collections of songs between 1868 and 1877.

After a successful five-week revival in the Commerce Street Christian Church in Dallas in the summer of 1879, Shaw left by train for another meeting in McKinney, Texas. Two miles south of McKinney a broken rail caused the derailment of the car in which Shaw was riding, and he was killed instantly.

The following year a Sunday school superintendent in the First Baptist Church in Richmond, Virginia, wrote a new tune for Shaw's words and published it with the text. So successful was this new tune that Shaw's original music has long been forgotten. But his words live on, firmly attached to the music of George A. Minor.

WORDS OF AN IRISH PREACHER

Spirit of God, descend upon my heart;
Wean it from earth; through all its pulses move;
Stoop to my weakness, mighty as thou art,
And make me love thee as I ought to love.

George Croly wrote the hymn in 1854. Born and reared in Dublin, he was the son of a highly respected physician. He was educated at the University of Dublin and ordained to the ministry. He moved to London at the age of thirty and devoted himself primarily to literary work, writing poems, dramas, satires, novels, and historical and theological works. An outspoken conservative both in religion and politics, he strongly opposed any form of liberalism.

In 1835 he accepted the pastoral charge of two Anglican churches. One of these, St. Stephen's, was located in a slum section of London where no services had been conducted for one hundred years. He "opened the pulpit," and the boldness of his preaching attracted large crowds to the services. At the urging of his congregations, Croly prepared a hymnbook that was published in 1854. It contained metrical psalms and original hymns, many of which were his own work, including this hymn. Only one edition was printed, and most of the copies were destroyed by fire.

"Spirit of God, Descend Upon My Heart" is filled with personal and emotional expressions. In the form of a prayer, it expresses the desire for the indwelling Spirit of God to take complete possession of one's soul and body. The last stanza contains one of the most beautiful figures of speech found in hymnic writing: "My heart an altar, and thy love the flame."

The tune most frequently found with Croly's hymn is called "Morecambe." Frederick C. Atkinson wrote the tune in 1887 as a musical setting for the hymn "Abide with Me," but it never became associated with those words. The tune is named for Morecambe Bay in western England, not far from Bradford, where Atkinson lived. Atkinson grew up in Norwich, England, and as a lad was a chorister at Norwich Cathedral. He graduated from Cambridge University and served as organist and choirmaster in several churches. In the areas of church music and music for the piano, he composed many anthems, hymn tunes, and songs.

INSPIRED BY A SERMON

Spirit of the living God, fall fresh on me.
Spirit of the living God, fall fresh on me.

Break me! Melt me! Mold me! Fill me!
*Spirit of the living God, fall fresh on me.**

Early in 1926, the George C. Stephans Evangelistic Party conducted a citywide revival in Orlando, Florida. Daniel Iverson, a Presbyterian minister from Lumberton, North Carolina, spent several days in Orlando visiting with the team members. They were friends from previous days and he coveted this opportunity for Christian fellowship with them. Greatly impressed by a sermon he heard on the subject of the Holy Spirit, Iverson wrote this chorus the same day and shared it with some of his friends.

E. Powell Lee, the music director for the Stephans team, was impressed with the song and introduced it that evening in the service. The immediate response of the people foretold the potential of the song. In later years Lee worked in music and education in several Southern Baptist churches and at the Home Mission Board in Atlanta, Georgia. He never forgot the emotion of that evening in Orlando when "Spirit of the Living God" was first sung.

Daniel Iverson pastored Presbyterian churches in Georgia, North and South Carolina, and Florida. During the twenty-four years he served as pastor of the Shenandoah Presbyterian Church in Miami, he led in the organization of seven other churches in the Miami area. His ministry in that area was held in the highest esteem.

Iverson retired from the active pastorate in 1951, and in 1962 he moved to Asheville, North Carolina. In this picturesque location he lived a quiet life, occasionally preaching in nearby churches. He died in 1977 when he was eighty-seven. The song he wrote in Orlando in 1926 lives on as Christians plead in song that the Spirit of the Lord will "fall fresh on me."

FROM A LUTHERAN PASTOR
IN STUTTGART

Spread, O spread the mighty word,
Spread the kingdom of the Lord,

That to earth's remotest bound
All may hear the joyful sound.

The German hymn on which this English translation is based was published in Germany in 1828. It was one of the first hymns of world missions in Lutheran hymnody. The first stanza exhorts us to take the gospel to earth's remotest regions; succeeding stanzas speak of God the Father, God the Son, and God the Holy Spirit. A strong appeal for evangelizing the world is made in the final stanza:

> *Word of life, more pure and strong,*
> *Word for which the nations long,*
> *Spread abroad, until from night*
> *All the world awakes to light.*

Jonathan Friedrich Bahnmaier, a Lutheran pastor, wrote the hymn in 1827 while serving a Lutheran congregation in a town about fifteen miles from Stuttgart, Germany. Bahnmaier had been a teacher and for a while served as head of a girls' school in Ludwigsburg. Later he was a professor of education and homiletics at the University of Tubigen. The last years of his life were spent in pastoral work.

Catherine Winkworth, who lived near Bristol, England, made an English translation of the German hymn in 1858. Of the nineteenth-century translators of German hymns, Winkworth was the most successful. Among her best-known translations sung in our churches today are "Now thank we all our God," "Praise to the Lord, the Almighty," "If thou but suffer God to guide thee," and "Wake, awake for night is flying." Arthur W. Farlander and C. Winfred Douglas made considerable alterations in Winkworth's English version of Bahnmaier's hymn for the 1940 Episcopal hymnal and their version is now commonly used in American hymnals.

A YOUNG MINISTER'S DYING REQUEST

Stand up, stand up for Jesus,
Ye soldiers of the cross;

Lift high his royal banner,
It must not suffer loss:
From victory unto victory
His army shall he lead,
Till every foe is vanquished,
And Christ is Lord indeed.

A wave of evangelical fervor swept through Philadelphia in 1858. Noonday meetings sponsored by the YMCA drew as many as five thousand people. The leading personality in this wave of spiritual renewal was Dudley Tyng, a young, very effective Episcopal minister who was held in highest esteem by his colleagues. His preaching of an antislavery sermon caused him to be ousted from his parish, so he established the "Church of the Covenant" in Jayne's Hall. Great throngs attended his services. His untimely, tragic death was the inspiration for this hymn.

One weekday afternoon Tyng went from his study to the barn where a mule was walking in circles powering a corn-shelling machine. As he patted the mule, the sleeve of his silk study jacket caught in the cogs of the wheel. His arm was torn from his shoulder, and despite all medical efforts and the prayers of his friends, he died five days later.

George Duffield was one of the ministers who stood by Tyng's bed in his last hours. When asked if he had any message to send to his people, Tyng replied, "Tell them, 'Let us all stand up for Jesus.'"

The following Sunday morning George Duffield preached to his Presbyterian congregation on the text, "Stand therefore, having your loins girt about with truth and having on the breastplate of righteousness" (Eph. 6:14). The sermon ended with this hymn, which Duffield had written, based on the dying testimony of his friend Tyng.

The hymn reflects the imagery of a Roman soldier's fighting equipment as described in Paul's letter to the Ephesians. Though the equipment is obsolete today, this hymn is still appropriate for congregational singing. The imagery of the Christian life as a warfare with evil is still valid. Personal strength and strong courage are imperative, and prayer is essential. Victory over evil is possible through Jesus Christ as one follows his teachings and trusts in him.

HYMNWRITER WAS
A BASEBALL PITCHER

Standing on the promises of Christ my King,
Through eternal ages let his praises ring;
Glory in the highest, I will shout and sing,
Standing on the promises of God.

This joyous hymn that rings with vitality and sings the praises of God was written in 1886. The martial rhythm reflects life on the campus of the military academy where the composer-author was a student and later taught. Russell Kelso Carter was an extraordinary person, gifted in many areas. He was in the first graduating class of Pennsylvania Military Academy at Chester. During his student days he was the best pitcher on the baseball team and the finest gymnast.

He joined the faculty of the academy and taught there for two decades except for a three-year period that he spent in California raising sheep. A prolific writer, he published works in the disciplines of mathematics, science, and religion; he also wrote several novels, one of which became a best seller.

Russell Carter and Albert B. Simpson compiled a hymnal, *Hymns of the Christian Life,* in 1891 for the churches of the Christian and Missionary Alliance. To this collection Carter contributed fifty-two hymns. (A 1978 revision of this hymnal includes seven tunes and five texts by Carter.) In 1887 Carter resigned his teaching position at the academy and became a Methodist minister. He was a highly respected leader in the Holiness movement of that denomination.

At that time camp meetings were extremely popular among the Methodists, especially in New York, New Jersey, and Pennsylvania. Carter attended often and maintained a warm friendship with many who were writing songs that reflected the evangelical fervor of the camp meeting services. After a number of years in the ministry, he studied medicine and spent his last years as a practicing physician in his hometown, Baltimore. He died in 1928 at the age of seventy-nine.

ENGLAND'S POET LAUREATE

Strong Son of God, immortal love,
Whom we, that have not seen thy face,
By faith, and faith alone, embrace
Believing where we cannot prove.

Alfred Tennyson was appointed poet laureate by Queen Victoria in 1850 when he was forty-one years old. His poetic gifts won for him high regard throughout England. Though he received several requests to write hymns, he graciously declined. He believed hymn writing was a difficult task for which he was not suited. Hymnal editors, however, have successfully used selections from Tennyson's writings as hymns.

His father was an Anglican minister; Alfred was the fourth of twelve children in the rectory in Lincolnshire, England. After three years at Trinity College in Cambridge, he became disillusioned and quit school. Although he composed some of the most exquisite poetry in the English language, he was anything but a delicate individual. So prodigious was his physical strength that he could hurl an iron crowbar farther than any person in his village. It was reported that he could bend horseshoes, and once he picked up an injured pony and carried it in his arms. His poetic works were in great demand, and people stood in long lines to buy copies of his newly published works. After he had twice declined knighthood, William Gladstone, prime minister, finally persuaded him to accept a peerage, and in 1884 he became Alfred, Lord Tennyson.

"Strong Son of God, Immortal Love" is a selection of stanzas from a larger work entitled "In Memoriam." The initial motivation for the poem came from the shocking death of a college classmate. Seeking to resolve the meaning of life and death, and reaching out for his own faith, Tennyson spent several years meditating on the realities of the Christian faith. The lines in this poem reflect his growing maturity.

A STRANGE STORY

Sweet hour of prayer, sweet hour of prayer,
That calls me from a world of care
And bids me at my Father's throne
Make all my wants and wishes known!
In seasons of distress and grief,
My soul has often found relief,
And oft escaped the tempter's snare
By thy return, sweet hour of prayer.

A strange mystery surrounds this hymn and its author. The poem of five stanzas appeared in a newspaper, *The New York Observer,* on September 13, 1845, with a statement that the poem had been submitted by a Rev. Thomas Salmon, who had come to America in 1842 following a four-year pastorate at Coleshill, Warwickshire, England. Salmon's account of the poem said that it was written by a blind preacher from Coleshill, W. W. Walford. Though lacking in formal education, Walford had a remarkable memory and a reputation for knowing the whole Bible by memory.

All efforts to identify the man described by Salmon have been unsuccessful. However, there was a Congregational minister, William Walford, who lived in England in the first half of the nineteenth century. Well-educated, William Walford was president of Homerton Academy, a Congregational school, and was the author of several books. There is no evidence that he was blind. All of this adds to the confusion about the true identity of the person who wrote "Sweet Hour of Prayer."

Somehow the poem came to the attention of William B. Bradbury, a New York composer, publisher, and piano manufacturer. He composed the tune that we associate with this hymn about 1860 and included it in one of the Sunday-school song collections he published.

Bradbury spent two years in Germany studying music under the finest teachers there. He arrived in Leipzig on September 11, 1847, and established his family just three doors from the home of Felix Mendelssohn, who was very ill. The whole city was greatly concerned about Mendelssohn's physical condition. To lessen the noise of the wagons on the cobblestones in front of Mendelssohn's home, straw was placed in the streets. Mendelssohn died on November 4, and Bradbury attended his funeral.

The success of Bradbury's hymn tunes may be judged by the number found in our hymnals today—"Savior, Like a Shepherd Lead Us," "Jesus Loves Me, This I Know," "He Leadeth Me, O Blessed Thought," "My Hope Is Built on Nothing Less," "Just As I Am, Without One Plea," and "Sweet Hour of Prayer."

THE JOY OF DISCIPLESHIP

Sweetly, Lord, have we heard thee calling,
"Come, follow me!"
And we see where thy footprints falling,
Lead us to thee.
Footsteps of Jesus that make the pathway glow;
We will follow the steps of Jesus where'er they go.

Strolling by the Sea of Galilee, Jesus first met Simon and his brother Andrew casting their fishing nets. He visited with them and, according to the account in Matthew 4, said to them, "Follow me, and I will make you fishers of men." Jesus also exhorted others to whom he spoke to follow him.

In this hymn Mary Slade draws upon the life and teachings of Jesus. Stanza two refers to the parable of the lost sheep (Luke 15) and to Christ's healing of the man blind from birth (John 9). Stanza three refers to Jesus' preaching in the temple in Jerusalem and ministering in the homes of the "poor and lowly." The final stanza refers to the Christian's hope for eternal life, "where the steps of Jesus end at his throne."

A native of Fall River, Massachusetts, Mary Bridges Canedy Slade became the wife of a New England minister. In addition to assisting her husband in his pastoral work, she taught school and worked on the staff of an educational journal. She wrote hymn texts for many contemporary composers, including Rigdon M. McIntosh, a prominent Methodist Musician in the South in the last part of the nineteenth century. Among Slade's best-known song texts are

"The Kingdom Is Coming," and "Who At My Door Is Knocking."

The music for Slade's hymn was composed by A. B. Everett in 1871. With his brother, L. C. Everett, he founded a successful music company in Richmond, Virginia. Before the Civil War this firm employed more than fifty music teachers throughout the Southern and Mid-Atlantic states.

COMPLETE CONSECRATION

*Take my life, and let it be
Consecrated, Lord, to thee.*

This two-line couplet was one of a dozen such couplets that came to the mind of Frances Havergal after a very unusual experience. In December 1874 she went to Worcester, England, with a group of friends for a five-day visit. She later wrote that in the group of ten people there were "some unconverted and long prayed for, some converted but not rejoicing Christians." She prayed that the Lord would use her to lead these to a joyful experience in Christian faith.

By the last day of her visit, her prayer had been answered. Because of the joy she felt, she was unable to sleep. She spent most of the night in praise and renewal of her own consecration, and the couplets of the hymn flooded her mind. Each of them expressed part of herself—time, hands, feet, voice, lips, wealth, mind, will, heart, love, and finally "myself."

Reared in a minister's home, Frances Havergal was an extraordinary person. Through her self-disciplined study and her travels throughout Europe, she became skilled in the biblical languages (Hebrew and Greek) and also in several modern languages. In her book *Swiss Letters,* she tells of hiking and skiing in the Swiss Alps. The challenge of the Alps provided great excitement for her, for she wrote, "The snow slopes were most entertaining to cross, and I enjoyed the scramble excessively."

Several years after the hymn was written, Havergal wrote that " 'Take my silver and my gold' now means shipping off all my ornaments, including a jewel cabinet which is really fit for a countess, to the Church Missionary Society where they will be accepted and disposed of for me. I retain only a brooch for daily wear, which is a memorial of my dear parents. I had no idea I had such a jeweler's shop; nearly fifty articles are being packed off. I don't think I need tell you I never packed a box with such pleasure."

In a real sense the hymn is autobiographical. It describes Frances Havergal committing her gifts and talents that "Christ may be all in all."

THE PRECIOUS NAME OF JESUS

Take the name of Jesus with you,
Child of sorrow and of woe;
It will joy and comfort give you,
Take it then where'er you go.
Precious name, O how sweet!
Hope of earth and joy of heav'n.

Lydia Baxter was an invalid for most of her adult life. She and her husband lived in New York City. Her home was a meeting place for preachers, evangelists, and Christian workers who came to seek her advice and counsel. In spite of lacking physical strength and having to spend much time in bed, she was a radiant person and a source of inspiration and encouragement to all who knew her.

Her conversations with friends frequently involved portions of Scripture. One such conversation centered around the name of Jesus, and Colossians 3:17 was mentioned: "Whatsoever ye do in word or deed, do all in the name of the Lord Jesus." Such discussions provided the immediate inspiration for the hymn, "Take the Name of Jesus with You," which Lydia Baxter wrote in 1870 when she was sixty-one years old.

The initial stanza of the hymn points out that Jesus' name brings joy and comfort. Stanza two states that Jesus' name is a protecting shield from danger and strengthens the Christian in the midst of temptation. The final stanza is based on Philippians 2:9–10: "Wherefore God also hath highly exalted him, and given him a name which is above every name; that at the name of Jesus every knee should bow."

William Howard Doane wrote the music we sing for the

hymn and published it in 1871 in a collection he compiled with Robert Lowry, a Baptist minister in Brooklyn, New York.

Translated into many languages, the hymn is sung around the world. In a Salvation Army leper colony in Indonesia, a patient with a beautiful voice sang the hymn in a gathering of patients in the ward. He sang the hymn with great meaning, then told of his joy in being a Christian. He concluded by saying he was glad he had become a leper, for he would never have heard the name of Jesus in his own village.

INSPIRATION AT
A KESWICK CONFERENCE

Take time to be holy,
  Speak oft with thy Lord;
Abide with him always,
  And feed on his Word;
Make friends of God's children,
  Help those who are weak,
Forgetting in nothing
  His blessings to seek.

First Peter 1:16, "Because it is written, Be ye holy; for I am holy" (the words of God recorded in Leviticus 11:44) provides the basis for the hymn. The writer, William D. Longstaff, was a wealthy shipowner who gave generously to charitable and philanthropic concerns. One of the first to welcome the evangelists Moody and Sankey when they arrived in England in 1872, Longstaff formed close friendships with them and frequently had them as guests in his home in Sunderland, England.

The immediate inspiration for the hymn came from a story about Griffith John, famed missionary to China, that was told at the Keswick Conference. The missionary had exhorted Christians to "take time to be holy." Longstaff completed the four stanzas that evening. The poem was published in several religious journals.

George C. Stebbins, a composer and music evangelist,

was associated with Moody and Sankey from about 1876 until the end of the century. He frequently traveled with them, and assisted other evangelists between Moody meetings. While working in meetings in Bombay, Calcutta, Madras, and other cities in India, Stebbins discovered Longstaff's poem among the papers he had with him. Someone had clipped the poem from a newspaper and had given it to him without his notice. Impressed by the poem, he quickly composed the tune now called "Holiness." The finished song was mailed to Ira D. Sankey in New York and was published in 1890.

FROM A DINNER CONVERSATION

"Take up thy cross and follow me,"
I heard my Master say;
"I gave my life to ransom thee,
Surrender your all today."
Wherever he leads I'll go,
Wherever he leads I'll go,
I'll follow my Christ who loves me so,
*Wherever he leads I'll go.**

In a hotel dining room in Clanton, Alabama, on January 15, 1936, two men sat together renewing their friendship of many years. R. S. Jones, a missionary to Brazil, explained that he had returned to the states because of poor health. B. B. McKinney, who had moved to Nashville, Tennessee, only a month earlier to be music editor for the Baptist Sunday School Board, sympathized with his friend for this unexpected crisis in his missionary career. With genuine concern McKinney inquired, "What do you plan to do now?" To which Jones replied, "I don't know, Mac, but wherever He leads I'll go."

Following dinner both men returned to their hotel rooms to prepare for a meeting that evening at the First Baptist Church. McKinney wrote down Jones's words, and a hymn began to formulate. At the church service, McKinney led several hymns and later Jones preached. McKinney completed the words and music of the hymn during the sermon. When Jones concluded, McKinney stood and related the dinner conversation, explaining how he had written the hymn. Giving his hurriedly written manuscript of music to the organist, he sang the hymn as a solo.

A few months later McKinney led the music at Oklahoma Baptists' Falls Creek Assembly, a summer camp meeting attended by thousands of people in the southern part of Oklahoma. There the new hymn, "Wherever He Leads I'll Go," was first sung publicly and was accepted with great joy and dedication. The tune is named "Falls Creek."

In 1941 McKinney became head of the newly formed Church Music Department of the Baptist Sunday School Board. He provided denominational leadership for promoting and encouraging music activities in Southern Baptist churches. He died on September 7, 1952, as a result of an automobile accident enroute to Nashville from Ridgecrest, North Carolina. He is credited with writing more than four hundred gospel songs; for many of them he wrote both words and music. At least ten pseudonyms were occasionally used by McKinney: Martha Annis, A. B. Cace, Howard Glenn, Hal Homer, John Mark, Otto Nellen, Fred Muller, Richard Radcliffe, Gene Routh, and Robert J. Snow.

A SUNDAY SCHOOL SONG

Tell me the stories of Jesus
I love to hear;
Things I would ask him to tell me
If he were here:
Scenes by the wayside,
Tales by the sea,
Stories of Jesus,
Tell them to me.

One summer Sunday afternoon in 1885, a Christian teacher reflected on his experiences at Sunday school earlier in the day. The oft-repeated inquiry from the children, "Teacher, tell us another story," lingered in his mind. As he pondered the keen interest of children in stories from the Bible, he began to write the hymn. It was first printed in a leaflet for use in his church and was published in a collection of hymns in London in 1905 by the National Sunday School Union.

The teacher, William H. Parker, lived in the village of New Basford in Nottingham, England. As a youth he was apprenticed to a machinist in a large lace-making plant in New Basford. Later he became the head of an insurance company. A member of the Chelsea Street Baptist Church in Nottingham, he was active in the Sunday school. Most of his hymns were written for Sunday school anniversaries. One of Parker's contemporaries described him as "quiet in demeanor, kindly in disposition, always trying to see the best in others—he was one of God's true gentlemen, respected and loved by all who came in contact with him."

In 1903, its centennial year, the National Sunday School Union sponsored a competition to secure new tunes for several new hymn texts. "Tell Me the Stories of Jesus" was one of them. Frederick Challinor's tune was judged the winner, and words and music were published in 1905. A prolific composer, Challinor claims more than one thousand published compositions. He died in England in 1952, at the age of eighty-six.

A BIBLE TRANSLATION INSPIRES
A HYMN

Tell out, my soul, the greatness of the Lord!
Unnumbered blessings, give my spirit voice;
Tender to me the promise of his word;
*In God my Savior shall my heart rejoice.**

The first edition of the New Testament of *The New English Bible* was published in 1961. Begun fifteen years earlier, the new translation sought to employ "a contemporary idiom rather than reproduce the traditional 'biblical' English." Timothy Dudley-Smith, then working with the Home Missionary Society of the Church of England, read the new translation with great excitement. Mary's Song (the Magnificat, Luke 1:46–55) in the King James Version begins "My soul doth magnify the Lord." Borrowing the opening line of the new translation, "Tell out, my soul, the greatness of the Lord," Timothy Dudley-Smith built a magnificent hymn of four stanzas, the first hymn to be inspired by *The New English Bible.* The worth and appeal of the hymn have been validated in that it now appears in more than one hundred hymnals and collections.

For more than a quarter century, Timothy Dudley-Smith has been writing hymns that have stood in the forefront of current hymn writing. He has sought to reflect the purity of scriptural truth in contemporary language that is clear and understandable. His sensitivity to human experiences and feelings comes from his own involvement as a Christian minister. His tenderness and sympathy, as well as his probing inquiry and exhortation, are found in his hymns.

Dudley-Smith's knowledge of poetic verse is the result of years of disciplined study and searching in this intriguing and fascinating area of literature. His 1984 publication, *Lift Every Voice* (Hope Publishing Company), includes not only more than 125 hymns and poems, but also a carefully written section revealing his understanding of the art of hymn writing. No other person has voiced so eloquently and clearly the framework of the language of Christian song.

A SONG OF GRATITUDE

Thanks to God for my Redeemer,
  Thanks for all thou dost provide!
Thanks for times now but a mem'ry,
  Thanks for Jesus by my side!
Thanks for pleasant, balmy springtime,
  Thanks for dark and dreary fall!
Thanks for tears by now forgotten,
  Thanks for peace within my soul.

August Ludvig Storm, a Salvation Army officer, wrote these lines in 1891. The poem was first published in *Stridsropet* (The War Cry) on December 5, 1891. Each line of the Swedish stanzas begins with the word "Tack" (thanks) and identifies one thing for which the author expresses gratitude to God— springtime, fall, peace, answered prayers, storms, pain, pleasure, comfort, grace, love, roses and their thorns, home, fireside, hope, joy, and sorrow.

Storm, born in Sweden in 1862, lived in Stockholm most of his life. Converted in a meeting by the Salvation Army, he later became one of its leaders in Sweden. In 1899 Storm was afflicted with a crippling back illness that caused constant pain. During his last fifteen years he continued his work with the Salvation Army, preaching with great effectiveness and writing religious verse for their publications.

The Swedish hymn was published in the United States in 1910 by J.A. Hultman, who provided a new tune for Storm's text. As a lad Hultman had come with his family from Sweden and settled on a farm in Iowa. A gifted singer, he directed church music, published music, and composed more than five hundred hymns. He pastored congregations of the Evangelical Mission Covenant Church and was held in high esteem.

For the *Covenant Hymnal* (1930) Carl E. Backstrom made an English translation of the Swedish hymn, and it was published with Hultman's music. Backstrom, also a native of Sweden, emigrated with his parents in 1907. Ordained in the Evangelical Mission Covenant Church in 1928, he pastored churches in Iowa, Ohio, and Nebraska.

"Thanks to God for my Redeemer" has appeared in a number of evangelical hymnals in recent decades. Congregational singing is greatly enriched by this and other Swedish hymns such as "How Great Thou Art," "Day by Day and with Each Passing Moment," and "Children of the Heavenly Father."

WRITTEN IN
A THEOLOGICAL STORM

The church's one foundation
Is Jesus Christ her Lord;
She is his new creation,
By Spirit and the Word:

> *From heaven he came and sought her*
> *To be his holy bride,*
> *With his own blood he bought her,*
> *And for her life he died.*

The musical score of a 1941 motion picture introduced this hymn to many people in our country. In the final scenes of *One Foot in Heaven,* starring Fredric March and Martha Scott, the carillon bells in the tall gothic tower of the church pealed forth this melody, furnishing a thrilling climax to the story.

The words of the hymn were written by a twenty-seven-year-old Anglican priest who was assigned to a mission church in a small community adjacent to Windsor, England, where the Royal Castle is located. Samuel J. Stone wrote more than fifty hymns during his eight-year stay at Windsor, but only this one is widely known.

The circumstances that prompted Stone to write this hymn involved a major controversy in the Church of England. Oddly, the focal point of the theological storm was in South Africa and involved two bishops of the church. Bishop John Colenso of the province of Natal in South Africa, in his published writings, critically questioned some Old Testament writings. Bishop Gray of Capetown, along with other Anglican bishops, charged him with heresy and demanded his resignation. The battle between fundamentalists and liberals soon involved Anglican leaders throughout the British Empire.

Stone sided with Bishop Gray and wrote this hymn in 1866 in strong defense of the fundamentalist position. His references to "toil and tribulation, and tumult of her war," and also "By schisms rent asunder, by heresies distressed" (from a stanza seldom found in today's hymnals), do not deal with generalities, but with the donnybrook stirred up by the liberals.

The tune we associate with this hymn was written in 1864 for another text. The composer, Samuel S. Wesley, a grandson of Charles Wesley, was an outstanding English organist.

Wesley was extremely fond of fishing and was accused of accepting or rejecting organist's positions that were offered him according to the fishing opportunities of the vicinity. On one occasion he was driving with a young assistant to a certain town where he was to play a dedication service for a newly installed pipe organ. Wesley could not resist the temptation of a beautiful stream they crossed. He stopped to fish and sent his assistant ahead to play the service, instructing him to say that Wesley had been unavoidably detained.

A JOYOUS NOWELL

The first Nowell the angel did say
Was to certain poor shepherds in fields as they lay;
In fields where they lay, keeping their sheep,
On a cold winter's night that was so deep.
Nowell! Nowell! Nowell! Nowell!
Born is the King of Israel!

This joyful Christmas carol is of unknown origin. The words are from a collection dated 1823, and the music was published a decade later. Its form has remained basically unchanged for more than a century and a half. The opening line of stanza two contains an error that seems to have bothered no one. "They looked up and saw a star" credits the shepherds with having sighted the heavenly body, yet Scripture says only the wise men saw the star (Matt. 2), not the shepherds (Luke 2).

Questions have been raised about the authenticity of the tune. Some suggest that it is a second melody, a counter-melody, or a descant to another melody. Nonetheless, the sweeping "Nowells" in the refrain make this an exciting carol to sing.

The word "Nowell" is the Old English form of the Old French "Nouel." The Latin form was "Natalis," the Spanish "Natal," and the Italian "Natale." It was an expression of joy, originally shouted or sung to commemorate the birth of Christ. Geoffrey Chaucer, the fourteenth-century English poet, mentions the term in his "Franklin's Tale," providing evidence of the early usage of the word. Writing in Middle English, the language then spoken in London, Chaucer wrote:

Biforn him stant braun of the tusked swyn,
And "Nowell" cryeth every lusty man.

The "Nowells" should be sung during the Christmas season with great joy, making the rafters ring!

HEARD IN A JEWISH SYNAGOGUE

The God of Abraham praise,
All praised be his name,
Who was, and is, and is to be,
For aye the same!
The one eternal God,
Ere aught that now appears;
The First, the Last; beyond all thought
His timeless years!

Sometime about 1760 Thomas Olivers, a preacher associated with the Wesleys in England, visited the Jewish Great Synagogue in London. During the service he heard Cantor Meyer Lyon chant the Yigdal, a doxology of thirteen articles of the Hebrew faith, attributed to Daniel ben Judah Dayyan, a fourteenth-century rabbi. Olivers fashioned a poetic version of the Yigdal that could be sung to the traditional melody he had heard. Olivers named the tune "Leoni" for Cantor Lyon and published the words and music about 1770.

In the 1880s Rabbi Max Landsberg of Rochester, New York, felt that Olivers' version was not faithful to the Hebrew original, that too much had been added by Olivers. So the rabbi asked Rev. Newton Mann, minister of Rochester's First Unitarian Church, to attempt a more faithful translation. Landsberg was pleased with Mann's efforts, but the lines would not fit the tune "Leoni." William C. Gannett succeeded Mann at the Unitarian church in Rochester in 1889, and Rabbi Landsberg asked him to recast Mann's version to fit the tune. Gannett made an acceptable version that sang easily, and the opening line was "Praise to the living God."

So, we have two English versions of the Yigdal—Olivers' "The God of Abraham Praise" and the Mann-Gannett version, "Praise to the Living God," published in 1910. The only problem with the hymn in the hymnals of today (the 1990s) stems from the actions of well-intentioned editors who transferred Oliver's opening line to the Mann-Gannett version in the 1933 Presbyterian hymnal. So now, in some hymnals, both versions begin the same way.

SWEETEST CAROL EVER SUNG

The great Physician now is near,
The sympathizing Jesus;
He speaks the drooping heart to cheer,
Oh! hear the voice of Jesus.

While the word physician occurs several times in the New Testament, it is not used to refer to Jesus. The name, however, is appropriate for one who brought the dead back to life, healed the sick, cured leprosy, restored sight to the blind, and drove out evil spirits. Surely Christ was no ordinary physician but the great Physician, with extraordinary powers to heal, restore, make whole, and speak the "drooping heart to cheer."

William Hunter wrote these lines in 1859. Born in Ireland, he came to the United States with his parents when he was six years old. The family settled at York, Pennsylvania. Hunter went to Madison College, was ordained to the Methodist ministry, and was admitted to the Pittsburgh Methodist Conference. He was appointed to churches at Beaver and Brighton, and later served in the Virginia and East Ohio Conferences. For fifteen years he taught Hebrew and biblical literature at Allegheny College.

The author of more than 125 hymns, Hunter compiled and published three collections of hymns that were widely used. He was on the committee to revise the Methodist hymnal, but died in 1877, a year before the *Hymnal of the Methodist Episcopal Church* was published.

Several years after Hunter published "The Great Physician," John Stockton, a Methodist minister of the New Jersey Conference, discovered the hymn and wrote the music so closely associated with this text. Stockton served a number of Methodist churches in New Jersey. Though often suffering poor health, he ministered faithfully to his congregation.

A POPULAR IRISH MINISTER

The head that once was crowned with thorns
Is crowned with glory now;
A royal diadem adorns
The mighty Victor's brow.

The contrast between the shame and suffering experienced by Christ during his life on earth and his ultimate victory and eternal glory is reflected in the lines of this hymn. The interweaving of New Testament writings about Christ makes the hymn a magnificent tool for believers to affirm their faith and to praise Jesus Christ the Savior.

Thomas Kelly, the author of the hymn, was familiar with the classical and Oriental languages. He studied the Bible daily in the original languages—Hebrew and Greek. From his daily devotions and his study of Scripture came hymns that reflected strong biblical truth. The son of an Irish judge, Kelly was educated at Trinity College in Dublin. He first intended to follow his father into the legal profession, but his keen spiritual conviction changed his mind. He was ordained in the Church of Ireland in 1792.

At that time the spiritual tides of the Irish church were at a low level. Kelly's evangelical enthusiasm was looked upon with disdain by his fellow clergymen. The Archbishop of Dublin, in an effort to stifle him, forbade churches in the diocese to allow Kelly to preach in their pulpits. By 1800 Kelly had left the Irish church and become an independent minister. Fortunately, he was a man of considerable means who had married a woman from a wealthy family. With his own money he built a number of chapels, which he generously supported. For these chapels he published several hymn collections, the first in 1802, and the last in 1853, two years before his death. Of his 765 hymns, only a few remain in common usage in England and America. His other most frequently sung hymn is "Look, Ye Saints! The Sight Is Glorious."

Kelly was generous and shared of his wealth with the poor. At the time of the Great Famine (1845–49), when thousands died of starvation and fever and thousands fled abroad, he gave unselfishly. During the famine one man cheered up his wife with the words, "Hold up, Bridget, there's always Mister Kelly to pull us out of the bog after we've sunk for the last time." Services are still held in one of Kelly's chapels in Ireland, and his hymns that have survived into the last of the twentieth century are a tribute to this Irish preacher who lived his faith magnificently.

THE COMFORT OF
THE SHEPHERD PSALM

The King of love my Shepherd is,
Whose goodness faileth never;
I nothing lack if I am his
And he is mine forever.

Psalm 23 has been put into poetic form for singing more than any other Old Testament psalm. The beauty and simplicity of the Shepherd Psalm have made it a universal favorite. It is, no doubt, the most frequently read and the most frequently quoted portion of Scripture.

"The King of Love My Shepherd Is" is an attempt by Henry W. Baker to paraphrase the psalm poetically in the language and spirit of the Anglican church in the middle of the nineteenth century. The excellence of his work, first published in 1868, may be measured in that this hymn is found in hymnals used today by English-speaking congregations around the world. The only other version of the psalm that approaches its popularity is that from the 1650 Scottish Psalter which begins, "The Lord's my Shepherd, I'll not want."

Baker drew on the New Testament in converting the Old Testament psalm into a hymn. The third stanza makes reference to the parable of the lost sheep as found in Matthew 18. The line "Thy cross before to guide me" in the fourth stanza borrows from traditional language of the church rather than from Scripture. The fifth stanza refers to Holy Communion in the word "chalice." And in the final stanza, "Within thy house for ever" provides a strong emphasis on the church.

Henry W. Baker, the son of Vice-Admiral Sir Henry

Baker, was ordained in the Church of England in 1844. He became vicar of Monkland, England, in 1851 and remained there until his death in 1877. The Monkland building was a twelfth-century church that Baker carefully restored. In 1855 he added a new pipe organ. The small parish that he served made few demands on Baker, and being a man of independent means, he was able to devote his energies and time to other worthy causes.

Out of his great interest in hymns and hymn singing, Baker wrote more than thirty hymns, some of which were excellent translations from the Latin. But his most significant work was the preparation and development of *Hymns Ancient and Modern* (1861), an unofficial Anglican hymnal that has become a benchmark for English hymnody.

A MAN OF GREAT TALENTS

The Lord will come and not be slow,
His footsteps cannot err;
Before him righteousness shall go,
His royal harbinger.

John Milton, a remarkable man in seventeenth-century England, became one of her greatest poets. As a scholar at St. Paul's School in London, his literary talent was evident. When he was fifteen he began writing psalm paraphrases, one of which is the hymn "Let Us with a Gladsome Mind." After his graduation from Christ's College in Cambridge in 1632, he lived at Horton in Buckinghamshire with his retired father and was totally immersed in his studies for six years.

Milton's disciplined daily routine at Horton involved rising at four in the summertime (five in the winter), reading a chapter from the Hebrew Old Testament, and studying until noon. Then he would take an hour for exercising, dining, singing, and playing the organ; after which he would study again until six. He visited with friends until eight, then had a light supper, and retired at nine.

In 1638 he settled in London and became involved in political activity, being sympathetic with Oliver Cromwell and the Puritan cause. In 1648, because of the religious tensions involved in the conflict between Charles I and the Parliament, Milton made a metrical translation of nine psalms (80–88) based on the original Hebrew text. "The Lord Will Come and Not Be Slow" includes portions of Psalms 85, 82, and 86.

Psalm 85 is a plea for God's forgiveness for sins; Psalm 82 pleads for God to end wrongs and injustices under which the people suffer; and Psalm 86 pleads for God's intervention in time of trouble. Capturing the trust and confidence of the psalmist, Milton's hymn concludes:

> *For great thou art, and wonders great*
> *By thy strong hand are done:*
> *Thou in thy everlasting seat*
> *Remainest God alone.*

Milton felt that these verses were most relevant to the tension and turmoil in England. A parliamentary victory resulted in the execution of Charles I, the exile of his heir, Charles II, and the establishment of the Commonwealth under Cromwell.

A HYMN SUNG AT THE WEDDING OF ELIZABETH II

> *The Lord's my Shepherd, I'll not want*
> *He makes me down to lie*
> *In pastures green; he leadeth me*
> *The quiet waters by.*

This is the first of five stanzas of a poetic version of Psalm 23 that appeared in the Scottish Psalter of 1650. Converting prose psalms into poetic verse had begun more than a century earlier on the European continent through the encouragement of Martin Luther and John Calvin.

King James, king of Scotland before he also became king of England in 1603, was responsible for the version of the Bible that bears his name, which was published in 1611. He wrote much poetry and made poetic versions of the psalms.

Of the poetic versions of the psalms that we sing from our hymnals, none is more frequently used or more dearly loved than Psalm 23. Some of the versions we have are faithful renderings of the biblical prose form. The King James Version of Psalm 23 is in six verses and 118 words. The 1650 Scottish Psalter version given here is in five verses with 114 words. Nothing is taken away, nothing is added.

More and more the tune associated with this psalm in our hymnals is the one composed by Jessie Seymour Irvine in 1871. It is called "Crimond" for a village in the northeast of Scotland where Irvine's father was minister for thirty years and where she wrote the tune. Much of the popularity of this tune can be attributed to the use of both text and tune in the wedding of Elizabeth II and Prince Philip, Duke of Edinburgh, at Westminster Abbey on November 20, 1947. Through radio transmission of the service and through the press, the world became aware of a Scottish psalm text and a Scottish tune.

AN INVITATION HYMN FOR HIS PASTOR

The Savior is waiting to enter your heart,
  Why don't you let him come in?
There's nothing in this world to keep you apart,
  What is your answer to him?
Time after time he has waited before,
  And now he is waiting again
To see if you're willing to open the door,
  *Oh, how he wants to come in.**

Ralph Carmichael set a new style for unique arrangements of original and traditional material. One of his first ventures while still a student at Southern California College in Costa Mesa was the production of a television series, "The Campus Christian Hour," which won an Emmy in 1951. In 1950 Carmichael made his first Christian recording, and the following year he wrote the musical score for his first Billy Graham film, *Mr. Texas,* which was followed later by *For Pete's Sake, The Restless Ones,* and *His Land.*

In the 1950s Carmichael served as minister of music for the Temple Baptist Church in downtown Los Angeles. Here he organized a brass choir and conducted his first performance of Handel's *Messiah* with a two-hundred-voice choir and a symphony orchestra. In his scoring for his choirs he freely experimented with harmonies, rhythms, and sonorities that met with some criticism from traditional minds. It was at Temple Baptist Church that he wrote "The Savior Is Waiting" as an invitation hymn for his pastor, Dr. J. Lester Harnish.

Soon after "The Savior Is Waiting" was written, Carmichael went with Dr. Bob Pearce to Japan for some evangelistic crusades. One of the new songs included in the choir book was "The Savior Is Waiting." First in Osaka and then in Tokyo, a choir of six thousand was enlisted and trained. The singers were organized to provide one thousand singers at each evening meeting. "The Savior Is Waiting" was an instant favorite and was sung each evening as the invitation hymn. Those Americans who assisted in the crusades returned to their churches and taught the song to their congregations. To Carmichael's surprise, the popularity of the hymn spread like wildfire. It now appears in many hymnals both in America and around the world and has taken its place as a well-known invitation hymn along with "Just As I Am, Without One Plea" and "Have Thine Own Way, Lord."

A STIRRING TUNE WITH A MILITANT TEXT

The Son of God goes forth to war,
A kingly crown to gain;
His blood-red banner streams afar;
Who follows in his train?
Who best can drink his cup of woe,
Triumphant over pain,
Who patient bears his cross below,
He follows in his train.

The stoning of Stephen (Acts 7:58–60) and the words of Jesus spoken to the multitude and his disciples (Matt. 23:34–36) were in the mind of Reginald Heber when he wrote the hymn early in the nineteenth century. The Anglican minister pictured the long line of Christian disciples who would follow Jesus and Stephen to a martyr's death. In stanza one Jesus is portrayed as going forth to conquer the world. Then Heber asks the question, "Who follows in his train?" The answer is those who "drink his cup of woe," are "triumphant over pain," and patiently "bear his cross."

Stanza two pictures Stephen, who saw the glory of God as he was stoned to death, and said, "Behold, I see the heavens opened, and the Son of man standing on the right hand of God." Then follows the probing question, "Who follows in his train?" The final stanza moves from those followers of Christ at Pentecost, to the apostles and those across the centuries who gave their lives for faith. What a challenge to us to be steadfast, true to the faith, that we might follow those who have gone before.

Reginald Heber developed a keen interest in hymn writing as he served his parish at Hodnet. In 1819 he compiled a book of hymns suited to the Christian year of the Church of England. But he was unable to secure the approval of the Bishop of London for this hymnbook, because the Church of England allowed only the singing of metrical versions of Old Testament psalms at that time. In 1823 Heber was appointed Bishop of Calcutta, but he served for less than three years before his untimely death at the age of forty-three.

"All Saints, New" was composed for Heber's hymn by Henry S. Cutler in 1872. During two years' study in Germany and England he was impressed with the English Cathedral choirs of men and boys. He became organist at Boston's Church of the Advent and organized a choir of men and boys in 1852, the first robed choir in America. In 1860, while organist at Trinity Church in New York, Cutler used the visit of the Prince of Wales as the occasion to bring his choir of men and boys into the chancel for the first time wearing vestments.

DECLARING GOD'S GLORY

The stars declare his glory;
The vault of heaven springs
Mute witness of the Master's hand
In all created things,
And through the silences of space
Their soundless music sing. *

Timothy Dudley-Smith wrote the hymn in 1970, basing it on Psalm 19. Singing it brings reminders of earlier hymns such as Joseph Addison's "The Heavens Are Telling the Glory of God," and Isaac Watts's "The Heavens Declare Thy Glory, Lord." The concluding lines of the first stanza remind us of the line from Maltbie D. Babcock's "This Is My Father's World":

All nature sings, and round me rings
The music of the spheres.

The hymn is a fresh setting of Psalm 19, and after referring to God's world in stanza two and his Word in stanza three, it concludes with a petition that God who guides all nature will guide the lives of his children.

So order too this life of mine,
Direct it all my days;
The meditations of my heart
Be innocence and praise,
My rock, and my redeeming Lord,
In all my words and ways.

Timothy Dudley-Smith was born and reared in Derbyshire, England. His father was a schoolmaster. When Timothy was eleven his father died, and this was a turning point in Timothy's life. He felt called to the Christian ministry. He inherited his father's love for poetry, and during his student days at Cambridge University began writing verse. He was ordained in the Church of England in 1950 and worked as an

*Copyright © 1981 by Hope Publishing Company, Carol Stream, Ill. 60188. All rights reserved. Used by permission.

assistant pastor in the outskirts of London. Later he was given charge of a mission boys' club in Bermondsey. In 1955 he became the editor of *Crusade,* a monthly Christian magazine which was started as part of the follow-up of Billy Graham's 1955 crusade at Wembley Stadium. From 1959 to 1972, Dudley-Smith worked for the Church Pastoral-Aid Society, a home missionary society of the Church of England. His friendship with Michael Baughen, a young Anglican clergyman, began about this time. He and Baughen were involved in publishing several venturesome collections of hymns.

During this time Timothy and his wife, Arlette, lived at Sevenoaks, a town within commuting distance of London. It was here that "The Stars Declare His Glory" was written. In January of 1981, at St. Paul's Cathedral in London, Timothy Dudley-Smith was consecrated Bishop of Thetford, a suffragan (assistant) to the Bishop of Norwich. With his family he lives in the village of Bramerton, a suburb of Norwich. He carries out his ecclesiastical duties with warmth and understanding and continually adds to his hymnic writings.

THE BALM THAT HEALS THE SINSICK SOUL

There is a balm in Gilead to make the wounded whole;
There is a balm in Gilead to heal the sinsick soul.
Sometimes I feel discouraged,
And think my work's in vain,
But then the Holy Spirit
Revives my soul again.

The distinctive characteristics of Negro spirituals bring a rich and rewarding dimension to Christian song. Beginning in the early nineteenth century, they have been sung by black Americans in their social and religious gatherings. Only recently have spirituals been found in hymnals used by white congregations. Fifty years ago they were used largely as "fun songs," for banquets, parties, and recreational singing. Now they are increasingly accepted as worthy expressions of worship, praise, and Christian fellowship in congregational services.

Origins of the spirituals, such as this one, are obscure. They were born in the hearts of the slaves who found that singing eased the burden of their labor. For generations they were passed from father to son, mother to daughter, and grandparent to grandchild without being written down. The tunes were shaped and reshaped as individuals and families sang them "in their own way."

"There Is a Balm in Gilead" is based on a reference in the writings of Jeremiah, the Old Testament prophet. The Lord speaks through the prophet to inquire, "Is there no balm in Gilead; is there no physician there?" (Jer. 8:22). The song provides the answer—the reviving work of the Holy Spirit makes the wounded whole and heals the sinsick soul.

In biblical times the mountainous country east of the Jordan River was called Gilead and is mentioned eighty times in the Old Testament. The tribes of Gad, Manasseh, and Reuben occupied it. Gilead was famous for the healing quality of the fragrant, transparent, pale yellow ointment made from the gum of a tree peculiar to that area. The balm of Gilead was in demand far and wide, for it seemed to have mysterious, miraculous powers to heal the human body.

A SONG OF SALVATION

There is a fountain filled with blood
Drawn from Immanuel's veins:
And sinners, plunged beneath that flood,
Lose all their guilty stains.

Long a favorite of evangelicals, this hymn was written about 1771 by William Cowper, perhaps the greatest English poet of the eighteenth century. He once was offered the post of clerk of the journals for the House of Lords, but the dread of appearing before the House to stand examination resulted in mental illness and deep melancholia from which he was never free.

"There Is a Fountain Filled with Blood" reflects Cowper's complete dependence for time and eternity on the atoning work of Christ at Calvary. The scriptural basis is Zechariah 13:1, "In that day there shall be a fountain opened to the house of David and to the inhabitants of Jerusalem for sin and for uncleanness," and Revelation 7:14, "These are they which . . . have washed their robes, and made them white in the blood of the Lamb."

Various alterations have been made in the hymn. James Montgomery completely rewrote the first stanza, because he felt that Cowper represented the fountain as being filled up instead of springing up. John Julian felt that these alterations changed the whole meaning and character of the hymn. "The sustained confidence and rapture of Cowper are entirely lost," Julian said.

"Cleansing Fountain," the tune we use to sing Cowper's hymn, is called a "Western Melody" in most of the nineteenth-century American hymnals. This usually meant that the hymnal editors in Philadelphia, New York City, or Boston thought it had originated beyond the Appalachian Mountains, "way out west" in eastern Kentucky or Tennessee. The hymn is quite characteristic of the camp meeting songs of that era, with much repetition of both tune and text.

FOLKLIKE CAMP-MEETING HYMN

There is a name I love to hear,
I love to sing its worth;
It sounds like music in mine ear,
The sweetest name on earth.

Frederick Whitfield wrote these lines in 1855 when he was a student at Trinity College in Dublin, Ireland. Four years later he was ordained in the Church of England, and he served his church well until his death in 1904. In less than ten years after the hymn was written, it appeared in hymnals and songbooks published in America. Cast in four-line stanzas, the hymn was in the metrical form of Common Meter—first and third lines with eight syllables and second and fourth lines with six syllables. By far the majority of hymns in the mid-nineteenth century were in this same structure and could be sung to any of the Common Meter hymn tunes. Also, most of the hymn collections were printed with words only. The leader would announce the hymn and the name of the tune, and the congregation would join in singing.

In many churches, particularly on the Western frontier and in the rural areas in eastern states, there would be only one hymnal available. It would be used by the preacher or "singing deacon." The lines of the hymn would be "lined out" to the congregation one line at a time before they sang them.

The tune we use for Whitfield's hymn is of unknown origin. A refrain is part of the tune and is repeated after each stanza. It was not part of Whitfield's original hymn.

> *Oh, how I love Jesus,*
> *Oh, how I love Jesus,*
> *Oh, how I love Jesus,*
> *Because he first loved me.*

The tune may be found in many nineteenth-century American hymnals with any one of several Common Meter hymns for the stanzas, and all with the refrain, "Oh, how I love Jesus." Among those hymns most frequently found are John Newton's "Amazing Grace! How Sweet the Sound," Isaac Watts's "Alas, and Did My Savior Bleed," and Whitfield's hymn. Because of its simplicity and lilting style, the tune is typical of the folklike camp-meeting songs which emerged in America in the early nineteenth century.

A WALK THROUGH THE PARK

> *There is sunshine in my soul today,*
> *More glorious and bright*
> *Than glows in any earthly sky,*
> *For Jesus is my light.*
> *O there's sunshine, blessed sunshine,*
> *When the peaceful, happy moments roll;*
> *When Jesus shows his smiling face,*
> *There is sunshine in my soul.*

A warm spring day in Philadelphia provided the inspiration for these lines. Eliza Hewitt found great joy in walking through

Fairmount Park in that city. The brightness of the sunshine and the joy of the day, following months of anxiety and physical pain, brought forth poetic expression. Miss Hewitt was a public school teacher in her mid-thirties. One of her students, an incorrigible boy, had struck her across the back with a heavy slate. She suffered a severe injury and was placed in a large cast for six months.

After her long confinement, the doctor permitted her to go for a short walk in the park. She returned home with her heart overflowing and wrote these lines. The second stanza refers to "unsung" songs:

> *There is music in my soul today,*
> *A carol to my King,*
> *And Jesus, listening, can hear*
> *The songs I cannot sing.*

The music is the work of a gifted musician, John R. Sweney. A cornet player of extraordinary skill, he directed the Third Delaware Regiment Band after the outbreak of the Civil War. Later he was professor of music for twenty-five years at Pennsylvania Military Academy. His unusual ability as a song leader is evidenced by the demand for his leadership as music director in the summer religious assemblies. He composed over one thousand gospel songs and shared in compiling more than sixty collections of gospel songs, Sunday-school songs, and other types of songs.

THE PROMISE OF SHOWERS OF BLESSING

> *There shall be showers of blessing:*
> *This is the promise of love;*
> *There shall be seasons refreshing,*
> *Sent from the Savior above.*
> *Showers of blessing,*
> *Showers of blessing we need:*
> *Mercy drops round us are falling,*
> *But for the showers we plead.*

The hymn reflects God's promise to the children of Israel as recorded in Ezekiel 34:26: "And I will make them and the places round about my hill a blessing; and I will cause the shower to come down in his season; there shall be showers of blessing."

The author of this hymn, Daniel Webster Whittle, was named for the American statesman when he was born in 1840. He grew up in New England, but in his youth could not resist the excitement and the opportunities of the Western frontier. He moved to Chicago and secured a job with the Wells Fargo Bank. He became active in the Tabernacle Sunday School meeting on Chicago's west side. During that time he was converted. He later recalled that he "went into the vault and in the dead silence of the quietest of places I gave my life to my Heavenly Father to use as he would."

After serving in the Union Army during the Civil War, Major Whittle returned to Chicago, and in 1873 began to devote his full time to evangelistic work. Philip P. Bliss served as his music director until his tragic death in 1876; James McGranahan then worked with Whittle for more than a decade. In addition to being an effective evangelist, Whittle is credited with writing about two hundred hymns.

Whittle wrote "There Shall Be Showers of Blessing" in 1883, and James McGranahan composed the music. Words and music were published that year in one of the popular collections of gospel songs used in the Moody-Sankey evangelistic meetings in the last decades of the nineteenth century.

AN INSTANT COMPOSITION

There were ninety and nine that safely lay
In the shelter of the fold;
But one was out on the hills away,
Far off from the gates of gold;
Away on the mountains wild and bare,
Away from the tender Shepherd's care.

The evangelist Dwight L. Moody and his song leader, Ira D. Sankey, had completed some meetings in Glasgow, Scotland, in 1874 and were on their way to Edinburgh to begin a four-month campaign. Sankey bought a newspaper in the station, and as the train left Glasgow, he pored over each page, looking for news from America while Moody read the mail he had received from Chicago.

Sankey found no news of interest, but he did notice a poem that began "There were ninety and nine" by Elizabeth Clephane. It impressed him immediately, and he read it aloud to Moody. When he finished reading, he realized that Moody had not heard a word he had said. He clipped the poem from the newspaper and put it in his notebook.

In the second day's meeting in Edinburgh, Moody preached on the subject of "The Good Shepherd." Then he called on one of the local ministers to speak briefly and asked Sankey to sing something appropriate to close the meeting. A sense of panic struck Sankey for he had nothing in his notebook to fit the situation. Suddenly he remembered the poem he had taken from the newspaper and was impressed to sing it, even though no musical setting then existed.

When the speaker finished, Sankey moved to the reed organ, placed the clipping on the music rack, struck an A-flat chord, and proceeded to make up the melody as he sang it. To his surprise he made it through the first stanza. He wondered if he could remember the tune to sing it again for the other stanzas. Miraculously he did just that.

Moody was deeply moved and came to the organ. "Where did you get that hymn?" he asked Sankey. Sankey replied, "Why, it is the hymn I read to you on the train yesterday!"

COMPOSED FOR AN EASTER SERVICE

There's a call comes ringing o'er the restless wave,
  "Send the light! Send the light!"
There are souls to rescue, there are souls to save,
  "Send the light! Send the light!"

Charles H. Gabriel wrote both words and music in 1890 while he was serving as music director for the Grace Methodist Episcopal Church, San Francisco. He wrote it for the Easter service of the Sunday school. An official from the Methodist Board of Missions was present at the service and he took a copy of the song back home and introduced it to others. The following year it was published.

Gabriel, a native of Wilton, Iowa, grew up on the family farm. His parents, with three older children, had moved to Iowa from Virginia in 1850 and had purchased a quarter section of virgin land for $6.00 an acre. Gabriel's music training began in the singing schools where he learned to read the "fa sol la" syllables of the shape-note system. A quick learner, Gabriel soon began teaching in singing schools and helping others to learn to read music.

For three years he enjoyed working in San Francisco as music director for Grace Church. Then he began to devote more and more time to writing new songs. As his output increased he felt he should leave California and move closer to a music-publishing center.

In October of 1892, with a wife, a baby, and $16.00, Charles Gabriel moved to Chicago, where he opened a music studio in the Methodist Book Concern Building. He remained there for twenty-three years. Chicago was then the major center of gospel-music publishing, and the publishers recognized Gabriel's creative gifts and welcomed his songs. Here he also met evangelists and singing evangelists who became helpful, supportive friends for years to come.

Among his best-known hymns still found in many hymnals are: "I Stand Amazed in the Presence," "He Lifted Me," "Higher Ground," "Just When I Need Him Most," "He Is So Precious to Me," "Since Jesus Came into My Heart," and "O That Will Be Glory For Me."

THE LITTLE BROWN CHURCH
IN THE VALE

There's a church in the valley by the wildwood,
No lovelier spot in the dale;
No place is so dear to my childhood
As the little brown church in the vale.

A young man was on his way to visit his bride-to-be in Fredricksburg, Iowa. The stagecoach in which he rode stopped at Bradford, fourteen miles east of Fredricksburg. As William Pitts joyously anticipated seeing his beloved, he strolled about enjoying the trees, the lush greenery, and the rolling hills.

Of particular beauty was a wooded area in the valley formed by the Cedar River. In his imagination Pitts envisioned a church building there. Later he could not seem to erase the vision from his mind. Days later, back at home, he wrote a poem about the imagined church that began "There's a church in the valley by the wildwood," and set it to music in 1857.

Seven years later Pitts returned to teach music at the Bradford Academy. To his surprise he discovered a small church building being erected on the very spot where he had imagined one years before. It was painted brown because that paint was the cheapest. Pitts dug out the copy of his almost forgotten song. At the dedication of the new church building, his singing class from the academy sang it for the first time.

In 1865 Pitts sold the song to a Chicago music publisher for $25.00. The money helped Pitts enroll in Rush Medical College, but the song was forgotten. After graduation in 1868 Pitts returned to Fredricksburg, where he practiced medicine until his retirement in 1906.

By the turn of the century the village of Bradford had almost ceased to exist. The railroad through the country bypassed it and went through Nashua, two miles to the west. Weeds grew in the churchyard, and the dilapidated building was closed. A few years later the congregation experienced revival, and the church was opened and repainted its original color. Traveling musicians discovered Pitts's song, and its popularity spread through the country.

The Little Brown Church in the Vale has become a famous tourist attraction in Iowa. Standing in a picturesque rural setting among the pine trees, it is a favorite place for weddings. Each year several hundred couples, young and old, are married there. Following each ceremony the bride and groom together pull the rope that rings the church bell.

A HYMN WRITTEN IN
A DRUGSTORE

There's a land that is fairer than day,
And by faith we can see it afar;

> *For the Father waits over the way*
> *To prepare us a dwelling place there.*
> *In the sweet by and by,*
> *We shall meet on that beautiful shore.*

Sanford Bennett and Joseph Webster were friends. They lived in Elkhorn, Wisconsin, about seventy-five miles northwest of Chicago. Bennett had served as a second lieutenant in the 40th Wisconsin Volunteers and after the Civil War had returned to Elkhorn to open a drugstore. Because of his strong antislavery convictions, Webster had settled in Elkhorn before hostilities had broken out. He was a music teacher and played the flute, violin, and piano.

A very sensitive person, Webster frequently experienced periods of depression. When Webster walked into Bennett's store, Bennett could sense immediately whether his friend was depressed. He found he could help Webster break out of his moodiness by giving him a new song to work on.

One day, Webster strolled in, obviously despondent. When Bennett inquired as to the difficulty, Webster replied, "It's really nothing. It will be all right by and by."

The words struck Bennett immediately, and he replied, "The sweet by and by. That would make a great hymn." Sitting down at his desk in the drugstore, Bennett wrote down the words as they seemed to pour from his mind. He handed the sheet of paper to Webster, who brightened quickly. Webster reached for his violin, tuned it, and began to compose a melody for the hurriedly written words. In a few minutes the tune was completed, and he wrote it down on paper.

In less than thirty minutes from the time Webster had walked into the store in a melancholy mood, he and Bennett—and two customers who happened to be in the store—were heartily singing the new song, "The Sweet By and By."

It was first published in 1868 in Chicago in a small songbook for Sunday schools entitled *The Signet Ring*, and became exceedingly popular.

A STAR AND A SONG

There's a song in the air!
There's a star in the sky!
There's a mother's deep prayer
And a baby's low cry!
And the star rains its fire while the beautiful sing,
For the manger of Bethlehem cradles a King!

Josiah Holland, who wrote these lines, gave up a brief career as a medical doctor to start a weekly newspaper that lasted only six months. Later he became one of the founders of *Scribners' Magazine,* serving as its editor until his death in 1881. This familiar Christmas carol reflects his keen imagination and his sense of lyrical beauty. The song of the angels heard by the shepherds and the star in the East that the wise men saw are the two focal points of the carol. Each stanza concludes with a tribute to the kingship of the child in Bethlehem's manger.

The use of the word "boy" with reference to the Christ child is most unusual in Christmas-carol literature. It occurs in the third line of the second stanza:

For the virgin's sweet boy
Is the Lord of the earth.

The terms "babe," "baby," "child," and "infant" are more common.

In the third stanza Holland turns from the manger of Bethlehem to ponder the effect and influence of the "song and the star" in his own day.

In the light of that star
Lie the ages impearled;
And that song from afar
Has swept over the world.
Every hearth is aflame, and the beautiful sing
In the homes of the nations that Jesus is King!

The final stanza becomes a doxology of sheer joy and praise for the salvation Christ brings "that comes down through the night"—not Bethlehem's night long ago, but our night, our darkness. What a delightful Christmas carol.

IN PRAISE OF THE HOLY SPIRIT

There's a spirit in the air,
Telling Christians everywhere:
   "Praise the love that Christ revealed,
   Living, working, in our world."
Lose your shyness, find your tongue,
Tell the world what God has done:
   God in Christ has come to stay.
   We can see his power today.*

Here are two of Brian Wren's seven stanzas written in 1969 for Pentecost, celebrating the Holy Spirit "working in our world." Lines three and four in the above stanzas alternate as refrains in the remaining stanzas. This poetic device ties together the seven stanzas urging Christians to "tell the world what God has done."

Brian Wren was born in 1936 in Romford, Essex, near London. He became a Christian at the age of fifteen, began attending Sunday school in a Congregational church, and sang in the choir. At New College, Oxford, he majored in French, then studied theology at Mansfield College. Feeling called to the ministry, he was ordained and accepted the pastorate of a Congregational church in Essex County. During this five-year pastorate he established a strong rapport with his congregation and was greatly impressed by their response when they were challenged to stronger faith and action. From 1975 to 1980 Wren worked for the British Council of Churches as a consultant for adult theological education in local churches. For more than a decade he was associated with Third World First, an Oxford-based organization publicizing the needs of poverty-stricken nations of the Third World. More recently he has devoted his time and energies as a free-lance lecturer, author, and clinician in the areas of worship and hymnody. He and his family live near Oxford.

Brian Wren's hymn writing began during his student days at Mansfield College when he was encouraged by his friends Erik Routley and Peter Cutts. His hymn writing increased during his pastorate in Essex County. His hymns provoke Christians to action, merging an awareness of the greatness of God and the needs of humanity around the world.

THE DIMENSION OF GOD'S MERCY

There's a wideness in God's mercy
Like the wideness of the sea;
There's a kindness in his justice,
Which is more than liberty.

In this hymn, written more than a century ago, Frederick W. Faber speaks of the dimension of God's mercy in most extravagant terms. He is saying that it is impossible for man to measure the mercy of God, its width, its height, its depth. What is true of God's mercy is true of the love of God.

For the love of God is broader
Than the measure of man's mind;
And the heart of the Eternal
Is most wonderfully kind.

Born in England of Huguenot ancestry, Faber was ordained in the Church of England in 1837. A decade later, under the influence of John Henry Newman and the Oxford Movement, he joined the Catholic Church. He was rebaptized, took the name Wilfred, and founded a religious community in Birmingham, England. He moved this group to London in 1854, and it became a part of what was later known as Brompton Oratory.

The music we sing with this hymn was composed by a high-school girl who wrote it for her graduation service to be used with other words. Lizzie S. Tourjee was the daughter of Eben Tourjee, the founder of the New England Conservatory of Music in Boston and one of the most respected musicians of his day. After graduation from high school in Newton, Massachusetts, Lizzie attended Wellesley College. She named the tune for the college, and her father included it in the 1878 *Hymns of the Methodist Episcopal Church,* which he helped compile.

MY FATHER'S WORLD

This is my Father's world,
 And to my listening ears,
All nature sings, and round me rings
 The music of the spheres.
This is my Father's world,
 I rest me in the thought
Of rocks and trees, of skies and seas,
 His hand the wonders wrought.

In a time when space flights and satellites were fantasies in the minds of only a few, a Presbyterian preacher started congregations singing about the "music of the spheres." Maltbie D. Babcock was a native of Syracuse, New York. At Syracuse University he was a champion baseball pitcher and an outstanding varsity swimmer. His magnetic personality, his friendliness, and his high marks as a student made him a dynamic leader. Following a distinguished ministry in Baltimore, Babcock succeeded Henry van Dyke as pastor of New York City's Brick Presbyterian Church. While on a Mediterranean tour eighteen months later, he died in Naples, Italy.

Babcock's poetic verses were published in 1901, shortly after his sudden and untimely death, but it is thought this hymn had been written several years earlier. Babcock's central theme in these lines is God the Father. "Father" is seldom used for God in the Old Testament, but Jesus used it for God almost exclusively. Babcock sees the Father's hand not only in the "rocks and trees," "the skies and seas," "the morning light, the lily white," but also in man's social and economic activities:

O let me ne'er forget
That though the wrong seems oft so strong,
God is the ruler yet.

WORDS FITTED TO A TUNE

Thou, my everlasting portion,
More than friend or life to me;
All along my pilgrim journey,
Savior, let me walk with thee.
Close to thee, close to thee,
All along my pilgrim journey,
Savior, let me walk with thee.

Fanny Crosby, the gifted blind poet, wrote many lyrics for the gospel songs of the last half of the nineteenth century. Her output was astounding. With great ease she wrote poems about ideas that came to her in various ways. Some phrase she had heard in casual conversation would bring a moment's inspiration, and she soon would complete some lines and stanzas.

Her publisher would occasionally ask for a poem on a given subject. Sometimes these requested poems were written with difficulty, for she really needed some spark of inspiration to open the channels of her imagination. Sometimes a composer would play an original tune for her and ask her to write appropriate words. "Blessed Assurance, Jesus Is Mine," "Safe in the Arms of Jesus," and "Thou My Everlasting Portion" came into being in this way.

One day in 1874, Silas Vail sought out Fanny Crosby and played for her a new tune he had written. As she listened, Fanny smiled and said that the melody of the refrain said to her, "Close to thee, close to thee." In a matter of minutes the rest of the words took shape and the song was complete.

Born in Brooklyn, New York, Silas Vail as a youth learned the trade of hatmaking in Danbury, Connecticut. Later he settled in New York, and established his own hat-manufacturing company. He was greatly successful in this venture, but his first love was music. He composed songs and engaged in publishing with Horace Waters and W. F. Sherwin and others.

In 1874, in collaboration with Sherwin, Vail published a collection of songs that included "Thou My Everlasting Portion," or "Close to Thee," as it is often called. While Vail wrote many songs, only this one remains in many hymnals today.

FINISHED IN AN EARTHQUAKE

Through it all, through it all,
I've learned to trust in Jesus,
I've learned to trust in God;
Through it all, through it all,
*I've learned to depend upon his Word.**

In 1971 Andraé Crouch's reputation and fame were beginning to grow. He and the Disciples were touring full time. They traveled in a new van with the words "Take the Message Everywhere" painted on both sides. People began to throng to their concerts and their future seemed bright.

Andraé had enjoyed his independence as a single person and thought little of marriage. But a young woman joined the Disciples, was featured as a soloist, and sang duets with Andraé. Before he realized it, he was in love with her.

One Saturday she quit the group and left immediately to go overseas with another singing group. Andraé was devastated by her sudden and unexplained departure. The Disciples were scheduled to leave for other engagements in a few days, but Andraé was ready to cancel the whole trip. While in the depths of depression over the experience, he had a call from a close friend who had formerly played with the California Angels baseball team. The friend provided the very support and encouragement Andraé needed. After much conversation and prayer, Andraé called his tour manager and said, "Tell the group everything's cool. We're going on, praise the Lord!"

With an extraordinary sense of awareness of God's healing in the midst of hurt and sadness, Andraé sat down at the piano and began playing music inspired by the moment. The tune came first, then the words, and before long "Through It All" was on its way. Three weeks later he wanted to add a third stanza to the first two. He asked the Lord for a third stanza, and in the early morning of February 9, 1971, it came to him. Just as he finished writing it all down, at five o'clock in the morning, the room began to shake and an earthquake rocked the San Fernando Valley, killing sixty-four people and leaving damages of one billion dollars.

TRUSTING JESUS IN GREAT STRESS

'Tis so sweet to trust in Jesus,
*   Just to take him at his word;*
Just to rest upon his promise,
*   Just to know, "Thus saith the Lord."*
Jesus, Jesus, how I trust him!
*   How I've proved him o'er and o'er!*
Jesus, Jesus, precious Jesus!
*   O for grace to trust him more!*

Louisa Stead stood on the beach with her four-year-old daughter and watched her husband drown as he tried to rescue a child in the waters off Long Island, New York. The loss of her husband and persistent health problems brought a testing time in her life. Out of these experiences came the writing of "'Tis So Sweet to Trust in Jesus," an expression of faith inspired by her confidence in a loving heavenly Father at a time of great sorrow and desperate need.

Born in Dover, England, Louisa came to the United States in 1871 to visit friends in Cincinnati, Ohio. At a camp meeting in Urbana, Ohio, she offered herself for missionary service in China, but her frail physical condition prevented her appointment. Left without sufficient support following the death of her husband, she and her daughter experienced poverty and hunger. One morning she found that someone had left food and money on her doorstep. The Lord had answered her prayer. She responded in poetic verse, "'Tis so sweet to trust in Jesus."

Later her health improved and, with her daughter, Lily,

she went as a missionary to the Cape Colony in South Africa, where she served for fifteen years. During this time she married Robert Wodehouse, a South African Methodist minister. They returned to the United States for a short time for the sake of Louisa's health but in 1901 were appointed to the Methodist Mission in Umtali, on the eastern border of Southern Rhodesia (now Zimbabwe). Years later Louisa Wodehouse retired but remained in Africa. She died in 1917 at her home in Penhalonga, about fifty miles north of Umtali. She was buried in a grave hewn out of solid rock, on the side of Black Mountain near her African home.

In some unknown manner, the words of the poem "'Tis So Sweet to Trust in Jesus" came to the attention of William J. Kirkpatrick, a Philadelphia music publisher and gospel song composer. He wrote the tune and published the hymn in 1882. It remains a favorite among many congregations around the world as an expression of praise to Jesus Christ and a prayer for "grace to trust him more."

A "NEWFOUND" SONG

To God be the glory, great things he hath done;
So loved he the world that he gave us his Son,
Who yielded his life an atonement for sin,
And opened the lifegate that all may go in.
Praise the Lord! Praise the Lord!
Let the earth hear his voice!
Praise the Lord! Praise the Lord!
Let the people rejoice!
O come to the Father, through Jesus the Son,
And give him the glory, great things he hath done.

In preparation for the 1954 Billy Graham Greater London Crusade, music director Cliff Barrows was compiling a songbook to be used in the singing by the participants. Someone in London suggested that "To God Be the Glory" be included. Barrows did not know the song, but on the strong recommendation of some English advisers, he included it in the songbook. At Harringay it became a favorite hymn. Delighted with this "newfound" song, Barrows returned to the states and later introduced it in the 1954 crusade in Nashville, Tennessee, where it was sung enthusiastically in Vanderbilt University's football stadium.

This was by no means a new song, and it did not originate in England. It is an American gospel song written by Fanny J. Crosby, with the music composed by William Howard Doane of Cincinnati.

Intended as a song for Sunday school children, "To God be the glory" was originally entitled "Praise for Redemption" and was first published in a small collection in 1875. Compilers of subsequent collections of gospel songs seemed to have overlooked this song, and for eighty years it was forgotten. Crosby's text is in an objective style rarely found in her gospel-song lyrics. Here is a straightforward expression of praise to God, rather than a poem in her usual subjective style. The refrain of Doane's tune, with the repeated "Praise the Lord! Praise the Lord!" provides the worshiper an opportunity for exuberant praise.

PRAISE HIM FOR HIS MIGHTY ACTS

To God be the glory,
To God be the glory,
To God be the glory,
 For the things he has done.
With his blood he has saved me;
With his power he has raised me;
To God be the glory,
 *For the things he has done.**

Andraé Crouch was born in Los Angeles. He and his family attended Emmanuel Church of God in Christ where his great uncle, Bishop Samuel Crouch, was pastor. When he was a lad, Andraé urged his parents to purchase a piano for the home, and soon his musical gifts became evident. He began playing for church services. During his high-school days he began a choir at Christ Memorial Church in San Fernando Valley, a church established by his father. After graduation, Andraé attended Valley Junior College for a year, then was employed by RCA Computers. All this time he continued playing and singing and directing the choir in his father's church.

For several years he worked with the Teen Challenge Center, a rehabilitation center for drug addicts in Los Angeles. There he directed the addicts' choir. He became a part-time student at L.I.F.E. Bible College and while there sharpened his technique of memorizing Scripture by setting it to music. He formed a group of singers called the Disciples and began doing programs in churches. Andraé had met Tim Spencer, president of Manna Music, and through him met Ralph Carmichael, president of Lexicon Music and Light Records. Carmichael heard Andraé and the Disciples sing and immediately set up a recording session. The album that resulted thrust Andraé and the Disciples into the spotlight, and soon they were nationally known. In the years following, Andraé and the Disciples toured the United States, Canada, England, Ireland, Europe, South Africa, Australia, and the Far East. Crouch received Grammy Awards from the National Academy of Recording Arts and Sciences in 1975, 1978, and 1979. The group has appeared in some of the great music halls of the world: Sydney Opera House in Australia, Carnegie Hall in New York City, and the finest halls of Europe and Asia.

"My Tribute" was written in 1971 and was published by Lexicon Music. It is the most popular of his compositions, which also include: "Bless His Holy Name," "Soon and Very Soon," "I've Got Confidence," and "Through It All."

BORN IN SLAVERY

Trials dark on every hand,
And we cannot understand
All the ways that God would lead us
To that blessed Promised Land;
But he'll guide us with his eye,
And we'll follow 'til we die;
We will understand it better
By and by.

The hymn "We'll Understand It Better By and By" was written, words and music, by Charles Albert Tindley in 1905. (See "Nothing between my soul and the Savior," page 189, for the details of his life.) The stanza beginning "Trials dark on every hand" was originally the third stanza; the first stanza began "We are often tossed and driven." Gifted as a songwriter, Tindley also wrote words and music for "Nothing Between," "Stand by Me," and "Leave It There."

Tindley became a prominent figure in the religious and community life of Philadelphia. He preached to throngs of people, both multiracial and multicultural. Always the climax of Tindley's services was the "altar call," when penitents were summoned to kneel and seek forgiveness for their sins. One time a young white man, his eyes bleary from drinking, knelt at the altar with Tindley, and the two whispered at length to each other. Then Tindley, with his arm around the young man, said to the congregation, "I want you to know this young man who has just given his heart to God. He is the grandson of the Maryland planter who once owned me as a slave!"

Tindley's song "I'll Overcome Some Day," written in 1901, served as a basis, in spirit and thought, for the popular civil rights song, "We Shall Overcome."

THE RADIANT FAITH OF
A LUTHERAN PASTOR

Wake, awake for night is flying;
The watchmen on the heights are crying,
Awake, Jerusalem, at last!
Midnight hears the welcome voices
And at the thrilling cry rejoices:
Come forth, ye virgins, night is past!
The Bridegroom comes, awake;
Your lamps with gladness take:
Alleluia!
And for his marriage feast prepare,
For ye must go to meet him there.

Advent anticipates Christmas, remembers the first coming of Christ, and claims the hope of his second coming. Appropriate for the Advent season is the hymn written by Philip Nicolai in the winter of 1597. As pastor of the Lutheran church in the town of Unna, Westphalia (now West Germany), he had witnessed the bubonic plague strike his town. In six months more than thirteen hundred people had died. Nicolai's parsonage overlooked the churchyard, where sometimes he conducted thirty funerals in a day. Faithfully ministering to his flock, he comforted them in their sorrow.

During these days Nicolai kept a record of his daily meditations and published them in 1599 under the unusual title, "Mirror of Joys." Three hymns were included in this book; one of them was "Wake, Awake for Night Is Flying." The radiant faith of this Lutheran pastor shines through these lines as one reads them against the background of the extraordinary circumstances in which they were written. With these hymns Nicolai wished to comfort his bereaved flock as the bodies of their loved ones and neighbors were borne to the churchyard for burial. For believers there is the promise of heaven in death and the reality of being in the presence of Christ, the Bridegroom.

The tune for the hymn, "Wachet Auf," was also composed by Nicolai and included with the text in the 1599 songbook. Long referred to as the "King of the Chorales," it is one of the choicest of the hymn tunes of Lutheran tradition. The English translation of Nicolai's German text was made in 1858 by Catherine Winkworth, one of numerous translations of this hymn.

THE WATCHMAN ON THE WALL

Watchman, tell us of the night,
What its signs of promise are.
Traveler, o'er yon mountain's height
See that glory-beaming star!
Watchman, doth its beauteous ray
Aught of joy or hope foretell?
Traveler, yes; it brings the day,
Promised day of Israel.

John Bowring's hymn is based on Isaiah 21:11–12. Isaiah's dramatic account involves a dialogue between a watchman standing on the wall of Jerusalem and an unseen inquirer. In the impenetrable darkness of night, a voice calls out for information. The watchman, with some uncertainty, reports signs of morning to come. He suggests that the inquirer leave and return later for more information.

Bowring was aware of the signs that predicted the end of a long night in human history and the dawning of a better day for humankind. Having served in Parliament beginning in 1835, he was appointed a government official in China, then became governor of Hong Kong. He was knighted by Queen Victoria in 1854. Drawing on the watchman incident reported by Isaiah, Bowring reflects his confidence in Christ's return to the world and in Christ's victory over Satan, the prince of darkness. Bowring's unswerving faith is evident in the final four lines of the third stanza of the hymn.

Watchman, let thy wanderings cease;
Hie thee to thy quiet home!
Traveler, lo, the Prince of Peace,
Lo, the Son of God is come!

Bowring's father was a manufacturer of woolen goods in England. At the age of fourteen, Bowring left school to help his father in the business. He had the opportunity to travel abroad because the business involved world trade. He became one of the outstanding linguists of his day. His extensive writings were published in thirty-six volumes.

CHRISTIAN FAITH OF THE DUTCH PEOPLE

We gather together to ask the Lord's blessing,
He chastens and hastens his will to make known;
The wicked oppressing now cease from distressing,
Sing praise to his name, he forgets not his own.

To fully understand this anonymous Dutch hymn, it is necessary to know its historical setting. Toward the end of the sixteenth century, the Dutch were praying to God for freedom from Spanish oppression. Philip II had become sovereign of Spain, the Netherlands, and some other parts of Europe and hoped to unify all this area, improve its financial status, and strengthen Catholicism. He did not consider the impact of the Protestant Reformation on all of Europe.

William the Silent, prince of Orange, led the revolt of the Netherlands against the demands of Philip II. Although he was quite eloquent in speaking, his adversaries called him "the Silent," accusing him of being secretive about his strategies and plans. In 1609 a truce was reached as the struggle for political freedom from Spain and religious freedom from the Roman Catholic Church came to a stalemate. The truce of twelve years gave the Protestants in the Netherlands opportunity to increase their strength and their resources. Frederick Henry became governor and commander-in-chief in 1625. A brilliant politician and a capable military leader, his leadership resulted in peace in the Netherlands in 1646.

The turmoil and turbulence of these early years can be read into the lines of the Dutch hymn that dates from the early seventeenth century. The Dutch were grateful to God and "gathered together to ask the Lord's blessing." The sturdy Christian faith of the Dutch people is clearly seen in the hymn. The opposition of the enemy only served to strengthen their trust in God's providence and care, as they exhorted each other to "sing praise to his name, he forgets not his own." This is the promise that they claimed.

The Dutch text and tune were included in a collection published in Haarlem, the Netherlands, in 1626. After this the hymn was forgotten for 250 years until a Viennese musician, Edward Kremser, discovered it and published it in Vienna in 1877. The English translation was made in 1894 by Theodore Baker, literary editor for G. Schirmer, Inc., a New York music publisher.

A HYMN INSPIRED BY RUINS

We meet you, O Christ,
In many a guise;

*Your image we see
   In simple and wise.
You live in a palace,
   Exist in a shack.
We see you, the gardener,
   A tree on your back.**

Fred Kaan wrote the hymn in 1966 when he was writing the script for a BBC television program as a part of the series "Seeing and Believing." Telecast on Passion Sunday that year, the program coincided with the twenty-fifth anniversary of the German air raid that destroyed the city of Plymouth, England. The program theme was "The Tree Springs to Life," and there was a photograph of the ruins of Plymouth's St. Andrew's Church, where a small apple tree had miraculously pushed its way through a heap of stones and rubble in the nave and was in blossom. At that time, Kaan was serving as minister of the Pilgrim Congregational Church in Plymouth.

Born in the Netherlands in the city of Haarlem, Kaan remembers vividly his childhood years during the Nazi occupation of Holland. At the age of eighteen Kaan came into the Netherlands Reformed Church and soon felt a call to the ministry. Through the Boy Scouts he became a pen pal with a boy living in the outskirts of London. The British boy's father, a devout deacon in the Congregational church was the influence that led Kaan into the Congregational ministry.

Ordained in 1955, Fred Kaan was called to the Windsor Road Congregational Church in Barry, South Wales. During his eight years at Barry he developed a growing interest in establishing friendships and relationships with people in many parts of the world. In 1961 he attended the International Congregational Council of Rotterdam and was caught up in a greater awareness of worldwide Christian fellowship. In the next two decades he visited more than seventy countries and established a network of friends around the world. *The Hymn Texts of Fred Kaan,* published by Hope Publishing Company in 1985, includes almost 150 hymns by this extraordinary person.

A HYMN OF THE ENVIRONMENT

We plow the fields and scatter
The good seed on the land,
But it is fed and watered
By God's almighty hand.
He sends the snow in winter
The warmth to swell the grain,
The breezes and the sunshine,
And soft, refreshing rain.
All good gifts around us
Are sent from Heaven above;
Then thank the Lord, O thank the Lord
For all his love.

In 1776 Matthias Claudius served as one of the commissioners of agriculture in Darmstadt, Germany. By 1782, when he wrote the hymn, he had become a newspaperman and literary editor in Wandsbek, near Hamburg. He loved the land and he loved the people. He loved the fall of the year when the crops are harvested. To picture this, he wrote a sketch entitled "Paul Erdmann's Fest," which described a scene in a farmhouse in northern Germany when the neighbors gather for a celebration. In the course of the festivities, the farm folk sing the "Peasant's Song." It consisted of thirteen stanzas, each sung by a different person, with the entire group joining heartily in the refrain "All good gifts around us."

Through this poem Claudius reminds us that God provides not only the land, but also the snow of winter, the warmth of spring, the sunshine and rain, all of which make the land productive. As an extra measure of blessing, Claudius points out in the second stanza, God provides the wayside flower and the evening star; he feeds the birds and "to us, his children, he gives our daily bread."

A respected man of letters, Matthias Claudius made his home in Wandsbek. He enjoyed the close friendship of the Danish crown prince (later King Frederick VI), who gave Claudius an annual grant. Because of the Napoleonic wars Claudius fled his home in 1813 but returned a year later and spent his final months in Hamburg. He died there in 1815 at the age of seventy-five.

By 1800, verses from Claudius' "Peasant's Song" were in the school hymnbooks and had become widely known in Germany. In 1861 Jane Campbell, daughter of an Anglican minister, discovered the German hymn and paraphrased it into English verse. Her paraphrase joyfully captures the rural simplicity and the folk quality of the original verse.

REVIVE US AGAIN

We praise thee, O God! For the Son of thy love,
For Jesus who died, and is now gone above.
Hallelujah! Thine the glory,
Hallelujah! Amen!
Hallelujah! Thine the glory,
Revive us again.

A Scottish minister wrote the words and a onetime choirboy at Westminster Abbey composed the music for the hymn. It has been identified with American revivalism for over a century. William Mackay studied medicine at the University of Edinburgh and became a successful physician. After several years, however, he felt God's call to the ministry and was ordained in the Presbyterian Church of Scotland. Mackay wrote the words of the hymn in 1863, about the time he entered the ministry. The hymn is based on Habakkuk 3:2, "O Lord, revive thy work in the midst of the years."

John J. Husband, composer of the tune, was a native of Plymouth, England. For six years he was a choirboy at Westminster Abbey and participated in the grand performances and magnificent music sung there. When he was forty he came to the United States and became a successful music teacher. In 1809 he settled in Philadelphia, where he taught music and led the singing at St. Paul's Protestant Episcopal Church until his death in 1825. He was highly respected as a churchman and as a music teacher.

Ira D. Sankey, whose name is synonymous with the gospel-song tradition of the late-nineteenth century, found this tune with these words to be extremely popular in his meetings. The music of the refrain lends itself to vigorous singing by throngs of people. The hallelujahs add much excitement to the song. In spite of some less than appropriate parodies of the refrain text, the song has retained much of its popularity and still serves well to emphasize the church's renewal.

NEW WORDS FOR AN OLD TUNE

We praise thee, O God, our Redeemer, Creator,
In grateful devotion our tribute we bring.
We lay it before thee, we kneel and adore thee,
We bless thy holy name, glad praises we sing.

Julia Cady Cory, who wrote the words of the hymn, was born in New York City. Her father was J. Cleveland Cady, a distinguished architect. The Cady family attended faithfully the services of the Church of the Covenant, and her father served as superintendent of the Sunday school for fifty-three years. As a student she had written a number of hymns and Christmas carols. Because of her writing, J. Archer Gibson, organist at the Brick Presbyterian Church in New York City, asked her to write a new text to fit an old Dutch tune called "Kremser." She completed the hymn and it was sung at the Thanksgiving services at both the Church of the Covenant and Brick Presbyterian Church. First published in a hymnal in New York in 1910, it is found in most hymnals today.

The earlier text for the Dutch tune was "We gather together to ask the Lord's blessing," an English translation of a German translation of the Dutch text. Through the last of the sixteenth century and well into the seventeenth century, the Low Countries had suffered much from Spanish oppression. The Dutch hymn expressed for these Christian people their trust in God and petitioned God to intervene with the enemy to relieve their suffering.

The hymn, published in Holland in 1626, remained virtually unknown for more than 150 years. In 1877 Edward Kremser, conductor of a men's singing society in Vienna, Austria, published a collection of six songs for men's chorus and orchestra. The Dutch tune with a German translation of the text, from the Dutch collection of 1626, was one of the six songs.

THE CIVIL RIGHTS
NATIONAL ANTHEM

We shall overcome, we shall overcome,
We shall overcome someday!
Oh, deep in my heart I do believe
We shall overcome someday!

The song that experienced almost instant popularity in the early 1960s civil rights movement had its roots in a song by Charles Albert Tindley, a Methodist minister in Philadelphia. Tindley wrote "I'll Overcome Someday" in 1901, and in spirit more than in words or music, it provided the basis for "We Shall Overcome." As Tindley's song was passed along in the oral tradition, it underwent many alterations so that the form in which it appeared in the early 1960s was quite different from the 1901 version.

A variant of the song was sung in 1946 on picket lines in Charleston, South Carolina, by members of Local 15 of the Food and Tobacco Workers Association. They were striking to increase their wages of forty-five cents an hour. Two members of this union came to the Highlander Folk School, then operating at Monteagle, Tennessee, and shared this song. From Tennessee the song spread quickly and many people altered the tune and the words. Folk singers, including Zilpnia Horton, Frank Hamilton, Guy Carawan, and Pete Seeger, added stanzas and shaped the notes. Among the many stanzas that were added are those beginning "The Lord will see us through," "The truth shall make us free," "We shall live in peace," "We are not afraid," "We'll walk hand in hand," "We shall all be free," and "The whole wide world around." Called "The Marseillaise" of the civil rights movement, it spread by word of mouth with phenomenal speed since there were at first no printed copies or recordings.

The Reverend Wyatt Tee Tucker, an associate of Dr. Martin Luther King, Jr., said in the summer of 1963 (as reported in the *New York Times*): "One cannot describe the vitality and emotion this hymn evokes across the Southland. I have heard it sung in great mass meetings with a thousand voices singing as one. I've heard half a dozen sing it softly behind the bars of the Hinds County prison in Mississippi. I've heard old women singing it on the way to work in Albany, Georgia. I've heard the students singing it as they were dragged away to jail. It generates power that is indescribable. It manifests a rich legacy of musical literature that serves to keep body and soul together for that better day which is not far off."

The tremendous appeal and power of the song, regarded by many as the greatest freedom song, is difficult to describe. One of the leaders of the Southern Christian Leadership Conference commented, "You really have to experience it to understand the kind of power it has for us. When you get through singing it, you could walk over a bed of hot coals, and you wouldn't even feel it!"

AN AWFUL MOMENT IN THE WORLD'S HISTORY

Were you there when they crucified my Lord?
Were you there when they crucified my Lord?
Oh! Sometimes it causes me to tremble.
Were you there when they crucified my Lord?

Here is one of the best-known and most widely sung Afro-American spirituals. This unique category of songs emerged in the South in the nineteenth century. "Were You There" was described by Marian Anderson as the most deeply emotional song she knew, for she felt that it captured "all the terror and tragedy of that awful moment in the world's history."

Today's hymnals include three or four of the several stanzas that have been associated with this spiritual. Some of these are: "Were you there when they nailed him to the tree," "Were you there when they pierced him in the side," "Were you there when the sun refused to shine," "Were you there when he bowed his head and died," and "Were you there when they laid him in the tomb." The stanza which begins "Were you there when he rose up from the grave" is not a part of spiritual tradition, for this is a song of the passion of our Lord, not his resurrection. There is no mention of the resurrection in this song in any of the early collections of spirituals. Nor does the resurrection stanza fit the mournful music and mood of the song.

Black slaves identified with Jesus' suffering and death on the cross. James Cone suggests that his death was a "symbol of their suffering, trials, and tribulations in an unfriendly world. They knew the agony of rejection and the pain of hanging from a tree." Though spirituals were known early in the nineteenth century, their popularity emerged after the Civil War. Groups of students from Fisk University, Hampton Institute, and Tuskegee Institute sang these songs around the world.

The version of "Were You There" most familiar to us first appeared in 1907 in a small collection of spirituals published in Nashville, Tennessee, by two brothers, John W. Work, Jr., and Frederick J. Work. We are indebted to them for this moving song of our Lord's crucifixion. As we sing it, we ponder thoughtfully what happened at Calvary.

A HYMN OF MISSIONARY ZEAL

We've a story to tell to the nations,
That shall turn their hearts to the right,
A story of truth and mercy,
A story of peace and light.
For the darkness shall turn to dawning,
And the dawning to noonday bright,
And Christ's great kingdom shall come on earth,
The kingdom of love and light.

The modern evangelical missionary movement emerged at the turn of the nineteenth century. William Carey went from England to India in 1793, Adoniram Judson went from America to Burma in 1813, David Livingstone went from England to Africa in 1841, and many others followed these pioneers. This missionary activity inspired the writing of numerous hymns that reflected the missionary spirit.

Henry Ernest Nichol of Yorkshire, England, felt the fervent missionary zeal and wrote both words and music for "We've a Story to Tell to the Nations" in 1896. It is based on the Great Commission that Jesus Christ gave his disciples: "Go ye therefore, and teach all nations" (Matt. 28:19).

Nichol planned to be a civil engineer, but his love for music was too strong to be denied. He received a music degree from Oxford University in 1888 and taught music and directed choirs for a number of years. He had great interest in the Sunday school movement and composed more than one hundred hymns and tunes for anniversaries. For most of these Nichol gave his name as the composer of the music, but for the author of the words he used a pseudonym, "Colin Sterne," a rearrangement of the letters of his middle and last name.

EVERLASTING ARMS

What a fellowship, what a joy divine,
Leaning on the everlasting arms;
What a blessedness, what a peace is mine,
Leaning on the everlasting arms.

Anthony J. Showalter was a young preacher and singing-school teacher active in several Southern states in revivals and singing schools. In 1888 he conducted a revival meeting in Hartselle, Alabama. While there he received letters from two men who had attended a singing school he had conducted in South Carolina a few weeks earlier. From the letters Showalter learned the tragic news that the wives of both of these men had died. Showalter thought he should write both of them to express his sympathy and love.

As he thought about what he might say, a biblical promise came to his mind: "The eternal God is thy refuge and underneath are the everlasting arms" (Deut. 33:27). He could think of no hymn based on this promise, so he began to piece together a song. The simple lines of the refrain and the melody took shape first.

Leaning, leaning,
Safe and secure from all alarms;
Leaning, leaning,
Leaning on the everlasting arms.

Showalter wrote the melody for the stanzas, but hard as he tried, he could not complete the stanzas for the hymn. He then wrote to Elisha A. Hoffman, a minister and writer of hymn texts, asking if he would supply the needed stanzas. Several weeks later, while Showalter was in a revival meeting at the Pine Log Methodist Church in Bartow County in northwest Georgia, Hoffman's letter containing the stanzas arrived. That evening in the revival service, Showalter sang the completed hymn for the first time.

A native of Virginia, Showalter received his early music training from his father, then attended the music normals conducted by the Ruebush-Kieffer Music Company in Singers Glen, Virginia. In 1880 he began teaching music schools, and after moving to Dalton, Georgia, to establish a branch office for the Ruebush-Kieffer firm, he began his own publishing business. He subsequently published more than sixty collections of music, of which more than two million copies were sold. In 1895 Showalter spent a year studying music in England, France, and Germany. A leading member of the First Presbyterian Church of Dalton, he served for many years as music director. He died in 1924 at the age of sixty-six.

A CANADIAN WHO HELPED
THOSE IN NEED

What a friend we have in Jesus,
All our sins and griefs to bear!
What a privilege to carry
Everything to God in prayer!
Oh, what peace we often forfeit,
Oh, what needless pain we bear,
All because we do not carry
Everything to God in prayer.

Joseph Scriven was ill in his little white frame cottage in Port Hope, Canada. A friend who came by to lend a helping hand happened to see a handwritten poem on the table. He asked Scriven if he had written it, and the elderly man replied, "The Lord and I did it between us."

Born in Seapatrick, County Down, Ireland, Scriven was educated at Trinity College in Dublin. His father was a captain in the Royal Marines, and young Joseph, dreaming of a military career, attended Addiscombe Military Seminary in London. However, poor health changed his plans. In 1844, at the age of twenty-five, he went to Canada. For a while he taught school; then he became a tutor to the Pengelley family who lived at Rice Lake, near Port Hope.

While he did not possess much of this world's goods, Scriven devoted his spare time to performing menial work for those who were physically handicapped and financially destitute. He was often seen striding along with a bucksaw over his shoulder on his way to cut firewood for someone in need.

Twice he experienced great personal tragedy. In England his bride-to-be drowned the evening before their wedding. It was to get away from this painful experience that he had gone to Canada. Then in Canada a romance developed, but before he and Eliza Roche could be married, she died suddenly after a brief illness in 1855.

Scriven wrote his mother in Ireland of the tragic death of Eliza and sent the poem "What a Friend We Have in Jesus," written in the time of his own grief, yet meant to comfort her.

In later years Scriven experienced considerable hardship. With failing health, meager income, and the fear of becoming physically helpless, he became very despondent. On October 10, 1886, the community of Bewdley, ten miles north of Port Hope, was shocked at the discovery of Scriven's body in the flume of a dam near Rice Lake. It was never known whether his death was an accident or suicide.

The widespread popularity of his hymn prompted the community to erect a large monument at Scriven's unmarked grave in the Pengelley family cemetery. The monument bears the stanzas of the hymn and stands as a tribute to this Irish-born immigrant whose hymn of the comforting friendship of Jesus is sung around the world in many languages.

A TUNE NAMED FOR A LADY

What Child is this, who, laid to rest,
On Mary's lap is sleeping?
Whom angels greet with anthems sweet,
While shepherds watch are keeping?
This, this is Christ the King,
Whom shepherds guard and angels sing:
Haste, haste to bring him laud,
The babe, the son of Mary.

William Chatterton Dix wrote these lines to fit the delightful English folk melody called "Greensleeves." Dating from 1580, the melody bears the name of Lady Green Sleeves and is used for both secular and sacred texts. It was mentioned by Shakespeare in *The Merry Wives of Windsor* and also by other writers, indicating that it was both well known and well loved.

Dix, a devout layman in the Church of England, possessed unusual talent for poetic expression and sought seriously to use his gifts for writing hymns and carols. The son of a surgeon in Bristol, England, he was educated at Bristol Grammar School for a mercantile career, but later became manager of a marine insurance company in Glasgow. Among his writings are hymns and carols, translations of Greek and Abyssinian works, two devotional works, and a book of instruction for children. "What Child Is This" was written about 1865.

In the second stanza Dix looks at the child in the manger, yet sees the cross at Calvary:

Why lies he in such mean estate,
Where ox and ass are feeding?
Good Christian, fear: for sinners here
The Silent Word is pleading;
Nails, spear shall pierce him through;
The cross be borne for me, for you;
Hail, hail the Word made flesh,
The babe, the son of Mary!

Dix anticipates the crucifixion, but returns in the final couplet to the child sleeping on Mary's lap.

WONDROUS LOVE

What wondrous love is this, O my soul, O my soul,
What wondrous love is this, O my soul;
  What wondrous love is this
  That caused the Lord of bliss
To bear the dreadful curse for my soul, for my soul,
To bear the dreadful curse for my soul.

There is a rich heritage of American sacred folk songs dating from before the American Revolution. The songs seem to be identified more with the southern states than with the New England or middle Atlantic states, but not exclusively. Some of them are folk melodies set to imported English hymns by such writers as Isaac Watts, John Newton, Samuel Stennett, and others, to make them theologically acceptable. Some of these are still sung in our churches: "Amazing Grace," "Come, Ye Sinners, Poor and Needy," "How Firm a Foundation," and "On Jordan's Stormy Banks I Stand."

Other sacred folk songs have indigenous words and music, both of unknown origin. Among these are "Where Are the Hebrew Children," "Our Bondage, It Shall End By and By," and perhaps the choicest American folk song, "What Wondrous Love Is This."

The words of "What Wondrous Love Is This" have been found in two collections of hymns published in 1811. One was a camp-meeting songbook, containing words only, published in Lynchburg, Virginia, the other, a hymn book compiled by a Baptist preacher in Frankfort, Kentucky. This indicates that by 1811 the song was known in those areas of Virginia and Kentucky. The tune "Wondrous Love" does not appear in print until the 1843 printing of William Walker's *Southern Harmony,* an oblong, shape-note tunebook, whose first edition is dated 1835. The name "Christopher" appeared on the page with it. Thirty years later Walker published the tune again, with the notation "Arranged by James Christopher, of Spartanburg, S.C.," a person who has remained unidentified.

OLD GLORY FACE

When all my labors and trials are o'er,
And I am safe on that beautiful shore,
Just to be near the dear Lord I adore,
Will through the ages be glory for me.
O that will be glory for me, glory for me, glory for me;
When by his grace I shall look on his face,
That will be glory, be glory for me!

The director of the St. Louis Sunshine Rescue Mission was a radiant Christian. His pent-up enthusiasm in praise of the Lord found expression both in his conversation and his preaching in the single exclamation, "Glory!" Ed Card's outburst was not a harsh, raucous one, but an expression of sincere and joyful praise. His prayers invariably ended with the phrase "and that will be glory for me." Such expressions became so much a part of the life and ministry of this remarkable man that his friends lovingly referred to him as "Old Glory Face."

In a moment of inspiration in 1900, Charles H. Gabriel, well-known gospel songwriter, took Card's expressions and wrote the hymn that became known as "The Glory Song." In the first decade of this century, a spiritual awakening occurred in many places throughout the world. Charles M. Alexander used the song repeatedly in his meetings with Dr. R. A. Torrey in the United States, Canada, Great Britain, Australia, Korea, China, Japan, and other places. "The Glory Song" became the most popular song of that decade as it went around the world. It was sung in shops and factories, whistled in the streets, hummed in trains, and played on hand organs and other instruments. Homer Rodeheaver also had great success with Gabriel's song. Robert G. McCutchan, editor of the 1935 Methodist hymnal, once said, "If you haven't heard Homer Rodeheaver lead five thousand people singing 'The Glory Song,' you haven't lived!"

Gabriel wrote singable songs that were very popular. Among his best-known hymns are "My Savior's Love," "He Lifted Me," "Send the Light," "Just When I Need Him Most," "Higher Ground," and "Since Jesus Came into My Heart."

LITTLE CHILDREN ARE
THE PRECIOUS JEWELS

When he cometh, when he cometh
To make up his jewels,
All his jewels, precious jewels,
His loved and his own.
Like the stars of the morning,
His bright crown adorning,
They shall shine in their beauty,
Bright gems for his crown.

William O. Cushing wrote these lines for the children in his Sunday school class. It is based on the promise of God to those who fear him: "And they shall be mine, saith the Lord of hosts, in that day when I make up my jewels" (Mal. 3:17). Malachi speaks of the righteous ones, but Cushing interprets the Lord's "jewels" to be children, according to the third stanza.

Little children, little children,
Who love their Redeemer,
Are the jewels, precious jewels,
His loved and his own.

Ordained in the ministry of the Christian Church, Cushing's first pastorate was in Searsburg, New York. In the years that followed he served faithfully other churches in New York state and was dearly loved by old and young.

During his lifetime Cushing wrote more than three hundred hymns. Those that are still well known are "Hiding in Thee," "There'll Be No Dark Valley When Jesus Comes," and "Under His Wings."

In the mid-1860s, Cushing sent his poem "When He Cometh" to George F. Root, a composer, nationally known music teacher, and music publisher who lived in Chicago. Root wrote the music for Cushing's poem and published it in 1855 in his collection "Chapel Gems for the Sunday School."

After a year's study in London and Paris about 1850, Root had returned to America, composed both secular and sacred music, and conducted musical institutes. Many of his early songs were secular, some of them written for Christy's minstrel troupe. For some of these he used his pseudonym "G. Friedrich Wurzel" (*wurzel* is German for "root").

JOY AT HIS APPEARING

When he shall come, resplendent in his glory,
To take his own from out this vale of night,
O may I know the joy of his appearing—
Only at morn to walk with him in white!*

There was much interest among Christian people in the second coming of Christ in the 1920s and 1930s. No doubt the misery and suffering of the Depression caused many to yearn and pray for Christ's return. The book of Revelation became the most popular text for study and interpretation. Some religious leaders divided sacred history into several periods, each with a special administration or dispensation. In this climate Almeda J. Pearce wrote both words and music for "When He Shall Come." Drawing inspiration from Revelation 3:4–5 and 7:9–15, she captured the spirit of these verses in the three stanzas of the hymn she wrote in 1934.

Born in 1893 in Carlisle, Pennsylvania, Pearce was reared in a Christian home. Her musical talents were evident at an early age, and her keyboard skills developed rapidly. Because of her ability in sight-reading and improvisation at the piano, she was in great demand as an accompanist for voice students at Dickinson College. One of the students was John Charles Thomas, a baritone who became world famous. For a while she studied voice at the Walter Damrosch School of Music in New York City. When she returned to Carlisle, she became soprano soloist in the Methodist church quartet and fell in love and married the bass soloist in that same quartet.

Sensing the Lord's leadership into full-time Christian ministry in 1929, the Pearces began a radio ministry on faith just before the Depression hit. The program, "Christian Voices," began at a small radio station in Camden, New

Jersey. It involved at one time the whole family—the Pearces, their daughter, and two sons. For thirty-five years the program grew, broadcasting each day at 7:00 A.M. The children sang and helped with the broadcast before they went to school. Because of the program's popularity, the father received invitations to speak at Bible conferences and meetings throughout many states. Almeda Pearce frequently traveled with her husband, playing the piano and singing. With unusual strength and ability she handled the housekeeping responsibilities, took care of their three children, and shared in the public services.

Bill Pearce, one of the sons, has continued in a similar ministry. First he developed the late evening program "Night Sounds" for Moody Bible Institute's radio station WMBI. Later he continued this format on an independent basis. On many Christian stations throughout the nation the program continues, featuring his distinctive voice, speaking and singing, and his trombone artistry.

The radiant influence of Almeda J. Pearce shines through the lines of her poem as a reminder to those who claim Christ as Savior of the time we shall "walk with him in white."

A HYMN OF THE WONDROUS CROSS

> *When I survey the wondrous cross,*
> *On which the Prince of Glory died,*
> *My richest gain I count but loss,*
> *And pour contempt on all my pride.*

To the churches in Galatia, the apostle Paul wrote that Christians were not obliged to observe the requirements of Mosaic Law, neither should they glory in performing these rituals. Then Paul exclaimed, "but God forbid that I should glory, save in the cross of our Lord Jesus Christ, by whom the world is crucified unto me, and I unto the world" (Gal. 6:14).

Inspired by these words, Isaac Watts wrote the hymn. He captures the essence of Paul's admonition to the Galatian churches in the first two stanzas. The hymn climaxes with a statement of commitment; such amazing love "demands my soul, my life, my all." Throughout the English-speaking world it is recognized as one of the greatest hymns of all time.

The use of the word "survey" in the opening line implies more than mere looking. Watts suggests contemplation, an awareness of the real significance of the cross. Rather than using an expected adjective such as cruel, tragic, or rugged, Watts describes the cross as wondrous. Such graphic language reminds us that an instrument of cruel torture and death became God's wondrous instrument for man's salvation.

In 1792, Isaac Watts, then twenty-eight years old, became pastor of the Independent Chapel on Mark Lane in London. Five years later he published a collection of hymns for his congregation that included "When I Survey the Wondrous Cross" along with "Alas, and Did My Savior Bleed," "Come, We That Love the Lord," and many others. Though he wrote his hymns in simple words that were easily understood by the people of his congregation, richness of language was his trademark.

In Westminster Abbey there is a monument to Isaac Watts, the Congregational preacher who is called the "Father of English Hymnody." In many respects Watts taught the world to sing songs of praise to God and songs of the gospel of Jesus in the fullest dimension.

MUSIC GLORIFYING GOD

When in our music, God is glorified,
And adoration leaves no room for pride,
It is as though the whole creation cried,
Alleluia!*

In the years immediately following World War II, Fred Pratt Green served as minister to Methodist churches in the Finbury Park Circuit in the north part of London. The congregations he served demanded all his time, so there was little opportunity for outside activity and no time to devote to his literary pursuits. One day he visited the home of one of the boys in his Sunday school. The boy's father, Fallon Webb, welcomed the minister and greatly enjoyed the conversation. When Webb learned that Pratt Green had some interest in poetry, he was extremely pleased for he also had a great interest in poetic writing. Webb suggested that each of them write a poem, and at their next meeting they could discuss and criticize each other's work.

Here was a challenge for Pratt Green, and out of the interaction with Fallon Webb came great inspiration and encouragement. Their friendship lasted for more than twenty years until Webb's death. They shared their poetry, counsel, and advice, and each gained new insights from the relationship.

Many of Pratt Green's hymns have been written in response to a specific request or occasion. John Wilson, a distinguished musician who was director of music at Charterhouse and later taught at The Royal College of Music, asked Pratt Green to write a hymn appropriate for a festival of praise or a choir anniversary. Wilson suggested the tune "Engelberg," composed by Charles V. Stanford in 1904. Pratt Green's completed hymn more than matched the challenge, for it is about the church's music and singing. The third stanza points out that across the centuries the church's song has "borne witness to the truth in every tongue." The fourth stanza reminds us that Jesus sang a psalm at the Last Supper and that we "for whom he won the fight" should sing. The final stanza brings the hymn to a resounding climax of praise with voices and instruments.

HYMN PREMIERED AT ST. PAUL'S CATHEDRAL

When morning gilds the skies,
My heart awaking cries,
*   May Jesus Christ be praised!*
Alike at work and prayer,
To Jesus I repair;
*   May Jesus Christ be praised!*

This hymn, as we know it, was first sung at St. Paul's Cathedral in London about 1868. Copies were distributed to the congregation in leaflet form and the organist and the choir led the congregation in this new hymn and tune.

The words of this joyful song of praise to Jesus Christ are rooted in a Roman Catholic hymnal prepared for the diocese of Würzburg, Germany, in 1828. The author of the German text is unknown. Edward Caswell translated it into English in 1854. A poet and linguist, Caswell wrote many original hymns and translated German and Latin hymns into English.

Fourteen years later the hymn appeared with the present tune by Joseph Barnby and then was sung at St. Paul's Cathedral. In public acceptance, Barnby's tune has surpassed all other tunes which have been written for this text.

Barnby, educated at the Royal Academy of Music, was one of the outstanding church musicians of his day. He served as organist and choirmaster in London churches, and his choirs were the finest in the city. He was knighted in 1892.

PEACE ATTENDS MY WAY

When peace like a river attendeth my way,
When sorrows like sea billows roll;
Whatever my lot, thou has taught me to say,
It is well, it is well with my soul.

In the middle of the Atlantic Ocean, the ship's captain called one of his passengers to the bridge and said, "To the best of my calculations, Mr. Spafford, this is where the tragedy occurred and your daughters were drowned." Weeks earlier Horatio Spafford had planned a family trip to Europe in November of 1873. Last-minute business developments made it necessary for Spafford to remain in Chicago for a few days. He sent his wife and four daughters—Anna, eleven; Maggie, nine; Bessie, seven; and Tanetta, two—on the ship *Ville du Havre* to France with a group of friends.

In midocean the *Ville du Havre* was struck by the *Lochearn,* an English ship, and twelve minutes later it sank. Mrs. Spafford was picked up among the survivors, but the four little girls perished. As soon as possible, Spafford left New

York to join his wife. At the place where the tragedy occurred, he stood on the bridge of the ship for some time, contemplating the loss of his girls. Then he went to his cabin and wrote the poem that begins "When peace like a river attendeth my way." In the midst of great sorrow and tragedy, he gave expression to the peace in his heart.

Sorrow and tragedy were no strangers to the Spaffords. The 1871 Chicago fire had wiped out Spafford's extensive real estate holdings on the north shore of Lake Michigan. In 1880 their fourteen-year-old son, Horatio, died of scarlet fever. Christian friends in the Presbyterian congregation to which the Spaffords belonged accused them of some great sin, causing these tragedies to be visited on them. The controversy grew until the Spaffords were asked to leave their church. With unwavering faith and trust in God, they departed.

Long interested in biblical archaeology, Spafford and his wife and several friends settled in Jerusalem in 1881. They made their homes and became part of the life and culture of that area. The people in the community called them "the American colony." After Spafford's death in 1888, his family and friends decided to stay in Jerusalem. His daughter, Bertha Spafford Vester, led the group in establishing the American Colony Hotel, which was well known into the twentieth century and provided a welcome oasis for travelers to Jerusalem. What a fitting tribute to one whose faith-inspired words we sing:

> *Whatever my lot, thou hast taught me to say,*
> *It is well, it is well with my soul.*

FOR A STEWARDSHIP RENEWAL CAMPAIGN

> *When the church of Jesus*
> *Shuts its outer door,*
> *Lest the roar of traffic*
> *Drown the voice of prayer:*
> *May our prayers, Lord, make us*
> *Ten times more aware*

That the world we banish
*Is our Christian care.**

In 1968 Fred Pratt Green was minister of the Trinity Methodist Church in the London borough of Sutton. The church was preparing for a Stewardship Renewal Campaign to encourage the congregation in their financial contributions for the coming year. The campaign sought support not only for the operating expenses of the church, but also for enterprises and social ministries designed to help people in need.

To communicate this emphasis more effectively to his people, Green utilized his poetic skills to voice the needs in a hymn. At the time there was criticism of the church for its self-centered concern for its own well-being, its lack of interest in world needs and the involvement of the gospel in social concerns. To prod his congregation to focus on these needs, Pratt Green wrote "When the Church of Jesus." This was within a year of his retirement from the ministry, and little did he realize that the writing of this hymn would mark the beginning of a new career in his life.

Now living in retirement in Norwich, England, Green is recognized as one of the outstanding hymnwriters of our time. His hymns and poems number about three hundred, most of which have been written since his retirement in 1969. In his hymnic writing he has provided avenues for Christians to express their feelings and beliefs about the Christian faith. The hymns are thoughtfully worked out, and should be sung with full awareness of the meaning of the words. Some of Green's lines are disturbing to Christians as they bestir their complacency and lethargy. Mark Borum has pointed out three paradoxes regarding Pratt Green's hymns: (1) they are panoramic, yet conservative; (2) they are terse, yet elegant; (3) they are provocative, yet reverent. These hymns demand to be sung repeatedly in the decades ahead.

TO TRUST AND OBEY THE LORD

When we walk with the Lord
In the light of his Word

What a glory he sheds on our way!
Let us do his good will;
He abides with us still,
And with all who will trust and obey.

Evangelist D. L. Moody was conducting a series of meetings in Brockton, Massachusetts, in the mid-1880s. Leading the music in these meetings was Daniel B. Towner, who, after fifteen years as a church music director in Methodist churches, entered the field of evangelism. In one of the services in Brockton, a young man spoke up in a testimony service saying, "I am not quite sure—but I am going to trust, and I am going to obey."

Impressed by the honesty and forthrightness of this statement, Towner wrote it on a piece of paper and put it in his pocket. Later, in a letter to his friend John H. Sammis, a Presbyterian minister, Towner related the incident and included the young man's statement. When Sammis read the letter, he wrote the following lines:

Trust and obey,
For there's no other way
To be happy in Jesus,
But to trust and obey.

Here was the refrain. Next he wrote the four stanzas.

Towner received the completed text from Sammis and soon composed the music that we sing with these words. In a collection of hymns he published in Chicago in 1887, Towner included the hymn.

From 1893 until his death in 1919, Towner was head of the music department at Moody Bible Institute in Chicago. In this strategic position he exerted an unusual influence on church music throughout the Midwest as he trained evangelical church music leaders and evangelistic singers.

THE THRONGING CITY STREETS

Where cross the crowded ways of life,
Where sound the cries of race and clan,

> *Above the noise of selfish strife,*
> *We hear thy voice, O Son of man!*

Times Square in New York City, Piccadilly Circus in London, Leipziger-Platz in Leipzig, and Place de la Concorde in Paris are great centers where throngs of people pass each day. Frank Mason North had such centers in mind when he wrote the lines of the hymn in 1903. His initial thoughts came while he was preparing a sermon on Matthew 22:9: "Go ye therefore into the highways." He was intrigued by the American Revised Version of this verse that begins, "Go ye therefore unto the partings of the highways," which presents quite a different picture from the King James Version.

North was a resident of New York City and wrote that he was familiar with the "jostling, moving currents of the life of the people as revealed upon the streets and at the great crossings of the avenues." He said that he had "watched them by the hour as they passed by tens of thousands."

The fourth stanza makes a prayerful appeal that Christ will "heal the hearts of pain," and with "restless throngs abide," and "tread the city's streets again,"

> *Till sons of men shall learn thy love*
> *And follow where thy feet have trod;*
> *Till glorious from thy heav'n above*
> *Shall come the city of our God.*

The tune we commonly sing to these words is called "Germany" (because it was attributed to German composer Ludwig van Beethoven). Actually, the man responsible for the tune was William Gardiner, a successful hosiery manufacturer in England in the early nineteenth century.

An avid amateur musician, Gardiner enjoyed the friendship of some of the most celebrated European musicians of his day. He frequently sent Joseph Haydn six pairs of stockings with Haydn's melodies woven into the design.

In 1815 Gardiner published a collection titled *Sacred Melodies from Haydn, Mozart, and Beethoven,* which contained the hymn tunes he had converted from the melodies of famous composers. While Gardiner attributed the tune "Germany" to Beethoven, he later wrote, "It is somewhere in the works of

Beethoven, but where I cannot now point out." No one else has been able to do so either.

FIRST SUNG
IN ROYAL ALBERT HALL

Why should I feel discouraged,
Why should the shadows come,
Why should my heart be lonely
And long for heav'n and home
When Jesus is my portion?
My constant friend is he:
His eye is on the sparrow,
And I know he watches me.
I sing because I'm happy,
I sing because I'm free!
For his eye is on the sparrow,
And I know he watches me.

Twice in the Gospels Jesus speaks of God's concern for his children and reminds us that God knows when a sparrow falls (Matt. 10:29; Luke 12:6). This illustration of God's love has been used many times in song and sermon. In 1905 Dr. and Mrs. W. Stillman Martin, well-known evangelists, were leading a series of services in Elmira, New York. During the days there, they visited in the home of a devout couple, both of whom had experienced much physical difficulty. Yet both were cheerful and radiant in their Christian faith.

Mrs. Martin enjoyed visiting with the woman and asked her the source of the radiant joy in her face and conversation. The woman smiled and replied, "His eye is on the sparrow, and I know he watches me." The line was an immediate inspiration to Mrs. Martin, and before the day was over she had completed the text as it now stands. She gave the words to Charles H. Gabriel, an experienced composer, and he provided the musical setting. Gabriel mailed a manuscript of the song to Charles M. Alexander, who was then leading the music in revival services with evangelist R. A. Torrey in London.

During these services in Royal Albert Hall, "His Eye Is on the Sparrow" was first sung publicly.

A native of Nova Scotia, Civilla Durfee Martin traveled extensively with her husband as he conducted Bible conferences and revival meetings throughout the United States. The Martins collaborated on a number of songs, the best known of which is "God Will Take Care of You."

Ethel Waters sang "His Eye Is on the Sparrow" many times at the services of the Billy Graham Crusades. On January 24, 1971, she sang the hymn at the White House, and President Nixon introduced her as "the most outstanding gospel singer in the world today." Her own autobiography is titled *His Eye Is on the Sparrow* because of her love for the song and because it became so closely associated with her.

IN TRIAL AND TRIBULATION

> *Ye servants of God, your Master proclaim,*
> *And publish abroad his wonderful name;*
> *The name all victorious of Jesus extol;*
> *His kingdom is glorious and rules over all.*

Charles Wesley wrote this hymn in 1744 and published it in a small pamphlet entitled "Hymns for Times of Trouble and Persecution." John and Charles Wesley were both ordained ministers in the Church of England, but because of their enthusiasm for the gospel, Anglican congregations closed their doors to them. They began to preach to small religious societies, hoping that their zeal would be contagious. For a year they continued speaking to these small groups, but the opposition to their work increased. When John Wesley returned to Epworth where he had grown up and where his father, Samuel Wesley, had pastored the local parish church, he was denied the privilege of preaching in the church. So John stood on his father's grave in the churchyard and preached heartily to the gathered throng.

Faced with growing hostility, John Wesley decided to preach to the unchurched wherever he could find them. He employed this new strategy first on Sunday, April 1, 1739, when he preached to three thousand persons at Bristol,

England, in an outdoor meeting. This method proved successful and throngs came to hear the fervent preaching of the Wesleys. Open-air meetings not only attracted many interested listeners, but also unruly gangs. Rocks, sticks, bricks, and curses were hurled at these who dared to preach in open places.

For such difficult times, Charles Wesley wrote several hymns—"Ye Servants of God" was one of these. Its scriptural basis is Revelation 7:9–12. It originally had six stanzas, but two that speak succinctly to trouble and persecution are omitted from our hymnals. One of these unused stanzas urges steadfastness of the faith:

> *Men, devils engage, the billows arise,*
> *And horribly rage, and threaten the skies;*
> *Their fury shall never our steadfastness shock;*
> *The weakest believer is built on a Rock.*

Here is strong Wesleyan courage that resulted in the survival of these who were called fanatics, and who dared to bring spiritual awakening in the eighteenth century. The indelible mark of the Wesleys stands today as a witness to their unswerving zeal and faith.

A HYMN WRITTEN BY
TWO PROFESSORS

> *Years I spent in vanity and pride,*
> *Caring not my Lord was crucified,*
> *Knowing not it was for me he died*
> *On Calvary.*
> *Mercy there was great and grace was free;*
> *Pardon there was multiplied to me;*
> *There my burdened soul found liberty*
> *At Calvary.*

William R. Newell was in his first year of teaching at Moody Bible Institute in Chicago in 1895. Not yet thirty years old, he had already earned for himself a reputation as an excellent

Bible teacher and preacher. The words to the song had been slowly taking shape in his mind for several weeks, but nothing had been written down. Then, one day on his way to class, the lines fell perfectly into place. He stepped into an unoccupied classroom and, on the back of an envelope, quickly wrote down the four stanzas.

Newell hurried down the hall to his class, and on the way met Daniel B. Towner, director of music at the Institute. With no time for an explanation, he simply thrust the envelope into Towner's hand. During the class hour Towner composed the tune and handed the completed manuscript to Newell when he returned from class. They stepped into Towner's office and sang together "At Calvary" for the first time.

Shortly before his death in 1899, D. L. Moody suggested that Newell begin teaching interdenominational Bible classes on successive weeknights in Chicago, Detroit, Toronto, and St. Louis. This involved much traveling for Newell, but the classes were well attended, especially in Chicago where the attendance reached several thousand.

Daniel B. Towner served on the faculty at Moody Bible Institute from 1893 until his death in 1919. His students became leaders in evangelical church music throughout many states. More than two thousand songs have been credited to Towner, and he was associated with the publication of fourteen collections of music. Two other hymn tunes by Towner that are widely known are "Grace Greater Than Our Sin" and "Trust and Obey."

Index of
Common Hymn Names

General Index

Songs of Glory was typeset by
the Photocomposition Department
of Zondervan Publishing House,
Grand Rapids, Michigan
Compositor: Susan Koppenol
Equipment: Mergenthaler Linotron 202/N
Designer: Ann Cherryman
Text type: 12 point Garamond No. 3
Paper: 50 Pound Pathfinder Natural Antique
Printer: R. R. Donnelley of Harrisonburg, Virginia

130